Monographien
Herausgegeben vom Deutschen Institut für Japanstudien
Band 39, 2005

Sven Saaler

Politics, Memory and Public Opinion

The History Textbook Controversy and Japanese Society

Monographien aus dem
Deutschen Institut für Japanstudien

Band 39
2005

Monographien Band 39
Herausgegeben vom Deutschen Institut für Japanstudien
der Stiftung Deutsche Geisteswissenschaftliche Institute im Ausland

Direktor: Prof. Dr. Florian Coulmas

Anschrift:
Kudan-Minami 3-3-6
Chiyoda-ku
Tōkyō 102-0074, Japan
Tel.: (03) 3222-5077
Fax: (03) 3222-5420
e-mail: dijtokyo@dijtokyo.org

Cover Photo:
Prime Minister Koizumi Jun'ichirō during a visit to Yasukuni Shrine
(Kyōdō News); the Great Monument to the Holy War in Greater East Asia
(Daitō-A Seisen Taihi) (Photo by Sven Saaler);
results from an opinion poll on "historical consciousness".

Bibliografische Information
Der Deutschen Bibliothek

Die Deutsche Bibliothek verzeichnet diese Publikation in der Deutschen
Nationalbibliografie; detaillierte bibliografische Daten sind im Internet über
http://dnb.ddb.de abrufbar.

© IUDICIUM Verlag GmbH München 2005
Alle Rechte vorbehalten
Druck: Kessler Verlagsdruckerei, Bobingen
Printed in Germany
ISBN 3-89129-849-8

TABLE OF CONTENTS

Foreword by the Director 7
Preface 9

INTRODUCTION 11

1. HISTORICAL REVISIONISM IN CONTEMPORARY JAPAN 23

1.1 The Revival of Historical Revisionism 23
1.2 The Formation of the Tsukuru-kai 39
1.3 The Tsukuru-kai's Aims and Agenda 42
    1.3.1 The Pilot Project: Kokumin no Rekishi...................42
    1.3.2 The Tsukuru-kai's "New History Textbook" and "New
         Civics Textbook" 51
1.4 Textbook Approval and Selection 2000/2001...................59
1.5 The Tsukuru-kai and Politics 69
    1.5.1 Historical Background: The Debates of the mid-1990s 69
    1.5.2 Contemporary Political Debates 80

2. HISTORICAL REVISIONISM AND THE POLITICS OF MEMORY 90

2.1 The Yasukuni Problem..94
2.2 The Historical Narrative of the Yūshūkan 97
2.3 Historical Interpretations Underlying Other Memorials 101
    2.3.1 Chidorigafuchi..101
    2.3.2 Shōwakan and Heiwa Kinen Tenji Shiryōkan................104
    2.3.3 Daitōa Seisen Taihi 110
2.4 The Debate over a New National Memorial to
    Commemorate the War Dead 116
2.5 Commemoration, the Nation, History and Memory 120

3. History and Public Opinion 124

3.1   Historical Consciousness..................................124
3.2   Changes in Views of History within Japanese Society 128
3.3   The Quest for an Historical Consensus in Movies,
      Novels and Museums 147
      3.3.1 Academic History and the Mass Media.................147
      3.3.2 Historical Novels....................................151
      3.3.3 Memoirs and Autobiography 157
      3.3.4 Museums...159

Conclusions and Outlook 165

References 171

Appendix 193

Foreword by the Director

In recent years, we have watched with growing fascination the powerful re-emergence of the question of coming to terms with the past. Far from applying only to Japan and Germany, this issue concerns many nations seriously involved in facing their collective past, their historical responsibilities, and the dark sides of their respective histories as well as the brighter ones. The issues of collective memory and of conflicting views of a common past have been studied intensively, and historians have done substantial research and presented striking evidence on many topics at the forefront of often heated public debate. As is well known, while scholarly research on history is one matter, public discourse is quite another—it is not necessarily based on the dispassionate findings of researchers and the objective study of documents and other sources. Public discourse functions, at least in part, according to other rules and motivations. Still another level of discourse is seen in history as it is presented to the younger generation at a basic level in the form of textbooks which, again, may serve other purposes than "simply" to present facts in their most objective form. Whether explicitly stated or not, textbooks also serve purposes such as identity-creation and the formation of a national consciousness and, as such, will in all probability play an important role in forming the "national identity" of the coming generation. The fact that history textbook issues have recently been subject to such extensive debate in Japan—as elsewhere—attests to an awareness of their overall importance in national life.

As a result, the textbook controversy does not concern Japan and its educational policy alone. On the contrary, it relates to issues shared in common with other nations, and in addition points to a fact which transcends the question of textbooks: in a world like ours at the beginning of the 21st century, no nation can negotiate its history alone or retain control of how its past is viewed by others. And so it will be no doubt helpful to Japan, as well as to others, to discuss matters such as the textbook issue under the new premises presented by a globalized world.

The present book is situated in the context of "Japan in Asia", the DIJ's research focus launched in 1997, and grew, among other projects, out of a DIJ workshop co-organized by the author in September 2001 titled "Making History: The Quest for National Identity through History Education". More specifically, it relates to our investigations into "Discourses of Cultural Uniqueness in East Asia", a project comparing manifestations of

Foreword by the Director

national self-assertion on the levels of intellectual, political, and everyday discourse in Japan, China, and Korea and documented, among other studies, in vol. 34 of the DIJ monograph series.[1] It seems that the location of the German Institute for Japanese Studies in the immediate vicinity of so many important Japanese institutions dedicated to national memory—the Yasukuni Shrine, the Shōwa-kan as well as the Chidorigafuchi National Cemetary—adds to an awareness of the importance of this topic. Sven Saaler, head of the DIJ Humanities Section, who in recent years has focused his work on issues of politics, memory and public opinion, working in close cooperation with Japanese colleagues and the wider international community of researchers, is to be congratulated on this timely publication. It will most certainly render good service to all of us in need of balanced and in-depth information on this important aspect of public life in Japan.

Irmela Hijiya-Kirschnereit
Director, German Institute for Japanese Studies
Tōkyō, Fall 2004

---

[1] Iwo Amelung, Matthias Koch, Joachim Kurtz, Eun-Jung Lee, Sven Saaler (eds): *Selbstbehauptungsdiskurse in Asien: China – Japan – Korea*. Monographien aus dem Deutschen Institut für Japanstudien 34. Munich: Iudicium 2003.

Preface

On 10 June 2004, on the initiative of the Nobel Prize winner for literature Ōe Kenzaburō, nine leading Japanese intellectuals including cultural critic Katō Shūichi, novelist Oda Makoto, and philosopher Umehara Takeshi gathered in Tōkyō to announce the formation of the "Association of Article 9" (9jō no Kai). Their aim was to protect Article 9 of the Japanese Constitution which they considered to be "in its deepest crisis ever." (*Asahi Shinbun* 11 June 2004: 37; cf. also *Sekai* 729: 46f) This initiative represents an attempt to give high-level expression to the broad opposition in Japanese society against the proposed revision of Article 9, against conservative-neonationalist tendencies in Japanese politics in general, and against certain policies supported by successive Cabinets since the late 1990s that are considered an expression of these tendencies. This broad-based opposition to resurgent neonationalism, however, has failed to translate into a strong parliamentary opposition that could challenge the dominance of conservative parties.

Nevertheless, resistance in the wider society remains strong. The so-called history textbook controversy has in recent years become another battlefield for the debates between Right and Left—which are also seen as a sign of resistance against the increasing claims of the state to strengthen its control over the individual citizen, implementing the "demand of the nation-state that we exist first and foremost as national subjects." (Duara 2003: 32, cf. also Kang 2001b: 56f) This study aims to provide insights into the current history textbook controversy by unveiling its backgrounds in politics and society, and by identifying the major actors and their respective motives and objectives. While the debate is set to enter a new round in 2005, the fundamental issues and the actors driving them are likely to remain largely unchanged, and this volume is also intended as a guide to understanding future developments in the Japanese debates over history, in particular the interpretation and political utilization of history and history textbooks.

The international dimension of the textbook controversy—its implications for Japanese relations with China and the two Koreas, as well as Japan's reputation in other countries—remains beyond the scope of this study. Particularly in Korea, but also in China, interest in the Japanese textbook question remains high. As other authors have pointed out in the case of Germany (Evans 1989: 175), Japanese history does not belong to the Japanese alone and it is only natural that neighboring states are interested in and concerned about the ways in which the Japanese view their recent history. The way history is taught in schools affects the ways in which future generations will think about their neighbors and thus contributes to the shaping of bilateral relations. It is surely no coincidence that in September 2003 in Jochiwon, South Korea, a "Textbook Museum" opened to exhibit Korean textbooks from the last 1,300 years (*The Korea Herald* 11 October 2003: 12). While the idea of building the museum originated in the 1960s, it was the recent controversy over Japanese textbooks that provided the impetus for its completion. Within Japan, interest in the issue also remains extremely high but, notwithstanding an array of academic symposia both in Japan and at the bilateral level (Chung 2003), publications on the subject are still scarce. This book is intended to fill the gap.

I could not have finished this monograph without the help of many friends and colleagues, whose cooperation I would like to acknowledge here. Above all I wish to thank Kimijima Kazuhiko, Yoshida Yutaka, Tawara Yoshifumi, Arai Shin'ichi, the late Sakamoto Takao, Steffi Richter and Chung Jae-Jeong for sharing their views with me, providing me with numerous insights into the various Japanese debates, and offering their comments and criticism on parts of the manuscript. I would also like to thank my colleagues at the German Institute for Japanese Studies (DIJ) for commenting on earlier drafts of the manuscript, and freelance editor Paul Sorrell for doing a marvellous job in knocking my English into shape. Above all, I wish to thank my wife Kayoko for her support and for being so patient during the last few years when this book was in preparation.

All names of Japanese, Korean and Chinese persons are given in the order: family name-personal name. Quotations from Japanese newspapers refer to the morning edition unless otherwise noted. And last—although this should be a matter of course—I follow a recent trend in academic writing on Japan and state that "all translations of quotations from Japanese sources are my own" unless otherwise noted.

Sven Saaler
Tokyo, October 2004

INTRODUCTION

Controversy over the history textbooks used in Japanese schools has been an important aspect of postwar Japanese politics and society. In recent years, however, the issue has taken center stage with politicians, academics and journalists alike. Recent developments mark a significant shift in the controversy and form the subject of this monograph. While the well-known textbook debate of the early 1980s has to be placed primarily in the context of international relations (Fuhrt 2002), the renewed debate since the late 1990s above all reflects changes taking place within Japanese politics and society.[1] Even though interpretations of history are at the core of the debate, the most recent textbook controversy is tied to discussions about Japan's *future*, such as the ongoing debates about revision of the Constitution and reform of the education system (Saaler 2003b). But the controversy is also linked to fundamental social and political issues such as the relationship of the individual to the state, the importance of national integration and national pride or patriotism, and the degree of control that the state can legitimately claim over the individual. These features of the textbook debate and other contested aspects of Japanese history are characteristic of the recent development of nation-states (*kokumin kokka*) and have been observed in many other countries.[2] Due to the intensity of the debate in that country, Japan, however, makes a particularly interesting case study.

This monograph takes a close look at recent developments in the Japanese textbook controversy (*rekishi kyōkasho mondai*) in order to understand the significance of this debate within the broader framework of Japanese society and politics.[3] Chapter 1 examines the re-emergence of neonationalist historical revisionism (*rekishi shūseishugi*)[4] since the 1990s, its role in the textbook debate in 2000/2001, and its significance in contemporary Japanese politics and society, where school textbooks have

---

[1] While it also remains an issue in Japan's relations with China and both Koreas, this aspect of the controversy has to remain outside the scope of this study. See Fuhrt 2002; Ducke and Saaler 2003.

[2] See Stille 2002 for the United States, and Lakshmi 2002; Sarkar 2003; Roy 2003 and Bhattacharya 2003 for India, where the "rewriting of history texts" by nationalist Hindus has aroused much opposition.

[3] Even though the textbook debate created immense interest in Japan in 2000/2001, with almost a dozen symposia and workshops in Tōkyō alone, in-depth coverage of the topic in the media was rare, and academic studies are still difficult to find (Richter and Höpken 2003; Hielscher and Horvat 2003; Nelson 2002; Nozaki 2003).

[4] For a detailed definition of "historical revisionism" see chapter 1.1.

become a major battlefield in what has been called a "civil war about historical memory" (Kang Sang-Jung in Tahara, Nishibe and Kang 2003: 40; Kang 2003: 101). In chapter 2, I discuss the question of "public memory" and the role of historical revisionism in official and other politically sanctioned interpretations of Japan's recent history as reflected in memorials, monuments, and public ceremonies; and chapter 3 sets the revisionist view of history against the "historical consciousness" (*rekishi ninshiki*) shared by many contemporary Japanese. Given that historical revisionism has received a great deal of attention recently (cf. AsiaSource 2001 for media coverage outside Japan), this study sets out to determine whether this current of thought reflects the understanding of history predominant in Japanese society, or whether it represents a minority view. A secondary task of this study will be to explore the origins and nature of historical revisionism, with a particular emphasis on the political background, to help explain the uproar it has created in Japan during the last decade.

The role of the state in Japan

As sociologist Anthony Giddens has pointed out, as a result of the high level of control and surveillance of society by the modern nation-state, "there is no type of nation-state in the contemporary world which is completely immune from the potentiality of being subject to totalitarian rule." (Giddens 1987: 302) Similarly, responding to the large-scale atrocities committed in World War II, Hannah Arendt blamed the "conquest of the state by the nation" for the widespread loss of human rights witnessed in the first half of the 20th century (Arendt 1986: 575f). Efforts to strengthen citizens' loyalty and allegiance to the state through the fostering of a strong national identity and patriotism are ubiquitous in modern nation-states (Suny 2001: 338; Nishikawa 1995; Hein 2003), and fears of increasing state control as a result of such developments lie at the heart of the recent textbook controversy in Japan and related issues. Although some observers have pointed out that "democracy is deeply linked to nationalism" and that "the key problem is to determine what kinds of nationalist values support democracy and what kinds of nationalist values undermine democracy" (Doak 2003: 22), recent Japanese discussions of nationalism and historical revisionism—concepts which are interlinked—indicate that such fine distinctions are rarely made due to the high degree of politicization and polarization of the debate.

Within this debate, two opposing camps have formed around questions of nationalism and the role of the state. What has been called the neonationalist or conservative side advocates a "strong state" and promotes the idea of the "natural" allegiance of the individual to the state, paralleling the theory of the "natural" development of nations which Ernest Gellner (1983; cf. also Billig 1995) has described as a core tenet of nationalism. This camp follows the assumption that the nation should be the primary focus of allegiance of the individual, and emphasizes that the individual's loyalty to the nation-state should eclipse all other individual or group interests. While this dogma has been central to the making of the modern nation-state (Suny 2001: 338), it also conceals a number of contradictions inherent in the nation-state's claims for absolute loyalty. The advocates of a strong "natural" allegiance to the state and a strong national consciousness in Japan regularly complain about the lack of readiness of "the Japanese" to identify with their country, to be proud on their nation, and to make sacrifices for the nation and the state. Conservatives are particularly alarmed by opinion polls that indicate that pacifism still is extremely strong in Japan and that the Japanese people's readiness to go to war for their country is low by international comparison (Dentsū Sōken and Yoka kaihatsu sentā 1995: 13; see chapter 1.1. and 1.4 for details). The representatives of this camp advocate fostering national consciousness and national pride or patriotism through education, in order to strengthen the "voluntary" allegiance of Japanese citizens to the state. One advocate of a strong nationalism is manga writer Kobayashi Yoshinori, who offers his fellow countrymen a stark choice on the cover of his notorious bestseller *About the War* (Sensō-ron): "Will you go to war? Or are you going to quit being Japanese?" (*Sensō ni ikimasu-ka? Soretomo Nihonjin o yamemasu-ka?*) (Kobayashi 1998).

This kind of argument is not unique to the Japanese context, but is rather an international phenomenon. As Tessa Morris-Suzuki has emphasized, in the "international nationalism" of the 1990s the perceived lack of commitment of citizens to the state is seen in each country "as a uniquely national [problem], as though 'our nation' alone were threatened by forces of disintegration from which all others were exempt." (Morris-Suzuki 2003: 34) She cites Bruno Mégret, the chief ideologue of the French National Front, who—ironically—admires *Japanese* values, which for him indicate "an acute sense of duty, a spirit of sacrifice towards the community, a patriotism conceived as a quasi-religion." (Morris-Suzuki 2003: 34) As with Kobayashi, for Mégret his country alone has fallen victim to disorder: "Only France seems plunged in a mortal lethargy." (cited in Morris-Suzuki 2003: 34)

The opposing camp of the nationalist debate in Japan rejects the idea of a "strong state" as the focus of allegiance for the individual and rather warns of the consequences of too great a control of society and the individual by the state—consequences which Japan has experienced in the recent past. Neonationalist efforts aimed at revising Article 9, the war-renouncing clause in the Japanese Constitution, and the anticipated slow drift of Japan towards becoming a "war-capable nation" (*sensō dekiru kuni*), cause alarm in the liberal camp (Tawara 2001: 157; Tawara 2002: 36; Takahashi and Miyake 2003: 46; Takahashi 2003: 128f; 170f; Ōuchi 2003: 89–93; Tanaka 2002a: 211–214; Obinata et al. 1999; Ōe Kenzaburō in *Asahi Shinbun* 11 June 2004: 37; *Kyōkasho Repōto* 2004: 8). This group challenges the fundamental "demand of the nation-state that we exist first and foremost as national subjects" (Duara 2003: 32). As with the conservative camp, the basic message of this group is proclaimed on the covers of their publications in slogans such as *Can the Individual Resist the State?* (*Ningen wa kokka ni kō shiuru-ka*, Oguma 1998) or *Resisting the Delusion of Empire and the Violence of the State* (*Teikoku no bōsō to kokka no bōryoku ni kō-shite*, Kang 2003).

HISTORY AND NATIONAL PRIDE

In these ideological debates, opposed conceptions of history have taken a leading role. History and the collective memory that shapes it have long been identified as central components in the creation of a national identity. As early as the 1840s, political philosopher John Stuart Mill stressed the importance of a shared historical consciousness in creating a sense of nationhood:

> [The] feeling of nationality may have been generated by various causes. Sometimes it is the effect of identity of race and descent. Community of language and community of religion greatly contribute to it. Geographical limits are one of its causes. But the strongest of all is identity of political antecedents: the possession of a national history, and consequent community of recollections; collective pride and humiliation, pleasure and regret, connected with the same incidents in the past. (Mill 1958: 229)

Mill's assessment has lost none of its validity and, if anything, the importance of history in re-affirming nationalism and national identity is increasing worldwide (Ōnuki 2003a; Morris-Suzuki 2003). As Tessa Morris-Suzuki has pointed out, particularly "in the context of the wealthier nations of the world, 1990s nationalism [...] is deeply obsessed with the relationship between globalisation, national identity, history and memory. It is the expression of a characteristic populism which seeks to defend 'natural' or 'commonsense' visions of the nation from the corrosive cynicism of a menacing 'cosmopolitan' elite." (Morris-Suzuki 2003: 28; cf. also

Introduction

Fulbrook 2004: 4) John Torpey has gone further and argues that this popular historical memory has come to play the role of a *substitute* for nationalism—not only a major pillar—in view of the contemporary dearth of future visions for the state. He argues "that preoccupation [with the past] is a substitute satisfaction that has arisen in response to the collapse of the future-oriented collective political projects of socialism and the nation-state. [...] Not since the Romantics has so much energy been spent on digging up the past, sifting through the broken shards and pondering what people think about them. [...] The pursuit of the future has thus been replaced by a veritable tidal wave of 'memory', 'historical consciousness', 'coming to terms with the past'." (Torpey 2001: Internet) Pierre Nora makes a similar observation in a recent essay (Nora 2002: Internet).

Although such popular neonationalism can be observed in many countries, the Japanese case has received particular attention in recent years, due not only to the exceptional intensity of the debate in Japan, but also to its possible consequences for Japan's foreign policy and international reputation. A key element of the debate on the role of history in Japan is the concept of "historical revisionism" (*rekishi shūseishugi*), vigorously promoted by the conservative advocates of a "strong state." They argue in favor of establishing a "bright" and "clean" historical narrative to counter a predominant "masochistic view of history" (*jigyaku shikan*) that is accused of wallowing in Japan's wartime past, alleged war crimes and postwar deficits in facing this past. Proponents of historical revisionism condemn this "masochistic view of history" as a product of the Tōkyō war crime trials (1946–48) as well as postwar Japanese historical research, which they allege has been dominated by left-leaning scholars. In order to re-affirm Japanese nationhood and counter the "erosion of national identities" due to "global competition, industrialization, urbanization, and other accelerating forces of transformation" (Duara 2003: 30), historical revisionists propose replacing the "masochistic" approach with a positive and "bright" view of Japanese history which fosters pride in the nation and allegiance to the Japanese nation-state.

This kind of historical narrative has become more and more influential since the late 1990s, and is increasingly reflected in popular media such as newspapers, magazines, books, movies and manga (Gerow 2000). A good example is the 1998 movie *Pride* (*Puraido – Unmei no toki*), which advocated the renewal of Japanese patriotism and national pride—an objective evident in the title alone. The cartoon strips of Kobayashi Yoshinori are even more outspoken in their advocacy of national pride and a strong allegiance of the citizen to the state: a recent series of his manga publications is entitled *A New Manifesto of Arrogance* (*Shin gōmanizumu sengen*), and is discussed further in chapter 1.1. A monthly magazine recently launched by Kobayashi carries the title *Washizumu*—which he provocatively explains as a combination of the words for "myself" (*washi*) and "fascism" (*fashizumu*). In the first issue, Kobayashi writes:

> Originally, 'fascism' (*fashizumu*) meant 'to bind something together' (*tabaneru*). The negative meaning [of the term], which people are unconsciously cautious about, is not the whole thing. I will defy this [prejudice] and work for the cause of *tabaneru* according to my own (*washi*) sense of values. (Kobayashi 2002a: 19)

The advocates of historical revisionism consider school history textbooks an important media to get their message across. Consequently, in late 1996 the Society for the Creation of New History Textbooks or Tsukuru-kai (Atarashii Rekishi Kyōkasho o Tsukuru-kai) was founded, and the new history textbook for junior high schools (literally: middle schools, *chūgakkō*) published by the Society in 2000 led to the renewal of the textbook controversy in 2000/2001.

It goes without saying that, within the framework of historical revisionism's efforts to fashion a "bright" national narrative, there is no room for reflection on Japan's wartime past or controversial topics such as war crimes. The central question in discussions between the historical revisionists and their opponents is whether Japan's wars on the Asian continent and in the Pacific between 1931 and 1945 were wars of aggression or rather wars of liberation (*Ajia kaihō sensō*) conducted for the sake of Asian "brother peoples" subdued by Western imperialism. Historical revisionism insists that the Asia-Pacific War[5] was a war of liberation, an interpretation that has provoked much criticism both within Japan and overseas. What makes the revisionist position particularly disturbing is the claim for exclusive knowledge of "the truth" (*shinjitsu*) about Japanese history (see for example publications such as Yasukuni Jinja Shamusho 2002;

---

[5] While the advocates of historical revisionism prefer the term "Greater East Asian War" (Daitō-A sensō), the official term for the war before it became part of World War II following Japan's attack on the United States, Great Britain and the Netherlands in December 1941, I follow the main trend of Japanese historical scholarship in using the term "Asia-Pacific War" (*Ajia Taiheiyō sensō*). This name covers the period designated by the older term "15-year war" (*Jūgo-nen sensō*), referring to Japan's military activities on the Asian continent starting with the Manchurian Incident (*Manshū jihen*) of 1931, escalating in 1937 with the outbreak of the (undeclared) Sino-Japanese War, expanding further in 1941 with the opening of hostilities against the western powers, and ending with Japan's capitulation in 1945 (cf. Maeda 2002: 3).

Maeno 2003; Nishio 1999). Regardless of whether or not it is always made consciously, however, this claim has been implicitly accepted by many observers: reviewing media coverage of recent developments in Japan, one could be forgiven for thinking that the majority of observers both inside and outside the country consider the revisionist perspective as embodying *the* authentic historical view of "Japan".

As will be shown in chapter 2, the growing expression of historical revisionism and neonationalism in the mass media, and its emergence in the public sphere in Japan—e.g. in memorials, museums, and ceremonies—is a major factor in raising the profile of this view of history in state and society. However, political-historical education conducted through popular media such as newspapers, magazines and movies (such as *Pride*), or through displays in historical museums, reach only a small part of the population. Since it is Japan's *future*, rather than the nation's past, that is really at stake in the revisionist debates, Japan's school history textbooks have a crucial role to play for all parties involved. All Japanese are exposed to prescribed textbooks, and, moreover, in their formative years.

HISTORY EDUCATION AND THE ROLE OF TEXTBOOKS

Education plays an important role in establishing a strong sense of national identity in any people. For the researcher, "one of the swiftest entrees to understanding any modern society is through listening to political discourse about education. Power struggles and ideological controversies about how to socialize and enculturate youth are at the heart of the processes by which a society is continually recreated." (Marshall 1994: 1) Again, this is a universal phenomenon that can be observed in any modern nation-state. In Germany, for example, a particularly strong obsession with "national education" was seen in the Imperial era (1871–1918). During the Weimar Republic (1918–1933) that followed the collapse of the Empire, conservative groups lobbied strongly on educational issues. From its foundation in 1891, the Pan-German League (Alldeutscher Verband) in particular was a major advocate not only of territorial expansion, but also of national integration and the strengthening of national consciousness and "Germanity" (*Deutschtum*) among the people. Like many conservative groups at the time, the League blamed the collapse of the Empire on the lack of national unity and national consciousness evidenced during World War I. In its Bamberg Declaration of 1919, the League demanded a reconstruction of the German school and education system in a national-German sense. The League will support all efforts in this direction. Particularly, it has to be stressed that the schools must systematically raise national consciousness and national pride among the youth, with whose future it is entrusted.[6]

In Japan, similar remarks have been made increasingly since the 1990s by conservative pressure groups and politicians who support historical revisionism. While some observers have questioned whether history textbooks actually play a major role in shaping popular views of history in contemporary Japan (and other countries), and question the amount of energy expended on this particular controversy, the evidence suggests that textbooks do play an important role in shaping the attitudes of Japanese to their past. Through history education in school, every citizen comes into contact with the past. Moreover, in response to the recent quarrels about textbooks, many schools are enforcing the role of prescribed textbooks in determining the content of history lessons. Some schools have warned teachers against teaching topics which are not covered in the textbooks. Teachers have even been suspended for covering details of Japan's war crimes which were not included in the textbook used in their schools.

Opinion polls also indicate that the importance of textbooks should not be underestimated. In a NHK (Nihon Hōsō Kyōkai) survey on "views on war and peace amongst the Japanese" (in which multiple answers were possible) (Makita 2000), out of 1,468 participants, 51% answered that they gained information on "the previous war"[7] mainly from television; 44% stated that "people close to them" (*mijika na hito*) were their main source of information; and 38% named the newspapers. After these three major sources, 37% named "school lessons" and another 36% "school textbooks" as their major source, while other media such as books (19%), movies (10%) and magazines (7%) were ranked relatively low (Makita 2000: 18; cf. also Chung 2004: chapter 2 for similar results).

These results help explain why the textbook debate is pursued so energetically in Japan, and why it has a dominant place in discussions

---

[6] *Alldeutsche Blätter*, March 1919. "Deshalb verlangt der Alldeutsche Verband eine Umbildung des deutschen Schul- und Erziehungswesens im deutschen Sinne und wird alle dahingehenden Bestrebungen fördern; dabei weist er auf die Notwendigkeit hin, daß die Schule die ihr anvertraute Jugend planmäßig zu stolzem Nationalgefühl erzieht."

[7] In this poll, "the previous war" (*saki no sensō*) was defined as "the war following the Manchurian incident up to the war against China and the Pacific War, during the years Shōwa 6 to 20 [1931–1945]." Makita 2000: 18.

about the relationship between the state and the individual in Japan, the right of the state to intrude into the individual's privacy and establish control over the individual citizen, and the state's right to shape the identity of its citizens. However, the main issues surrounding the textbook controversy also lie at the center of discussions about history in other media, in "the culture of memory" and in the mass media, and the relation of the textbook issue to these other debates is explored in chapters 2 and 3 of this study. While the influence exerted by prescribed textbooks on Japanese perceptions of history is relatively strong, other factors that contribute to the shaping of historical consciousness or historical identity should not be neglected.

HISTORY TEXTBOOKS AND HISTORICAL REVISIONISM IN MODERN JAPAN

While this discussion of the Japanese textbook controversy focuses on recent developments, the textbook dispute in Japan has been closely intertwined with debate about the character and purpose of the nation-state since its foundation. As early as the Meiji period (1868–1912), we find discussions about state intervention in education and the degree of state control of the contents of textbooks.

> Education has to be separated as much as possible from the control of the government and has to be practiced independently. If education is subject to the control of the government, the holy purity [sic] of education will be dishonored. [....] There is no need for the Ministry of Education to edit textbooks; on the contrary, such interference will become even more unnecessary in the future, since it is reasonable to expect that the people's wisdom will increase further. (cited in Kajiyama 2001: 413f)

This complaint from writer Fujii Uhei, published in the magazine *Taiyō* (*The Sun*) in 1896 [!], shows that opposition to state control of education and the contents of textbooks goes back a long way. The issue's long pedigree also demonstrates that the textbook question is not, as conservative lobbyists and the historical revisionists argue, a tool recently adopted by Japan's neighbors to exert diplomatic pressure, nor is it a device for the "extreme left" (*sayoku*, literally left-wing) to wield against the conservative establishment which has dominated Japanese politics in the postwar period. Resistance to state control of education, of which the textbook issue is one aspect, is rather a phenomenon linked to the emergence of the nation state itself—a phenomenon observed in Japan as elsewhere.

Although the protests of Fujii Uhei and others failed to prevent the introduction of state-issued textbooks (*kokutei kyōkasho*) for primary schools in 1903 (Kajiyama 2001: 409), resistance against state control of education remained strong. In postwar Japan, the name of historian Ienaga Saburō (1913–2002) stands as a synonym for the textbook problem and resistance against state scrutiny or examination (*kentei*) of history textbooks. For over 30 years Ienaga fought the state examination system through the Japanese courts, a system which he and his supporters described as censorship of historical writing. In 1982, the textbook problem first assumed an international dimension when South Korea and China condemned what they regarded as efforts to replace the word "aggression" (*shinryaku*) with the word "advance" (*shinshutsu*) in textbook treatments of Japan's military expansion in the 1930s. The increasing "moralization of international politics" (Fujiwara 2002; cf. also Morris-Suzuki 2003: 32f) gave Korea and China the leverage to utilize history as a diplomatic weapon against Japan over these allegations, and the pressure has been maintained ever since.[8]

However, since the 1990s, the Japanese textbook problem has once again returned to the domestic stage. The changes in the content of Japanese school textbooks which began in the 1980s had by the early 1990s expanded to include more or less detailed explanations of problematic chapters in Japan's war past, such as the Nanjing massacre (also Nanjing incident or rape of Nanjing), the history of the infamous Unit 731, and the so-called "military comfort women" (*jūgun ianfu*) (mostly Korean, but also Japanese and women from other Asian countries forced into sexual slavery by the Japanese military) (Tawara 2000; Chung 1998; 2003a; 2003b; Barnard 2001). In reaction, resistance to what conservatives labeled a "masochistic" (i.e., self-critical) view of history (*jigyaku shikan*) swiftly emerged, and today an increasing number of critics advocate a kind of history education that creates pride in nation and country—a role that "masochistic" views of history are considered unable to perform. These "historical revisionists" dismiss the predominant "masochistic" interpretation of history as a product of the "victors' justice" meted out by the prosecution in the Tōkyō war crimes trials (e.g. Maeno 2003; Rekishi Kentō Iinkai 1995). Rejecting what he regarded as a "masochistic" view of history, Fujioka Nobukatsu, one of the forerunners of what has since grown into a "movement" (Tawara 2001: 46; Richter 2001) to revise

---

[8] For a more detailed overview over the textbook controversies before the 1990s, which can not be dealt with in detail in this study, see Fuhrt 2002; Foljanty-Jost 1979; Nozaki 2002; Yang 2001; Orr 2001: chapter 4.

Japanese history along neonationalist and conservative lines, claimed that the way history is taught is crucial in determining national identity:

> It is precisely its way of teaching its modern history that is the crucial determinant of the constitution of a people as a nation. The people that does not have a history to be proud of cannot constitute itself as a nation. (cited in McCormack 2000: 53)

The Society for the Creation of New History Textbooks (Atarashii Rekishi Kyōkasho o Tsukuru-kai) founded in 1996 is the organizational expression of recent historical revisionism in Japan and receives increasing academic and media attention.

In addition to analyzing the growing influence of historical revisionism in Japanese politics and in official and semi-official views of history reflected in public spaces, ceremonies, museums and memorials, this study aims to contrast the revisionist perspective with views about their recent past held by the Japanese population in general with the "historical consciousness" (*rekishi ninshiki*, *Geschichtsbewußtsein*) of the Japanese people. The increasing acknowledgement of the so-called "dark" chapters of Japan's wartime past in school textbooks since the 1980s, and the consequent improvement in the level of historical education, has led to a situation where revisionist views of history are not widespread in Japanese society. Notwithstanding often-repeated truisms regarding the Japanese reluctance to acknowledge responsibility for the war, most Japanese citizens, and especially the majority of young people, are not in denial over any part of their nation's past including the aggressive nature of Japan's wars in the 1930s and 1940s, and Japanese war crimes in Korea and China. They neither reject Japan's responsibility for the past, nor are they uninterested in their national past—in contrast to the conclusions of most studies of the historical consciousness of the Japanese (see chapter 3). Beliefs and attitudes such as embracing revisionist thought, denying or concealing indisputable facts regarding Japan's wartime past and war crimes, and re-interpreting Japan's wars on the Asian continent as wars of liberation and rejecting responsibility for these wars, are held by only a minority of Japanese. Such views also face an uphill battle to increase their influence, as the events of 2001 proved (see chapter 1.4).

Most importantly therefore, the recent textbook controversy reflects a significant—and insufficiently acknowledged—discrepancy between the views of conservative politicians and supporters of historical revisionism on one side, and the majority of Japanese people on the other. While it is difficult to express concepts like "historical consciousness" or a public consensus on the understanding of history in concrete terms, in what follows I draw on information gained from recent public opinion polls as well as my own research in order to gain a clearer picture of the predominant views on history in contemporary Japanese society. Despite the inherent difficulties of the data, the results indicate that even though there is no consensus on the interpretation of Japan's war past, revisionist views which see the Asia-Pacific War (1931–1945) as a defensive act (*jiei sensō*) or a "war of Asian liberation" (*Ajia kaihō sensō*) are held by only a small minority and can in no way be regarded as the consensus view of history in Japan—despite their domination of the public sphere.

In many ways the textbook debate reflects the state of the Japanese body politic. The next examination and adoption of junior high school textbooks is scheduled for late 2004 and spring/summer of 2005. Since, as the results of the 2000 NHK poll indicated, history textbooks play a very important role in shaping Japanese citizens' views on history, the upcoming round of the textbook controversy will act as a barometer for the future course of Japanese politics and the development of the Japanese state and Japanese society as a whole. Since the textbook controversy is also intimately connected to political debates on other issues such as the reform of the Constitution and the education system, its importance for the future shape of Japanese politics and society can hardly be underestimated.

1. Historical Revisionism in Contemporary Japan

1.1 The Revival of Historical Revisionism

"Revising" history is a completely normal process. Indeed, the writing of history *is* revision, since historians continually re-evaluate sources in order to revise existing theories or present new information or perspectives. While the methods of individual historians might differ, there are generally accepted rules of historical inquiry that are regarded as fundamental to the discipline (Rekishigaku Kenkyūkai 2000: xi). However, what has been called "historical revisionism" (*rekishi shūseishugi*) in the context of postwar Japanese intellectual and political discourse does not follow these basic assumptions, but is rather a highly politicized version of historiography that subordinates scientific method—however defined—to the achievement of political aims. These aims are the re-assertion of national identity and the strengthening of citizens' allegiance to the state, and, as a basis for these goals, the construction of a "bright" or exculpatory historical narrative of Japan's recent past.

The proponents of historical revisionism decry the self-critical view of Japanese history predominant in mainstream Japanese historiography (and Japanese society) as "masochistic", describing this view as a product of "victor's justice", i.e. of the judgement of the Tokyo war crimes trials, and the one-sidedness of postwar Japanese historical studies, allegedly dominated by Marxist historians and leftists or *sayoku* (literally: leftwing), as the revisionists generally label their opponents. Historical revisionism proposes to replace the "masochistic" view of "leftist" historians by a "bright" historical narrative as the basis for a "healthy nationalism" (*kenkō na nashonarizumu*) or patriotism (*aikokushin*). The opponents of historical revisionism, however, characterize these objectives as ultraconservative, neonationalist, or even right-wing extremist (*uyokuteki*) and frequently complain about a trend to the right (*ukeika*) (Tawara 2001; Irie 2004: 201; Obinata 2004: 13; Umehara 2004: 72 and others) triggered by the increasing prominence of historical revisionism in the media. In its efforts to reshape the past, historical revisionism resorts to constructivist methods, involving an arbitrarily selective memory of historical fact and the suppression, denial or re-interpretation[9] of certain chapters of contempo-

---

[9] The question whether the historical revisionist movement in Japan aims at "denying" parts of history or "merely" ignoring them to construct a "bright" narrative to further historical education along national lines; whether it aims at

rary Japanese history that—allegedly—hinder the construction of a "bright" narrative. Although the revisionist project seeks to rewrite the national narrative *in toto*, the "positive" re-interpretation of the Asia-Pacific War—as a war of Asian liberation (*Ajia kaihō sensō*) rather than a war of aggression—lies at the center of its claims and interest.

While the scientific character of "history" as a discipline has often been contested, and while it is clear that historical data "can be put together in a number of different and equally plausible narrative accounts of 'what happened in the past'" (White 1973: 283), the claims of historical revisionism in Japan are especially problematic in several respects. The first involves international relations. While Japan's acknowledgement of its recent history has played a large role in reconciliation with its Asian neighbors after the war, and particularly since the 1980s (Fuhrt 2002; Saaler 2003a; Chung 2002), historical revisionism jeopardizes this ongoing normalization of relations. Secondly, since historical revisionism is intimately connected with politics, it has issued a fundamental challenge to historiography as an established (if at times contested) *science*, and demonstrates the problematic of the "uses and abuses of history". Third and most important, the rise of historical revisionism has become a political issue—one that lies at the center of this study. While mainstream historiography served as a vehicle for "political enlightenment" in state and society in postwar Japan[10], and was an important aspect of what we

---

stressing certain aspects of history at the expense of others; or whether it "merely" engages in selective memory is a philosophical issue which is discussed *within* the revisionist movement itself. Such a discussion certainly lies beyond the scope of this study. The questions raised by historical revisionism have occupied philosophical historians for centuries. Nietzsche was one of the first to characterize the difference between "animal oblivion"—which cannot be defined as forgetting since an animal has no prior impulse to remember—and "human forgetting", which entails the suppression of aspects of one's own past, particularly those that might undermine self-confidence (cf. White 1973: 347–350). Ernest Renan had claimed even earlier that, for nation-states, "forgetting" is inseparably linked to "remembering" and the creation of the nation (Renan 1967 [1882]: 11). Cf. also Assmann 1999: chapter 1.IV; 1.VI and passim.

[10] The same is true of postwar Germany; cf. Kleßmann 2002; 2003; Cornelißen 2001: 17; Wehler 1988; Beier de Haan 2000: 54; 59; Iggers 1997: 70f. German historian Christoph Kleßmann claims that contemporary German history "understands itself as the antipodes of unreflective memory. Its objective is the rational control of memory and the disciplining of remembrance." (Kleßmann 2002: 9) However, in Germany—as in Japan—also exists an "extraordinarily close relationship [...] between historical approaches and positions on the political spectrum." (Fulbrook 2004: 4; cf. also Evans 1989: 25)

might call the "extraparliamentary opposition" to the dominant conservative establishment in politics, historical revisionists support conservative political forces and have formed close personal and organizational alliances with them, as I show in chapter 1.5.[11] Some critics regard historical revisionism as a tool used by conservatives to promote statist nationalism and see its continuing influence as the product of purely political initiatives (Watanabe 2002; Ōuchi 2003: 25).

Certainly the revisionist movement shares with conservative and neonationalist political forces an emphasis on strengthening citizens' allegiance to the state by fostering national consciousness, national pride, and patriotic sentiment, and the construction of a "bright" national history to achieve these ends. A proud future for the nation is at stake. "It is possible (if rare) for a nation to embrace and assume responsibility for previous crimes and errors as a foundation for establishing new directions." (McCormack 2001: xviii) The revisionists and their political allies cannot envisage embracing Japanese war crimes and integrating them positively into the national narrative and collective memory—even if this involves discarding previous historical research and jeopardizing efforts for international reconciliation. In constructing this "bright" narrative, it is essential for them to exclude the "dark" chapters of Japan's wartime history and to re-interpret the war in a positive way. Because this way of "revising" history clearly serves an established political agenda—and is not a re-interpretation following new developments in historiography or historical research, or even the discovery of new historical documents—it has elicited harsh criticism from academic historians, educators and philosophers alike (Uesugi et al. 2001; Takahashi 2001; Net 2001; Kimijima 2001).

The re-interpretation of the Asia-Pacific War as a "glorious" war, a war of self-defense or a war undertaken to liberate Asia from Western imperialism is a major theme of publications issued by the major revisionist organization, the Atarashii Rekishi Kyōkasho o Tsukuru-kai (Tsukuru-

---

[11] Although the term "conservatism" suggests a "conserving" of the status quo in state and society, in the Japanese debate the "conservative camp" is associated with advocating historical revisionism and the *revision* (*kaisei*) of laws on education, i.e. Guidelines for School Lessons, the Basic Law of Education and even the Japanese Constitution (see 1.5.2 for details). On the other hand, the "liberal" or "progressive" camp usually *opposes* the revision of these laws—at least a revision in the sense demanded by "conservatives", seen by progressives as a "revision for the worse" (*kaiaku*) that would involve a partial or gradual return to prewar conditions in education and societal attitudes.

kai).¹² On the other hand, the so-called "dark" chapters of modern Japanese history, such wartime atrocities as the Nanjing massacre, the activities of Unit 731, the issue of the "military comfort women" (*jūgun ianfu*),¹³ or the Japanese colonization of Korea are either excluded from the narrative, relativized or simply denied. The foundation of the Tsukuru-kai was a direct result of political developments related to these issues—the group sprang out of conservative efforts to deflect blame aimed against Japan for its "unilateral" responsibility for the "outbreak" of the war in Asia and the Pacific (see chapter 1.5).

The recent growth of historical revisionism is not peculiar to Japan. In India, references to the assassination of Mahatma Gandhi have been dropped in some textbooks which have been broadly rewritten to serve by-now familiar aims: national integration, national unity, and the construction of an "Indian" national historical narrative. And critics have observed that textbooks in Western countries are not particularly outspoken in their treatment of the history of colonialism and imperialism (cf. Bhattacharya 2003; Cave 2002: 631, 636). As critics of historical revisionism point out, this writing and rewriting of history to enforce national consciousness and national pride undermines the "scientific objectivity" prized by professional historiography. Neither does it allow critical approaches that aim at "political enlightenment" in opposition to a given political authority. The recent growth of historical revisionism has sharp-

---

[12] Historian Eguchi Keiichi (1995) has divided affirmative views of the war held by the wartime generation into four categories: a war of Asian liberation (*kaihō sensō shikan*); a defensive war (*jiei sensō shikan*); the sacrifice of participants for the homeland as "heroic souls" (*junkoku shikan* or *eirei shikan*); and the view that the war was a conventional imperialist war, with the USA and Great Britain sharing the blame with Japan (*bei-ei dōzai shikan*). The rise of the revisionist movement has given predominance to the view of the war as a war of Asian liberation (Kimijima 2001), sometimes incorporating aspects of the other perspectives (cf. Yoshida 1997; Yoshida 1995: 208–211).

[13] For a summary of scholarship on the Nanjing massacre see Fogel 2000; Yoshida Takashi 2000; Yang 1999; 2000; 2001; on Unit 731 see Gold 1996; on the comfort women see Tanaka Yuki 2002; Yoshimi and Kawada 1997. See Tanaka Yuki 1996 for Japan's war crimes in general. The explosion of research on the "comfort women" actually was a major stimulant for the growth of historical revisionism and the foundation of the Tsukuru-kai. In the English version of its inaugural declaration, the Tsukuru-kai claimed that "the widespread adoption of the irresponsible, unsubstantiated argument that the 'military comfort women' were forcibly transported to war zones can be traced to [...] the perverse, masochistic historical view. This is a prime example of the steady decline of national principles due to the loss of a national historical perception." (Tsukuru-kai 1996: Internet)

ened international debate about historiography and exacerbated the crisis of history and the role of the historian experienced in many countries.[14]

In postwar Japan, a sanitized national history was already under construction during the Tōkyō war crimes trials (formally known as the International Military Tribunal for the Far East, hereafter IMTFE). It has resurfaced over the years in a variety of guises in politics, the media, and academia. In 1963, for example, Foreign Minister Shiina Etsusaburō characterized Japan's prewar policies and colonial rule in Taiwan, Korea and Manchuria as "glorious imperialism" in his autobiography (cited in Fuhrt 2002: 70). The publication of Hayashi Fusao's infamous "Affirmation of the Greater East Asian War" in the 1960s (first as a series in the magazine *Chūō Kōron* [1963–1965] and later as a multi-volume book) marked the first climax of postwar efforts aimed at rejecting war guilt and responsibility for war crimes and substituting an affirmative view of Japan's war past. Many of Hayashi's controversial claims are still at the center of contemporary debate.

One of Hayashi's major claims was that, prior to 1945, Japan had fought a "100-year war" as a *defensive act* against Western aggression in East Asia. Building on prewar writings by Marxist scholar Takahashi Kamekichi (cf. Sakai 1991), Hayashi denied that Japan was an imperialist power (in a Leninist sense) and therefore could not be described as an aggressor. Rather, Japan's (initial) victories against Europe and America were a catalyst for national liberation movements in Asia in the years following 1945. Hayashi identified the Opium War (1840–1842) as the starting point for the penetration of East Asia by Western imperialism and, in opposition to these incursions, a rise in pan-Asian sentiments. Following the foundation of the modern nation-state in Japan in 1868, pan-Asian sentiments were indeed common in certain political circles in Japan (Saaler 2002a). Despite this, Hayashi fails to explain why it was necessary for Japan to colonize Korea and invade China in order to "liberate" Asian nations. He is also wrong to assume a direct connection between Pan-Asianism in Meiji Japan (1868–1912), which was primarily a

---

[14] One Indian historian has summarized the issues at stake very sharply: "Rewriting of history is […] undoubtedly necessary. It is an act that infuses history writing with life and energy. But it is not a project that can be given over to those who seek to destroy the very conditions of its possibility. The political moves to stop the publication of the volumes of the Towards Freedom project, delete passages from the existing NCERT [National Council of Educational Research and Training, New Delhi] textbooks and to rewrite these texts do not reveal a will to explore new horizons. They are declarations of a war against academic history itself, against the craft of the historian, against the practices that authenticate historical knowledge." Bhattacharya 2003: Internet.

tool of political opposition to the Tōkyō government, and pan-Asian propaganda in the war years (1937–1945)—a tool for legitimizing Japan's continental expansion which was criticized by many of the original pan-Asianists, not to mention opposing voices in other Asian countries (Hatano 1996). While emphasizing that a number of Asian nations gained their independence after the "100-year war" as a result of nationalist movements inspired by Japanese victories over the Western powers, Hayashi fails to explain Asian nations' postwar insistence on Japanese apologies and compensation. And while he stresses the "unavoidable" (*yamuoezu*) character of Japan's external wars, he fails to consider counter-examples of nations like Thailand which succeeded in securing its (at times tenuous and restricted) independence without recourse to expansionism, even though expansionism as a political device had precedents in Thai premodern history.

Since Hayashi's works were first published, the twin notions of Japan's wars in the first half of the 20th century as "wars of Asian liberation" (*Ajia kaihō sensō*), and of a defensive "unavoidable war", have become articles of faith in conservative Japanese interpretations of the wartime past. While the 1980s and the early 1990s saw changes in the historical consciousness of the Japanese (see chapter 3), a series of formal apologies by Japanese prime ministers and even the Diet,[15] and changes to school textbooks which, by the early 1990s, covered most aspects of Japan's wartime past (Tawara 2000; Chung 1998; 2003a; 2003b), since the 1990s historical revisionism has again been in the ascendant. A reaction against "progressive" developments in historical writing and education, it adopts an aggressive stance to Japan's wartime past and advocates an "affirmative" view of the war, which is, once again, labeled a "war of Asian liberation".

Although the international dimension of the textbook debate, which was central to the 1982 controversy (Fuhrt 2002; Saaler 2003a), largely lies outside the scope of this study, conservative claims are also directed against what is perceived as "undue interference in Japanese domestic affairs" by China and South Korea (Kobayashi 2002b: 65; cf. also Nishio

---

[15] High-level apologies to South Korea and other Asian nations have been made by Prime Minister Suzuki Zenkō (24 August 1982), Kaifu Toshiki (25 May 1990), Miyazawa Kiichi (17 June 1992), Hosokawa Morihiro (11 August 1993), Murayama Tomiichi (15 August 1995; "Murayama danwa", see appendix), Obuchi Keizō (8 October 1998) and others. However, most of these apologies were undermined by statements issued by conservative politicians and/or organizations insisting, for example, on the "legal correctness" and benefits of Japanese colonial rule in Korea. See chapter 1.5.1.

2001: Internet). Against this view, political scientist Fujiwara Kiichi argues that, in a time of increasing "moralization of international politics" (Fujiwara 2002), bluntly rejecting foreign input on domestic issues with historical implications can only lead to isolation. In an era of increasing regionalization and globalization, controversial textbooks are unlikely to remain strictly domestic matters, but spill over national boundaries—as occurred in East Asia after 1982 and in Europe after World War II (Kondō 2001). In the case of Japan, while pressure from abroad (*gaiatsu*) has been an important aspect of the textbook controversies since 1982, recent developments indicate that today foreign voices are barely heeded on this issue (Saaler 2003a; cf. also Ha 2002: 76f; Uesugi 2002). The Tsukuru-kai has recently demanded the deletion of the "paragraph regarding neighbouring countries" (*kinrin shokoku jōkō*) from the Ministry of Education's guidelines for history textbook examination (Tsukuru-kai 2004b: Internet), a requirement that was introduced in 1982 to promote understanding and improve bilateral relations with South Korea and China (cf. Tawara 2001: 143; Watanabe 2002: 5; Kondō 2001: 86; Tawara 2002: 24). This objective has clearly lost priority in the last decade, partly due to pressure from conservative neonationalists who insist that Korean and Chinese protests over school history textbooks constitute "interference in domestic matters". Manga writer Kobayashi Yoshinori, for example, considers modern history education as "brainwashing of Japanese children by South Korea" (Kobayashi 2002b: 71). A result of "undue pressure" on Japan and "interference in [its] domestic affairs", Kobayashi believes that the Japanese education system is teaching Japanese children a Korean view of history—rather than a Japanese one.[16]

As a result of the changes made to school history textbooks in the wake of the 1982 controversy—until the 1990s they still contained all the controversial topics—historical revisionists set their sights on history education and the contents of history textbooks as their first priority. But at the same time, apologetic views of Japanese history gained increasing exposure in the public sphere, tolerated or even sponsored by politicians and the administration (see chapter 1.5 and 2). And since the mid–1990s, historical revisionism has had increasing publicity in the mass media, further differentiating it from conventional history—but also from older forms of neonationalism and established conservative pressure groups. Commentators have observed that in many societies the media are taking the place of academic history in terms of influencing the historical con-

---

[16] See also the greeting message of Tsukuru-kai president, Tanaka Hidemichi (Tanaka 2004: Internet), the "Letter to the Korean People" by Nishio Kanji (Nishio 2001: Internet) and Maeno 2003: 260f for similar remarks.

sciousness of society at large (Steinbach 1999: 32f). While, for example, the German *Historikerstreit* (historians' debate) of the 1980s—which has been recently compared to the ongoing discussions in Japan (Richter and Höpken 2003)—had a certain spillover into the wider society, giving people a greater awareness of academic historiography, today public perceptions of history are being formed to a much greater degree by historical fiction and history recycled through the media in documentaries, movies and manga, as well as public exhibitions and memorials.[17] In Japan, historical revisionism constantly reproduces itself in the mass media, leading observers to conclude that it "should be considered a threat"; whereas the old right-wing (*uyoku*) groups touched only the margins of society, this new "consumerist nationalist" movement is reaching a broad sector of the population (Gerow 2000: 93; cf. also Oguma and Ueno 2003: 3).

One example of this new phenomenon is the 1998 movie *Pride – The Moment of Fate* (*Puraido – unmei no toki*), which even in its title reaffirms the basic claim of historical revisionism, the necessity for strong national pride. The movie depicts wartime Prime Minister Tōjō Hideki, who was convicted as a class A war criminal and executed in December 1948, as a loving family man and a brave patriot who fulfilled his duty by loyally serving his country, the nation and the Emperor. His conviction as a war criminal is presented as mere victor's justice, wholly unjustified by the policies pursued by the wartime Tōjō cabinet. Dwelling upon the judicial inconsistencies of the IMTFE, the movie casts doubts on the illegality of Japanese conduct during the war. It follows the story of Indian Justice Radhabinod Pal who recalls the wartime links between Japan and India and his own role in the IMTFE. Indeed, Pal was the only judge on the IMTFE to dismiss the charges against Japan and deny that Japan could be pronounced guilty based on the technical legal charge of conducting a war of aggression. However, the movie neglects to mention that Pal, although questioning the legitimacy of the trial, did not doubt that Japan had actually conducted a war of aggression or committed war crimes.

Pride stirred up controversy both within Japan—where a "Society to Criticize the Movie Pride" (Eiga Puraido o Hihan Suru-kai) was founded—and abroad.[18] The movie was widely discussed, and the production company, Tōei (Tōkyō Eizō Seisaku), succeeded in attracting almost 1.3 million visitors to the set during 1998—probably as many critics of the

---

[17] On the term "historical consciousness", see further chapter 3.1.
[18] See for example *Der Spiegel* 23/1998 ("Pride of the Nation") for German coverage of the movie, and *Mainichi Shinbun* 17 May 1998, p. 25, for a summary of critiques made inside and outside Japan.

movie as supporters of historical revisionism. In response to media criticism of the project, Tōei president Asano Katsuaki asserted that he saw it as his "duty to restore the pride of the Japanese and transmit a correct image of history (*tadashii rekishi ninshiki*)." (cited in *Mainichi Shinbun* 17 May 1998: 25) *Pride*'s première was accompanied by academic symposia and by academic as well as journalistic publications (e.g. Tanaka 2001), confirming the legitimacy of the IMTFE as a central issue for revisionists. In 1997, the same year in which historical revisionists began organizing themselves as a movement, a memorial was built acknowledging his role in the IMTFE in a Kyōto cemetery attached to the Gokoku-Shrine, one of the local branches of the Yasukuni-Shrine established as monuments to the war dead in each prefecture (see chapter 2.1).

Ill. 1:   Memorial to Justice Pal at the Gokoku-Shrine in Kyōto (Photo: Sven Saaler).

Even more influential than movies that transmit revisionist messages are the publications and regular media appearances of Kobayashi Yoshinori, one of the founding members of the Tsukuru-kai. Above all, Kobayashi is famous for his manga, which are particularly popular with Japanese youth. One of his regular series in the biweekly journal *Sapio* is titled "A New Manifesto of Arrogance" (*Shin gōmanizumu sengen*), and is also recycled in book form, both hardcover and paperback. His (in)famous bestseller *On War* (*Sensō-ron*), published in 1998, is a collection of manga from this series in *Sapio*. As the title suggests, this book is all about war—Japan's wars in the past and the attitudes of contemporary Japanese towards war. *Sensō-ron* takes a broadly affirmative stance toward Japanese wars of the past as well as to war in general, both in the present and future. With his provoking mix of graphics and hard-hitting text, Kobayashi sets out to "cure" the young generation of Japanese of their passivity and to change social attitudes from what he sees as rampant individualism (*ko*) to an emphasis on the common good (*kō, ōyake*), with loyalty to the state taking first place.[19] Kobayashi accuses the Japanese of evading responsibility towards state and society and an unwillingness to make sacrifices for their country, or to go to war on its behalf (Kobayashi 1998: 18, 287, 346–349, chapter 21). As we have seen, on the cover (*obi*) of *On War* Kobayashi confronts the potential buyer with the provocative question: "Will you go to war? Or will you quit being Japanese?" The book's success prompted a group of leftist historians to produce a volume entitled *Can you Really Die in War? A Critique of Kobayashi Yoshinori's 'On War'* (Obinata et al. 1999), in which they critique Kobayashi's logic as a hangover from prewar attitudes when those unwilling to go to war were considered anti-Japanese or non-Japanese, no longer part of the national community (*hikokumin*) (Obinata et al. 1999: 110).

In his provocative writings, Kobayashi sets out to tackle what he considers the belief of many Japanese that peace and prosperity come for free (*sābisu*) and are delivered as a matter of course to the citizen who pays his taxes. This belief, according to Kobayashi, is the product of an undue emphasis on individualism in postwar Japan:

> In today's Japan, there is nobody who would die for his ancestors' country (*sokoku*). It is only one's own life that matters. The country and the public come last. People are keen to claim their rights, but accept no duties beyond paying their taxes. […] Peace is expected to come with paying taxes. The Japanese individual is nothing more than a consumer. (Kobayashi 1998: 18)

---

[19] Although, in recent years, Kobayashi's manga have increasingly targetted both the "extreme left" (*sayoku*) and the LDP-led Koizumi administration, his views regarding history and the role of the state have remained largely unchanged (cf. Kobayashi 2002b: 29–36, 48–56, 64–73). However, an increasing anti-Americanism has marked his work since the war in Afghanistan along with criticism of the pro-US policies of the Koizumi cabinet (Kobayashi 2002b: 17–24, 138–156; Kobayashi and Nishibe 2002).

In his manga, Kobayashi's main objective is to strengthen the "voluntary" allegiance of the people to the state. He expects Japanese to sacrifice individualism and individual rights for the sake of the state or the nation—Kobayashi never really clarifies the distinction. For Kobayashi, the "one-sided and guilt-laden historical narrative of postwar Japan" must carry chief responsibility for the alienation of the individual from the public sphere in today's Japan (Kobayashi 1998: 54, chapter 20). It is also the reason why so few Japanese are willing to go to war for their country—a perception backed up by statistical fact (see below). Kobayashi aims to counter this perceived lack of patriotism with the propagation of a "bright" national history, a goal which has led him to side with the revisionist camp. So in *Sensō-ron* and other manga, Kobayashi advocates an interpretation of Japan's recent wars as defensive campaigns and wars of Asian liberation:

> At that time, Asians did not even believe in their dreams that they could win against the Whites. They were completely subdued and living in slavish conditions. [...] Somebody had to prove that it was possible to fight Euro-American white imperialism. This is what Japan has done. (Kobayashi 1998: 31, cf. also 311)

Criticizing historical novelist Shiba Ryōtarō (1923–1996),[20] whose writings contrast a "bright Meiji" era (1868–1912) with the "dark Shōwa" (1926–1945) period, Kobayashi further insists:

> There is of course glory (*eikō*) in wars that were won, but there is also glory in wars that were lost. (Kobayashi 1998: 311)

For Kobayashi, who borrows much of his message from Hayashi Fusao (Kobayashi 1998: 37), Japan's wars in the 1930s and 1940s were "conventional" (*futsū*) imperialist wars, not acts of aggression. They were acts of self-defense with the ultimate aim of liberating Asian nations from the imperialist yoke. Kobayashi stresses that the annexation of Korea took place at the request of Korea's largest political party, the Isshin-kai; and the Manchurian Incident of 1931 could not be called an act of aggression against China, since Manchuria was not then considered an integral part of China, even by Chinese leaders such as Sun Yat-Sen. A war conducted with such noble aims as the liberation of Asia could not, of course, sustain accusations of war crimes and atrocities. Kobayashi therefore takes pains to relativize or deny Japanese war crimes, comparing alleged atrocities to

---

[20] On Shiba Ryōtarō and the impact of his historical novels on the historical consciousness of the Japanese, see chapter 3 and Narita 2003; Nakamura 1998.

German war crimes in order to play them down (Kobayashi 1998: chapter 10)—a strategy common among Japanese revisionists (Nishio 1999: chapter 33; Nishio 1994; Rekishi Kentō Iinkai 1995: 231–248), but also among historical revisionists of other nationalities, and, interestingly, conservative German historians who took part in the "historians' debate" of the 1980s (cf. Evans 1989: chapter 2).[21] Kobayashi also reasserts the revisionist claim that the prevailing view of postwar Japanese history is the product of victor's justice and the monopoly of historical writing by leftist historians. In addition to manga, Kobayashi propagates his views in public lectures, television appearances and speeches—such as the one he gave in Kanazawa city in August 2002 to mark the second anniversary of the construction of the "Great Monument to the Holy War in Greater East Asia" (Daitō-A Seisen Taihi).[22]

Ill. 2: **Speech of Kobayashi Yoshinori at the Great Monument to the Holy War in Greater East Asia (Photo: Sven Saaler).**

---

[21] The standard response to such attempts at relativization is given by Hagen Schulze: "Is mass murder even just a little less despicable, is the obligation of the Germans to draw a lesson from the atrocities of the Nazi era less urgent, if comparable atrocities have been committed at other times and at other places, too?" (Hagen Schulze, cited in Evans 1989: 149)

[22] See chapter 2.3.3 for further discussion of this monument.

In his enthusiasm for Japan's "holy" wars against Western imperialism, Kobayashi neglects to mention that Japan herself had colonized Asian nations and fought an expansionist war in China, in the north from 1931 and in central China from 1937. Even though the war in China had been designated a "holy war" by the Imperial Army as early as 1934 (see chapter 2.3.2), after 1941 Japanese propaganda sought to legitimize Japan's war against the United States and Great Britain as a "holy war" conducted for the sake of Asian liberation. In his groundbreaking study of Japanese foreign policy during the Pacific War, historian Hatano Sumio (1996) showed that the alleged aim of "Asian liberation" formed a major part of Japanese wartime propaganda, but had little basis in reality. "Many official declarations were little more than political propaganda designed to evoke the sympathies of Asian peoples." (Hatano 1996: 51) Documents of the period confirm Hatano's analysis: the term "Asian liberation" was not used in official documents before the 1943 Tōkyō Declaration (*Daitō-A kyōdō sengen*) and, even after that date, was never given high priority according to Hatano. Even when the war situation worsened, the Japanese leadership never considered granting independence to *all* Asian nations "liberated" from Western colonialism, but only to those areas whose raw materials were not needed to supply the Japanese war machine. Thus while Burma and the Philippines were granted independence in 1943, Indonesia[23] and Indochina, which were rich in required raw materials, were denied independence or autonomy of any kind, and remained occupied territories until the capitulation of the Japanese Empire in August 1945 (Hatano 1996: 218–228; cf. also Obinata et al. 1999: chapter 2). Moreover, the circumstances in which Burma and the Philippines were granted independence suggests that Japan was more interested in maximizing the mobilization of manpower for war than in upholding any principle of "Asian liberation" or even in responding to claims for independence from the countries concerned (Hatano 1996: 4, 103f, 197). Assessing Japan's situation near the end of the war, Hatano confirms the view of prominent political scientist Robert S. Ward:

> With the war situation clearly becoming untenable, the chief priority for Shigemitsu [Mamoru] and the bureaucrats in the Foreign Ministry, who had been the main driving force behind the Greater East Asia Proclamation [1943] and the 'new policies' that resulted, was to

---

[23] Malay, Sumatra, Java, Borneo and the Celebes were considered particularly vital to the continued supply of raw materials and were envisaged as becoming an integral part of the Japanese Empire after the war. See Obinata et al. 1999: 61f. Furthermore, immediately after its occupation Singapore was integrated into the Japanese Empire as "Shōnan Island".

prepare a 'case' (*Nihon no 'iibun'*) for Japan that would serve an apologetic (*benmei*) view of history. (Hatano 1996: 208, cf. also 296f)

Although Hatano Sumio is not regarded as a leftist historian in Japan, his research has effectively countered the revisionist claim of Japan's spearheading of a "war for Asian liberation". However, due to the strong political character of historical revisionism, for neonationalists like Kobayashi historical inconsistencies revealed by careful scholarship carry little weight.

Reading Kobayashi's manga[24] prompts the question whether the Japanese really display such a poor sense of national identity and duty to the common good as he alleges—leaving aside the question whether, in a time of shifting identities and individual interests, a stronger allegiance to the state is desirable in the first place. There is some evidence to back up Kobayashi's assertion that Japanese would refuse to go to war even if Japan were attacked by foreign military forces. According to an international opinion survey carried out by the research institutes Dentsū Sōgō Kenkyūjo and Yoka Kaihatsu Sentā between 1989 and 1991, the willingness of Japanese to fight "for their country" was the lowest among the 37 countries included in the survey (Dentsū Sōken and Yoka kaihatsu Sentā 1995: 13). Only 10% of Japanese interviewed expressed a readiness to fight for their country in the event of war (*susunde kuni no tame ni tatakau*), well behind Italy with 26%, Belgium and West Germany with 31% each, Brazil with 33% and former East Germany with 38%. Progressively higher scores were recorded for France (52%), Britain (65%), Russia (67%), the United States (70%), Denmark (82%), Norway and Korea (85%) and India (86%), while Turkey with 89% and China with 92% were the top batters.

While Kobayashi is clearly disturbed by these kinds of figures, his disquiet is shared by certain politicians, sections of the media and some of the self-appointed cultural "critics" (*hyōronka*) (Rekishi Kentō Iinkai 1995: 67; *Sankei Shinbun* 27 August 2000: 3; Nishibe Susumu, cited in Tahara, Nishibe and Kang 2003: 5). The survey was quoted in a speech by historian and influential Tsukuru-kai member Takahashi Shirō to the members of the LDP's notorious "History Examination Committee";[25] he blamed the results on policies implemented by the U.S. occupation authorities aimed at indoctrinating the Japanese with war guilt after 1945 (Rekishi Kentō Iinkai 1995: 297f). However, the survey seems to reflect not so much a lack of national identity as deep-rooted *pacifist* attitudes in

---

[24] For a more detailed discussion of Kobayashi, including the techniques used in his manga, see Obinata et al. 1999.
[25] *Rekishi Kentō Iinkai*; see chapter 1.5.1 for details.

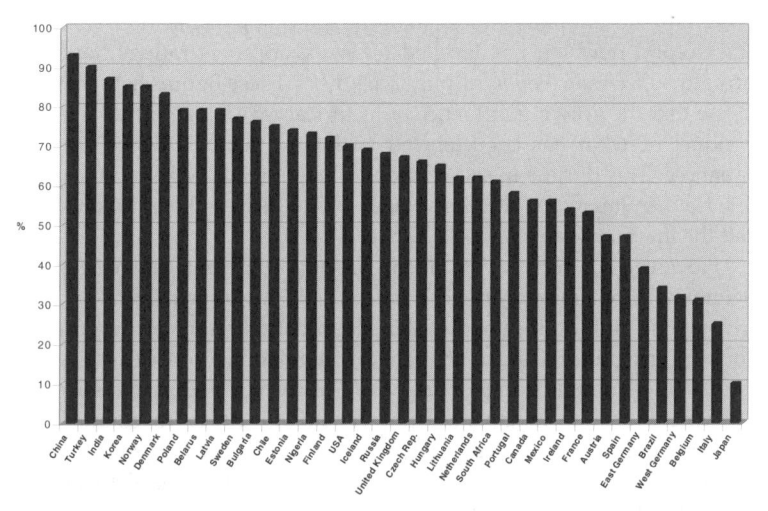

Ill. 3: Opinion survey 1989–1991: "Would you fight for your country in the event of war?" Affirmative responses by percentage of respondents by country. Source: Dentsū Sōken und Yoka Kaihatsu Sentā 1995: 13.

postwar Japan—criticism of which is still considered a "direct challenge to the collective identity of Japan as a peaceful country." (Katzenstein 1996: 151; cf. also Obinata et al. 1999: 165–178)

Although the survey was taken around the end of the Cold War, it still reflects Japanese values and attitudes characteristic of the Cold War era. Commentators have argued that historical revisionism would gain strength as a result of worsening economic conditions and an accompanying decline in national self-confidence experienced by Japanese since the 1990s. However, Japanese self-confidence and trust in their country were already in decline *before* the so-called bubble economy burst in the early 1990s. Notwithstanding continuing economic troubles, national self-confidence has been on the rise again recently, if national opinion polls are anything to go by. Every five years, Japan's semi-public broadcasting station NHK (Nihon Hōsō Kyōkai) commissions surveys aimed at defining the "values" of the Japanese and clarifying Japanese attitudes towards the state. The NHK surveys show that the Japanese sense of national identity and confidence in the state was already in decline in the early 1980s, at a time when Japan's "bubble economy" had reached new heights. While in 1983 a record 71% of Japanese answered that they felt "confidence in their country" (*jikoku ni tai-suru jishin*) and 57% considered Japan a first-rate country (*ichiryū-koku*), already by 1988, *before* the burst of the "bubble economy", these figures had declined to 62% and 50%

respectively. They continued to decline, with 57% expressing confidence in their country in 1993 and 51% in 1998, while those considering Japan a first-rate country plummeted to 49% in 1993 and to 38% in 1998 (NHK 2000: 116). Recent polls indicate that the sense of pessimism revealed by this second question has levelled off, with approval ratings hovering around 50% (*Asahi Shinbun* 1 May 2004: 17).[26] These figures help demonstrate that the growing influence of historical revisionism is not a direct product of what has been labeled a "loss of self-confidence" by the Japanese. This decline in self-confidence had already begun in the early 1980s when Japanese economic power was at its height and Japan strutted the international stage as "Number 1".

However, a perceived "decline in national consciousness" due to the economic problems experienced since the 1990s is usually taken as a given by Japan's political establishment and often presented as a pretext for increasing efforts aimed at strengthening national consciousness and pride. The economic slump of the 1990s was seen by politicians as accompanying a decline in Japanese power and influence. To counter this decline, a large sector of the political elite favors greater utilization of "hard power" by Japan, including increased Japanese participation in military activities, either within the framework of UN operations or as a partner of the U.S. By choosing this option, the conservative establishment implies that Japan's "soft power" is inadequate to further its international prestige although, at least in Asia, Japan's standing depends on its reputation as a "cultural power"—home of Hello Kitty and Miyazaki Hayao's anime movies—rather than as an active military power.[27] In their demand for the increasing utilization of "hard power", Japanese politicians also face strong opposition within Japan, in the form of widespread pacifist sentiments that oppose the militarization of Japanese foreign policy. It is in this context that historical revisionism has come to play an active political role, since the construction of a "bright" historical narra-

---

[26] Supporting the theory that pacifism is an important facet of postwar Japanese national self-confidence and even (not-statist) nationalism is the fact that, when survey respondents were asked *why* Japan was considered a "good country", the most frequent answer was "because it is a peaceful country" (*Asahi Shinbun* 1 May 2004: 17). This view reflects Japan's foreign policy and constitutional military restraints, but also the comparatively high security of daily life in Japan.

[27] One politician who advocates a shift in emphasis from the manic quest for "hard power" to a concentration on the "soft power" acknowledged in large parts of Asia is Matsui Kōji of the Democratic Party (Minshutō). He laments the fact that Diet members and the bureaucracy "ignore changes in lifestyle and political views as well as 'values' in society" (*Asahi Shinbun* 12 August 2003).

tive celebrating a strong Japan is seen by some politicians as a means to counter pacifism and generate support for Japanese participation in military activities on the international stage. In the long run, the movement could also create the conditions for the revision of Article 9 of the Constitution—a major issue for conservative politicians whether in the LDP or the opposition Democratic Party (DP). I will return to this important issue in chapter 1.5.2.

In sum, while there is no evidence of a direct connection between the vagaries of economic development, fluctuating levels of national self-confidence and the rise of historical revisionism in Japan, some politicians are using a perceived decline in national self-confidence as a pretext for realizing their political objectives. This strengthens the assumption made in this study that the explanation for the recent growth of historical revisionism is to be sought in shifting political interests and priorities rather than in any crisis of national identity and attitudes towards state and nation within Japanese society. However, with the formation of the Tsukuru-kai, conservative politics has found an ally within the wider society to organize support for its drive for a strong state and a stronger statist nationalism. The next chapter takes a closer look at the Tsukuru-kai, its objectives and membership.

1.2 THE FORMATION OF THE TSUKURU-KAI

Founded in late 1996, the Tsukuru-kai was the successor to the Association for the Advancement of a Liberal View of History (Jiyūshugi Shikan Kenkyūkai), a more academic enterprise established by Fujioka Nobukatsu, professor of education at Tōkyō University (cf. McCormack 2000: 56–65; Gerow 2000: 74; Obinata et al. 1999: 21). The original association is still quite active, as witnessed by a website which also contains a substantial amount of information in English.[28] On the website, the association informs readers that its main objective is the "escape from the 'masochistic view of history' that produces contempt for your own country", and the "promotion of historical research and historical education based on a

---

[28] http://www.jiyuu-shikan.org/. According to the website, the association offers seminars for teachers and "upskilling programs for teaching modern and contemporary history;" publications including "bestselling books on Japanese history;" lectures by historians on controversial issues; "a media watch, which surveys reporting of historical issues with contemporary relevance involving Japan in major Western newspapers;" and information in Japanese and English via the internet "as a basis for stimulating debate and constructive dialogue."

healthy nationalism (*kenkō na nashonarizumu*)." (Jiyūshugi shikan kenkyūkai 2000: Internet) Its successor organization, the Tsukuru-kai, makes similar claims:

> Since ancient times, Japanese soil has bred civilization and produced unique traditions. In every age, Japan has kept pace with the advance of civilization throughout the globe, and stepped forward steadily throughout history.
> When in the era of imperialism the Euro-American countries aimed at swallowing East Asia, Japan emerged on the world stage by reviving its own traditions and harmonizing them with the ways of Western European [*seiō*] civilization.
> However, this was also a violent time that involved tension and friction with other countries. Today Japan is the safest and wealthiest [country] in the world [sic], the product of the persistent efforts of our fathers and mothers and their ancestors.
> However, historical education in the postwar period has neglected the culture and traditions that Japanese are duty bound to pass on to following generations, involving a shameful loss of national pride. Especially in the field of modern history (*kingendai-shi*), the Japanese are treated like criminals who must continue apologizing [for the past] for generations to come [*shishi sonson*]. After the end of the Cold War, this masochistic [*jigyaku*] tendency continued to increase, and in current history textbooks the propaganda of former war enemies is included and treated as if it were the truth. There is no other country in the world where history education is taught in such a way.
> On the other hand, the textbook produced by our organization offers a balanced and dignified portrait of Japan and the Japanese in the larger framework of world history. […]
> Our textbook enables children to take pride and responsibility in being Japanese and to contribute to world peace and prosperity. (Tsukuru-kai 1997b: Internet)

Although the shorter English version goes into less detail, it stresses that "each nation has its own perception of history, which differs from those of other nations. It is impossible for nations to share historical perceptions." (Tsukuru-kai 1996) This position is diametrically opposed to mainstream textbook research and practice in the international context, which, in the words of Wolfgang Höpken, director of the German Georg-Eckert Institute for International Textbook Research, aims above all at the "'decontamination' of textbooks and historic concepts" from being "poisoned by nationalistic misuse of history." (Höpken 2003: 3; cf. also Chung 2002; 2003a) By contrast, the Tsukuru-kai claims that the society's objective is "to develop

1. Historical Revisionism in Contemporary Japan

and disseminat[e] history textbooks founded on common sense, textbooks that will assure us that we have transmitted the correct version of *our* history to Japan's future generations." (Tsukuru-kai 1996; italics added) While the controversies of the 1980s focused primarily on high school textbooks, in 1997 the Tsukuru-kai announced plans to produce a new history text for Japanese junior high schools (literally middle schools, *chūgakkō*). At the same time, it announced its intentions of producing a textbook for civic studies (*kōmin kyōkasho*), thereby revealing a clear political objective—influencing the attitudes of young Japanese to the state.

In its first major publication, based on the society's inaugural symposium held in March 1997 and issued in July that year, the Tsukuru-kai announced the "beginning of a new Japanese history". (Tsukuru-kai 1997a) This volume contains articles by the central figures of the Tsukuru-kai[29] and repeats the basic tenets of historical revisionism including the necessity of an historical narrative that serves as a basis for national pride and the pressing need "*not* to teach the topic of 'comfort women' to junior high school students." (Tsukuru-kai 1997a: 76, 100) The book claims that postwar historical education has helped spread "distorted" views of history by putting too much emphasis on Japan's war past and treating what it calls the "persecution" of military and civil leaders at the Tōkyō war crime trials as the "truth" about Japanese history (Tsukuru-kai 1997a: 82–86). A level of popular support for historical revisionism was demonstrated by the inclusion in the book of dozens of postcards from supporters and participants in the original symposium encouraging the Tsukuru-kai in its activities (Tsukuru-kai 1997a: 305–312).

Like Fujioka's original association, since its foundation the Tsukuru-kai has engaged in a variety of activities designed to disseminate its views. Each year the society organizes around 150 symposia, conferences and lectures which attract up to 1,500 participants. In 1999 they reportedly organized 230 public events, although the true figure is probably three times higher since only a small percentage of their events are announced publicly (Net 2000: 110). Moreover, the society and its members have published dozens of books, some of which have become bestsellers—not least due to their character as "feel-good narratives about 'great' men and women in modern Japanese history" (Gerow 2000: 74).[30] These activities

---

[29] Most of the articles had been published previously in magazines such as *Seiron*, *Shokun!*, *Voice*, *Bungei Shunjū*, *Ronza* and in the newspaper *Sankei Shinbun*. In the book, the association calls itself (in English) the Japanese Institute for Orthodox History Education.

[30] See Gerow 2000: 74–78 for an analysis of one of the first of these publications, *Kyōkasho ga oshienai rekishi* (The History That isn't Taught in Textbooks). Al-

generate a considerable income for the Tsukuru-kai, and it is no secret that the society's finances have been boosted by supporters in the business world (cf. Tawara 2001: 175; see for example Maeno 2003).

Among the society's membership—which peaked at 10,000 in 1999—a number of prominent personalities have boosted the Tsukuru-kai's influence in society and politics. The first leader of the Tsukuru-kai was Nishio Kanji, professor of German Studies [sic] at Electro-Communications University. His deputy was Fujioka Nobukatsu, professor of education at Tōkyō University and the founder of the Jiyūshugi shikan kenkyūkai. Other founding members included former chairman of BMW Tōkyō Tanegashima Kei, manga writer Kobayashi Yoshinori, columnists Izawa Motohiko and Nishibe Susumu,[31] art historian Tanaka Hidemichi of Tōhoku University, honorary Tōkyō University professor Haga Tōru, ethnologist Ōtsuki Takahiro, newscaster Sakurai Yoshiko and—the only prominent historians in the society—Takahashi Shirō and Itō Takashi. Historian and political scientist Sakamoto Takao, who died in 2002, was also a founding member. Despite its involvement in a range of activities, the Tsukuru-kai remained true to its name ("Society for the Creation of New History Textbooks") and in 2000 a draft history textbook for junior high schools was submitted for examination to the Ministry of Education (Monbushō, abbreviated as MOE[32]).

1.3 THE TSUKURU-KAI'S AIMS AND AGENDA

1.3.1 The Pilot Project: Kokumin no Rekishi

In the fall of 2000, the Tsukuru-kai completed a history textbook along with a civic studies text which were submitted to the MOE for examination. This double submission was a clear sign of the society's political intentions and its major concern—the relation of the citizen to the state. Although rumours had already spread about the contents of both text-

---

though some Tsukuru-kai publications indeed became bestsellers, Tawara (2001: 66–70) stresses that others achieved this status by artificial means by being printed in bulk to be given away and distributed to politicians.

[31] Nishibe was originally trained as an economist. He is the co-author of the Tsukuru-kai's civics textbook (see chapter 1.3.2) and author of *Kokumin no Dōtoku* (Morals of the Nation; Nishibe 2000), which, together with Nishio Kanji's *Kokumin no Rekishi* (History of the Nation; Nishio 1999) form part of an informal series published by Sankei Shinbun News Service.

[32] As the result of a restructuring of Japan's ministerial administration in early 2001, the Ministry of Education (Monbushō) was renamed the Ministry for Science and Education, Monbu Kagakushō.

books, earlier publications by Tsukuru-kai members left little doubt as to what kind of historical narrative the new history textbook would convey.

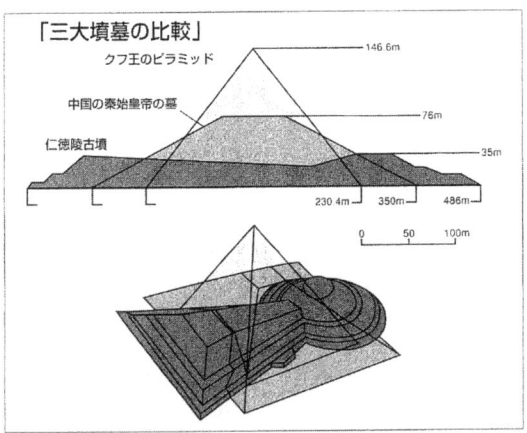

Ill. 4: Comparison of Japanese kofun tombs with the Egyptian pyramids (used by permission of Fusōsha).

In 1999, founding president Nishio Kanji had published his *History of the Nation* (*Kokumin no rekishi*, Nishio 1999), widely seen as a "pilot version" of the 2000 junior high school text, anticipating many of the claims to be made in the textbook. Throughout his voluminous book, Nishio describes Japan as a distinctive civilization (*dokuji no bunmei*) (Nishio 1999: 18) and stresses the equality (or even superiority) of Japanese cultural achievements with those of "the West", as well as Japan's neighbors Korea and China. Commentators such as Oguma Eiji claim that the Tsukuru-kai's insistence on comparing Japan to the West in order to establish Japanese "equality" is based in a "hefty inferiority complex" (Oguma and Ueno 2003: 64). In his book, Nishio describes the earthenware civilization (*doki bunmei*) of the prehistoric Jōmon period[33] as "the oldest civilization in the world" (Nishio 1999: 55f, 64), comparable in its long-term stability and unchanging character only to ancient Egypt (Nishio 1999: 66)—but eventually surpassing Egypt in the grandeur of its monuments, with the tombs of the Kofun period (300–600 a.d.) dwarfing even the pyramids (Nishio 1999: 291f; see ill. 4).[34]

---

[33] Most dictionaries of Japanese history date the Jōmon period from around 10,000 b.c. to 300 b.c.
[34] For further examples of Nishio's obsession with monumentality and (literally) "large" advances in civilization, see Nishio 1999: chapter 13. For a critical discussion of Nisho's thought in general, see Mishima 2000; 1999.

This "striving for the oldest" has been a facet of nationalist discourse since earliest times, and today is particularly popular in Asia where ancient pedigrees are readily attached to modern nations and a continuous "national tradition" of thousands of years is proclaimed even in states as young as Pakistan (Hobsbawm 1997: 5). Throughout history, historical reconstructions of this kind have often led to territorial conflicts and civil wars and are still sources of international friction. As early as the late 19th century, August Bebel, a social democratic member of the German Reichstag (parliament) argued against the pursuit of irredentism in foreign policy:

> Of course, we have sufficient [historical] reason to annex the German provinces of Russia along the Baltic Sea. We also have reason to make even larger annexations of French territory. We also could go back further in history and claim the whole of Switzerland, which once belonged to Germany; also Holland, a part of Belgium and so on. [...] Gentlemen, if you consider it as the chief principle of the theory of nationality that every country has the right to conquer back territory that once belonged to it—centuries or even longer ago—Germany would be in a state of constant warfare without any end in sight. (Bebel 1889: 44f)

Historian Eric Hobsbawm in retrospective makes a similar point:

> Few of the ideologies of intolerance are based on simple lies or fiction for which no evidence exists. After all, there was a battle of Kosovo in 1389, the Serb warriors and their allies were defeated by the Turks, and this did leave deep scars on the popular memory of the Serbs, although it does not follow that this justifies the oppression of the Albanians, who now form 90 per cent of the region's population, or the Serb claim that the land is essentially theirs. Denmark does not claim the large part of eastern England which was settled and ruled by Danes before the eleventh century, which continued to be known as the Danelaw and whose village names are still philologically Danish. (Hobsbawm 1997: 6f)

Hobsbawm's argument seems self-evident, even to a pro-Danish observer of world politics. As political scientist Dieter Senghaas (1994: 85f) has stressed, after the end of the Cold War it was particularly in the Balkans that the "discovery of national history" required the construction of "mystifying and glorifying narratives. Pasts are phantasized, empires long collapsed are brought back to life, and often, they become identical with future goals: Greater Serbia, Greater Aserbaichan, Greater Macedonia, Greater Romania, etc." Contemporary neonationalists often quite irrationally link the alleged antiquity of a nation to a glorious national past, and in many cases this leads to an ideological use of antiquity to stress the uniqueness or superiority of a given nation in the present—as in the writings of Nishio and Japanese neonationalism in general. Although some commentators have stressed the differences between traditional nationalism—with its strong emphasis on nostalgia and primordial antecedents for the nation—and the rise of historical revisionism or neonationalism in Japan as a manifestation of "urban populism" (Oguma and Ueno 2003: 3), the borders between the two are clearly permeable.

Certainly, in *Kokumin no Rekishi* Nishio lays particular emphasis on the prehistoric and early period of Japanese history in order to claim historical continuity—and by implication superiority over its neighbors—for the Japanese "nation". Exploiting the many gaps and uncertainties revealed by modern research into ancient Japanese history (cf. Hudson 1999), Nishio devotes a whole chapter (6) to the relationship of *myth* and history and stresses the role of myths as a source of knowledge of Japan's early history and the necessity of incorporating mythology into the construction of a national history. Of the 34 chapters in the book, ten deal with early Japanese history prior to the Nara period (710–794). To "prove" Japanese "equality" or even "superiority" to the West, Nishio frequently compares Japanese and European cultural and civilizational achievements, as at the beginning of the book where he equates Japanese art of the Kamakura period with the European Baroque. And in a chapter on the early modern period, an unidentified medieval Chinese [!] ship (120m long)—interpreted in a broadly Asian context and therefore seen as a legitimate example of *Japan's* superiority over the West—is pictured side by side with the much smaller but well-known "Santa Maria" sailed by Columbus (25,7m long) (Nishio 1999: 421). Comparisons with the West also extend into the modern period, when Nishio characterizes the Meiji Restoration (*Meiji ishin*) of 1868 as "more revolutionary than the revolutions of the West" (Nishio 1999: 475), and describes American militarism as "in a sense more aggressive than that of [wartime] Japan" (Nishio 1999: 585).

Even stronger than Nishio's resentment against the West are his contemptuous views of Japan's Asian neighbors. Nishio never passes up the opportunity to slap China and Korea in the face, whether he is criticizing the "low level of historical writing in China" (Nishio 1999: 152); characterizing China as a backward country (e.g. Nishio 1999: 419); or accusing Korea of ignoring disturbances in East Asia and reacting too slowly to the threat of Western imperialism, while Japan alone had the ability "to help herself" (Nishio 1999: chapter 23). His attitude to Korea is made all too clear at the beginning of chapter 32: "Contemplating Japanese-Korean relations has never been a pleasant task. Most Japanese probably feel this way." (Nishio 1999: 705) Nishio's claim to speak for the majority of Japanese conveniently ignores developments such as the recent "Korea boom" in Japan, particularly among Japanese youth (Saaler 2003a).

Nishio's ignorance about Korea becomes even clearer in his treatment of Japanese colonial rule in Korea and Japanese foreign policy in the early 20th century. Nishio stresses the role of Japan as a "liberator" in Asia, in particular of non-White peoples suppressed by Western imperialism—for example, in a detailed discussion of the "racial equality proposal" which Japan tabled for the charter of the League of Nations at the Paris peace conference in 1919 (Nishio 1999: 571–573). However, he fails to mention *Japanese* colonial rule in Korea which, in the same year, led to the brutal suppression of anti-Japanese uprisings known as the First March Movement (*san-ichi undō*). In passing over inconvenient facts such as these, Nishio brushes aside the background to the difficulties that characterize present-day Japanese-Korean relations, an ignorance which proceeds from wishful thinking about creating a national narrative of Japanese history. In an open "Letter to the Korean People" written in 2001, Nishio laments:

> The Japanese have their own history, just as the Koreans have theirs. Have we so far even once complained about Korean textbooks? Moreover, [Japan and Korea] are independent countries and sovereign states, and therefore interference in domestic affairs cannot be tolerated. This is the most minimal condition for talking about bilateral problems, and, moreover, it is only good manners. When I look at Korea's requests to Japan (*tai-Nichi yōkyū*)[35], I see [Koreans] as failing to understand even this [point], and most Japanese (*taitei no Nihonjin*) shrug their shoulders or shake their heads. (Nishio 2001: Internet)

A further controversial aspect of Nishio's book relates to the revisionist claim that "history is not a science." (Nishio 1999: 41) Nishio starts chapter 6 with this statement and, throughout his book, he justifies his claim for the creation of a "proud" national narrative by citing the recent emphasis in historiography on the character of history writing as construction or even as fiction. In 1973, Hayden White summarized modern doubts about the validity of history as a science:

---

[35] Here Nishio must be referring to the Korean government's request to revise the Tsukuru-kai textbook (see above), a request which was sent to the Ministry of Education and Science, not to "Japan".

1. Historical Revisionism in Contemporary Japan

What does it mean to *think historically*, and what are the unique characteristics of a specifically *historical method* of inquiry? These questions were debated throughout the nineteenth century by historians, philosophers, and social theorists, but usually within the context of the assumption that unambiguous answers could be provided for them. 'History' was considered to be a specific mode of existence, 'historical consciousness' a distinct mode of thought, and 'historical knowledge' an autonomous domain in the spectrum of the human and physical sciences. In the twentieth century, however, considerations of these questions have been undertaken in somewhat less self-confident mood and in the face of an apprehension that definite answers to them may not be possible. Continental European thinkers—from Valéry and Heidegger to Sartre, Lévi-Strauss, and Michel Foucault—have cast serious doubts on the value of a specifically 'historical' consciousness, stressed the fictive character of historical reconstructions, and challenged history's claims to a place among the sciences. (White 1973: 1f; italics in original).

White concluded that "history is *not* a science, or [...] at best a protoscience with specifically determinable nonscientific elements in its constitution." (White 1973: 21) In his view, historical facts exist only as a function of prior concepts and problems.[36] These points have a particular resonance in the case of Japan, where *historical fiction* has had a considerable influence on the historical consciousness of postwar Japanese. The historical novels (*rekishi shōsetsu*) of Shiba Ryōtarō have been considered particularly important in this regard, as Nakamura Masanori (1998) has pointed out. "Shiba's works of historical fiction and criticism have had unparalleled influence on the historical consciousness of the Japanese people." (Nakamura 1998: 26; cf. also Kang 2003: 109) Not only are his novels bestsellers (and longsellers), but they are also continuously recycled in TV series, movies and new media such as the internet and on CD-ROMs (cf. Saaler 2002b; see below chapter 3.3). In view of the popularity of historical novels and their recycling in the mass media, commentators have recently drawn attention to the similarities between professional history writing ("historical science"[37] or academic history) and historical

---

[36] See Iggers 1997 for an overview over this debate in general.
[37] Georg Iggers has pointed out that "English speakers are not comfortable with the term 'historical science' (*Geschichtswissenschaft*), commonly used in continental European but also East Asian languages to distinguish history as a discipline from history as literary pursuit." (Iggers 1997: 17) Such linguistic differences reflect different perceptions of and ideas about history in English-speaking countries and countries like Japan and Germany.

fiction. Narita Ryūichi (2003) has traced these links in the writings of Shiba Ryōtarō:

> The act of combining 'historical facts' (*shijitsu*) with other 'historical facts' and thereby creating an historical portrait (*rekishi-zō*) is called historical narrative (*rekishi jojutsu*). Although the aim of historical narrative is to provide a real picture of history, in a given historical portrait the 'interpretation' of the author also comes to the fore. [...] It is obvious that there are differences between the interpretation and the narrative of Shiba on the one hand and the interpretation and narrative of historians on the other. However, on the level of presenting a real portrait of history in which rival interpretations are weighed against one another, neither historians nor historical novelists can claim superiority or inferiority. (Narita 2003: 37)

However, notwithstanding the fact that academic history "uses many of the methods of fiction and often aspires to be literary", it still "claims a particular relation to truth that is different from fiction" (Suny 2001: 336; cf. also Hobsbawm 1997: 339f; Cornelißen 2001: 21; Abe 2004: 175; Assmann 1999: 143f; Iggers 1997: 2f, 12, 118f). As Eric Hobsbawm has argued in his book *On History*:

> It has become fashionable in recent decades, not least among people who think of themselves as on the left, to deny that objective reality is accessible, since what we call 'facts' exist only as a function of prior concepts and problems formulated in terms of these. The past we study is only a construct of our minds. [...] I strongly defend the view that what historians investigate is real. The point from which historians must start [...] is the fundamental and, for them, absolutely central *distinction between establishable fact and fiction*, between historical statements based on evidence and subject to evidence and those which are not. (Hobsbawm 1997: viii, 337f; italics added)

Hobsbawm elaborates in another essay in the same volume:

> We have a responsibility to historical facts in general, and for criticizing the politico-ideological abuse of history in particular. [...] The rise of 'postmodernist' intellectual fashions in Western universities [...] impl[ies] that all 'facts' claiming objective existence are simply intellectual constructions—in short, that there is no clear difference between fact and fiction. But [...] we cannot invent our facts. Either Elvis Presley is dead or he isn't. The question can be answered unambiguously on the basis of evidence, insofar as reliable evidence is available [...]. (Hobsbawm 1996: 6, cf. also chapter 9, 337f)

Mary Fulbrook moreover argues that

> professional history is generally held [...] to be something other than politics by other means. It is supposed to be telling us something true about the past—not something that is convenient from one or another political standpoint in the present. Historians [...] are supposedly pursuing the reconstruction and representation of the past 'as it really was', and not constructing a 'usable past' for the present. (Fulbrook 2004: 1)

Hobsbawm and Fulbrook would find much support from Japanese professional historians—whose political "neutrality" is, however, compromised in the eyes of their opponents as a result of their methodological connections with Marxism. Japanese historians themselves admit that they have a long road yet to travel since, while "Western European academic history aims at verifying historical fact vis-à-vis 'historical myth', in the controversy over Japanese history textbooks the appraisal of historical facts is the actual problem." (Abe 2004: 178) However, Japanese professional historians also have to contend with a blurring of historical fact and fiction. Historical fiction and especially historical novels (*rekishi shōsetsu*) are very popular in Japan and since the 1960s have reached a wide audience. Such dramatized history is also recycled in television programs such as the annual series *taiga dorama* in NHK, which in its most recent season has taken up the history of the Shinsengumi, a group of masterless samurai (*rōnin*) active at the end of the Tokugawa period (1600–1867) (cf. Miyachi 2004).

While some Japanese historians, including some of the most fervent critics of historical revisionism, would subscribe to the "inventive" and "fictive" character of professional historiography (Narita 2003), the position of academic history in Japan has also been challenged by historical revisionists utilizing "post-modern" and constructivist methods, claiming that they are doing nothing more than constructing one historical narrative—that of the proud nation—in opposition to the prevailing masochistic narrative. However, in doing so, they are self-contradictory. For although revisionists take pride in constructing a narrative that excludes Japan's wartime atrocities without openly denying them,[38] the number of revisionist writings that lay claim to "the truth" (*shinjitsu*) about modern Japanese history—and the exclusive truth—is astonishingly high (Maeno 2003; Yasukuni Jinja Shamusho 2002; Rekishi Kentō Iinkai 1995: 29).

---

[38] While some revisionists flatly deny wartime atrocities, the extent of this depends on the individual writer and the topic under discussion.

Although some chapters of Japan's wartime history, such as the Nanjing massacre, "challenge the limits of positivist empiricism" (Yang 1999: 863, c.f. also Yang 2000: 136f) that characterized mainstream Japanese history in the postwar period, and indicate the necessity of a "reconsideration of some of the most basic tenets of historical inquiry" (Yang 1999: 864), historical revisionism is ill-equipped to offer solutions to these problems. There can be no common ground in exploring, for example, the reasons for the Asia-Pacific War—a central topic of discussion between revisionists and mainstream historians. Such an impasse should not keep Japanese from seeking a consensus on their collective history—such as was found in a postwar Germany struggling to "come to terms with the past" of the Nazi era with its atrocities. However, the difficulties of arriving at a balanced view of history are formidable, as Reinhard Koselleck has pointed out: "Whoever gets involved in causal explanations will always find reasons for what he wishes to demonstrate, but, at the same time, any history, because it is ex post facto, is subject to final constraints." (Koselleck 2002: 11f) The question, therefore, seems to be whether the "new" causality set up by historical revisionism against established historical causalities is going to be *convincing* enough to a majority of Japanese to replace established interpretations of history. This seems unlikely at present, since the revisionist narrative depends to a high degree on wartime rhetoric and previously deconstructed (and long discredited) narratives, and also on denying or playing down certain wartime atrocities that are by now deeply embedded in the Japanese collective memory (see chapter 3).

The main problem therefore seems to lie not so much in the academic question whether or to what degree history is a "real" science or only a "protoscience", but rather in the resurfacing of a close relationship between history and the nation. When history was first constituted as a "science" in the mid 19th century, Leopold von Ranke and his followers considered the "nation" to be the "sole possible unit of social organization" and "national groups [...] the sole viable units of historical investigation"—providing a legacy which still haunts professional history today (White 1973: 175; cf. also Koselleck 2002: 11). Academic history now stands at a crossroads in its relation to the concept of the nation-state: while contemporary historians aim for an "objective" understanding of political, social and cultural processes, in many countries history cannot escape its legacy as a byproduct of the development of the "nation" and a tool for legitimizing nations and nation-states. Ronald Suny summarizes the issues:

> Historians participate in the active imagination of those political communities that we call nations as they elaborate the narratives

that make up national histories. Yet as historians helped generate national consciousness and nationalism, their own discipline acquired the task of 'discovering' or 'recovering' the 'national' past. Even as history as a discipline helped constitute the nation, the nation-form determined the categories in which history was written and the purposes it was to serve. At the same time historians sought to render an objective understanding of the past and propose a critique of what they considered to be 'mythological' formulations. Though they often provided a base for the legitimation of nations and states, historians also questioned the metanarratives of nationalism and the restriction of history to national history. (Suny 2001: 335)

The complex task of providing the Japanese state and nation with a legitimization built upon prewar assumptions and rhetoric is the crucial challenge presented to mainstream Japanese historians by the rise of historical revisionism. The "New History Textbook" is a major tool adopted by revisionists to disseminate their views, and we turn now to examine the textbooks—both in history and civic studies—issued by the Tsukuru-kai in fall 2000 and submitted to the Monbushō for examination.

1.3.2 The Tsukuru-kai's "New History Textbook" and "New Civics Textbook"

Although the examination process (*kentei*) at the Monbushō is usually kept secret, it took only a few weeks before an early version of the Tsukuru-kai history textbook, the "white-cover book" (*shiro-byōshi-bon*), was leaked and circulated amongst scholars and other interested parties. As I discuss more fully in chapter 1.4, both of the Tsukuru-kai textbooks passed the Monbushō examination and were approved in revised versions (*shūsei-bon*) identical to those later sold in bookstores (*shihan-bon*).[39] Since access to the version submitted for examination (*shiro-byōshi-bon*) was restricted (at least in theory), the following discussion refers to the published editions (Nishio et al. 2001; Nishibe et al. 2001). It is important to note that the contents of the Tsukuru-kai history textbook did not change in *character* from the first version to the second, but only in terms of phrasing and degree. The contents of the revised version still came in

---

[39] Normally, junior high textbooks are not available in bookshops but are distributed exclusively to schools after orders have been placed at the Ministry for Education and Science (see chapter 1.4). More than 750,000 copies of the "bookshop edition" (*shihanbon*) of both Tsukuru-kai textbooks had been sold by the end of 2001. Uesugi 2003a.

for some harsh criticism both within Japan (Rekishigaku Kenkyūkai 2001) and abroad.

The two Tsukuru-kai textbooks generally followed the "guidelines" outlined by Nishio Kanji in his *Kokumin no rekishi*. The following points summarize the criticisms that have been directed against them (cf. also Kimijima 2001: passim; Tawara 2001: chapter 1; Chung 2003a: 96–98; Nelson 2003; Irie 2004: chapter 2 for detailed criticism):

- The history textbook presents Japan as a closed cultural entity with a strong emphasis on continuity from the pre-historic period until the present. No attempt is made to distinguish between Japan as a nation, as the name of a state, and as a geographic term.
- It presents Japanese history as centered on the Emperor (*kōkoku shikan*) in order to stress historical continuity.
- It places strong emphasis on the equality of Japan's development with the West and the superiority of Japan's historical development compared to other Asian countries.
- It conveys discriminatory and condescending views of Japan's neighbors who are presented as inferior and lagging behind in development throughout their history.
- It presents Japan's imperialism in the 1930s and 1940s as a purely defensive measure directed against the penetration of the European powers and the U.S. into East Asia.
- It presents the wars conducted by Japan from 1931–1945 as wars for the liberation of Asia; it makes no mention of war atrocities and the consequences of Japanese colonialism, or of resistance to Japanese colonization and occupation within the Asian nations affected.
- Both the history and civics textbooks are in general affirmative of war as a legitimate tool of the state to solve international conflicts.
- The civics textbook questions some of the central principles of the Japanese Constitution, such as the war-renouncing Article 9 and gender equality.
- Both textbooks are written at too high a level for junior high school (grades seven to nine).
- Both textbooks—in the first as well as the revised editions—contain many errors of detail and present one-sided, arbitrary or distorted views of history as well as of contemporary Japanese polity and society.

In what follows, I briefly raise some general questions and discuss a few examples to illustrate the problematic character of the Tsukuru-kai textbooks. The question of their suitability as textbooks for junior high school can be gauged by comparing them with texts already prescribed for junior high school or even high school.

In their treatment of just a single example of modern Japanese history, it is clear that for the Tsukuru-kai educational objectives take second place to the propagation of their political aims and their views about history. My example is the conflict known as the Siberian Intervention (1918–1922), a relatively unknown but large-scale war and a significant part of Japan's modern history. In most Japanese history textbooks designed for use in high schools, this episode is usually dealt with in a short paragraph of five to eight lines (it is given seven lines in the 1984 edition of Yamakawa Shuppansha's *Nihonshi*), typically matched with a photograph of Japanese troops marching down the streets of Vladivostok. In the seven textbooks distributed by mainstream publishers for *junior* high school, the Siberian Intervention is treated even more briefly. By contrast, the Tsukuru-kai textbook contains a detailed account that is nonetheless difficult to understand—even for adults, as I have confirmed by showing the passage to laypeople without any specialist historical knowledge. The Tsukuru-kai history text—which is aimed at 13 to 15-year-olds—has eleven lines on the Siberian Intervention, illustrated by a map and a photograph, supported by a further paragraph of 15 lines on the Russian Revolution as background to the Siberian Intervention. The text on the Russian Revolution is glossed as follows:

> According to Marxism, revolutions[40] occur in countries in which capitalism is highly developed, and capitalism is inevitably replaced with Socialism. However, the first revolution occurred in Russia [sic], where capitalism was not yet developed. Moreover, in later history no revolutions occurred in countries with a civil society that guaranteed the freedom of the individual and (or?) where capitalism had succeeded. (Nishio et al. 2001: 246)

According to the book's index, the term "Marxism" occurs here for the first time, and the terms "Socialism" and "Capitalism" occur only once previously,[41] but only in fleeting references. In the absence of basic information about terms and concepts like these, the above paragraph seems hardly suited for young teenagers. Indeed, few Japanese adults could make sense out of this passage when asked to comment. And the bald reference to the Russian Revolution as the "*first* revolution" is positively misleading.

---

[40] The text refers here to "revolutions" in general—not to communist revolutions, socialist revolutions or any specific kind of revolution.
[41] Although their occurrence on page 246 fails to appear in the index.

This and many other factual errors in the Tsukuru-kai history text can be explained by the priority given to the group's political agenda over pedagogical or academic issues. Many errors remain even in the revised edition, notwithstanding the numerous revisions requested by the Monbushō (see chapter 1.4) and the fact that a number of reputable historians, such as Itō Takashi or Sakamoto Takao, contributed to the book. Many of these errors and distortions are listed in various publications (Rekishigaku Kenkyūkai 2001) and websites.[42]

A further example illustrates the tendency of the Tsukuru-kai to identify myth with proven fact. This time, the setting is Japanese prehistory or the "dawn of Japan" (*Nihon no akebono*) (Nishio et al. 2001: 20)—here presented as a primordial, eternal entity. In chapters 2.6 and 2.7, the legendary conquest of the Yamato area in central Japan by the mythical first Emperor Jimmu (page 36), and the legendary Yamatotakeru's conquest of the Kantō region (page 42–43) are presented as historical facts, rather than as myths that probably contain a core of historical truth. Maps showing details of both conquests are provided (Nishio et al 2001: 36, 43), and Yamatotakeru, Jimmu Tennō, the sun goddess Amaterasu Ōmikami, the wind god Susanoō, and Japan's creator gods Izanami and Izanagi appear without further comment in the "Index of Persons" (*jinmei sakuin*) at the end of the book. The objective is clear: the origins of the nation are projected back into remote antiquity in order to evoke the legitimacy of the current order which is considered a natural product of historical continuity and antiquity.

The Japanese myths *Kojiki* and *Nihongi* have long been considered by conservatives as "the soul, the home (*furusato*) and the identity (*aidentitī*) of the Japanese (*Nihonjin*). [...] The 'Japanese myths' are the spiritual inheritance of the Japanese race (*Nihon minzoku*)." (Rekishi Kentō Iinkai 1995: 385f) In Japanese prewar textbooks, the myths and Japan's character as the "land of the gods" was very much emphasized, and the Tsukuru-kai textbook for history in many places reminds of the contents of prewar textbooks (Irie 2001). To put more emphasis on Japanese tradition, Japan's origins as the 'land of the gods' therefore always has stood in the center of postwar historical revisionism, and with the appearance of the Tsukuru-kai textbook, the quest for "a correct history textbook based on the 'Japanese myths'" (Rekishi Kentō Iinkai 1995: 397) therefore seems to have been fulfilled. The above example nicely illustrates the group's claim that history is not a science, but rather offers

---

[42] See for example http://www.h2.dion.ne.jp/~kyokasho/0_con004.htm (last accessed on 10 August 2004).

materials to construct a narrative that will contribute to the formation of a national identity.

The Tsukuru-kai history textbook has also come in for criticism for omitting unpalatable and inconvenient parts of Japanese history. Of course, history writing always involves selecting facts and assembling them into a plausible and logical account. However, there are limits to the historian's legitimate task of selection—it would be impossible to write the history of modern Germany without referring to Germany's colonial empire or the atrocities committed during World War II; or a history of Spain that failed to mention the civil war; or an Indian history that omitted the assassination of Mahatma Gandhi. Yet the Tsukuru-kai textbook contains scarcely any reference to Japanese colonial rule in Korea (Nishio et al. 2001: 240f), not to mention such issues as Unit 731 or the "military comfort women".[43] It is understandable that Korea would protest the teaching of this version of history to Japanese youngsters—just as Poland would object to German textbooks that omitted all mention of the Nazi massacres committed in Poland during World War II.

As in the writings of Nishio, Korea is treated with particular disdain in the Tsukuru-kai textbook. The Japanese colonization of Korea is described as contributing to the development and modernization of the country, while Japan's assimilation policies and the brutal suppression of resistance are not mentioned at all. The colonization of Korea is described as a "natural" process arising from geographical factors, and made unavoidable by the impact of European imperialism in East Asia. In this view, Korea lacks any will of its own and is a mere appendage of Japan, subservient to Japanese security needs:

> Japan is an island country (*shimaguni*) surrounded by oceans, not far distant from the Eurasian continent. The Korean peninsula juts out towards Japan from the continent like an arm. If in those days the Korean peninsula had come under the control of a power hostile to Japan, it would have made a suitable base for an attack on Japan which, as an island country lacking hinterland, would have had great difficulty in defending the nation. (Nishio et al. 2001: 216)

Lacking any subjectivity of its own, Korea is seen only as a potential base for an attack on Japan by an unnamed "large power" and therefore, the

---

[43] The Nanjing Incident is actually mentioned in the book, but in relation to the IMTFE rather than the war (Nishio et al. 2001: 295). The text stresses that although accusations of a massacre in Nanjing were made at the IMTFE, the ongoing debate on the issue does not allow a final judgment (Nishio et al. 2001: 295).

logic goes, became the subject of an unavoidable and preemptive colonization by Japan. This is what the passage suggests, although the intended audience would have difficulty grasping its significance, a difficulty exacerbated by its isolated place in the textbook. The phrase "in those days" (*tōji*) is particularly obscure. The previous chapter ends with the Rescript of Education 1890, and the passage in question begins a chapter headed "The Sino-Japanese War and the Breakdown of the Sinocentric World System". A map on the same page showing "East Asia in the second half of the 19th century" (Nishio et al. 2001: 216) assumes a fair degree of background knowledge in the book's audience. Leaving Korea behind, the text moves swiftly on to describe the Russian thrust for an "ice-free port" as the main reason for the impending Japanese-Russian conflict—implying, once again, the "natural" causes of Japanese military intervention in East Asia and the unavoidable character of Japanese expansion on the Asian continent.

The civic studies text drawn up by the Tsukuru-kai raises similar contentious issues.[44] The presentation of both history *and* civics textbooks demonstrates the organization's political aim of fostering pro-state attitudes and strengthening allegiance to state and nation (which are treated almost synonymously in the textbooks) in young Japanese. However, a closer look at the civics textbook suggests that, far from fostering an understanding of the existing state structure, the Tsukuru-kai rejects many of the established features of postwar Japan and remains ambiguous about aspects of the Constitution and other laws. Instead, the text puts a heavy emphasis on the type of moral education (Nishibe et al. 2001: 43) common in prewar Japan,[45] stressing the difference between the "individualist citizen" (*shimin*) who leads "a private existence (*shiteki sonzai*) and pursues his own, private profit (*shiteki rieki*), his own rights and his own desires" and the "society-oriented individual (*kōmin*)" who leads "a public life (*kōteki sonzai*) dedicated to the good of the whole society and primarily motivated by [the common] interest (*kanshin*)" (Nishibe et al. 2001: 24). The textbook laments the "egoism" of Japanese youth, illustrated by such examples as illegally parked bicycles in front of a bus stop or young people sporting brand-name goods (*burando-hin*) (Nishibe et al. 2001: 34, 149). While the book makes the by-now familiar demands for loyalty to the state and readiness to make sacrifices for it, including

---

[44] As a result of the stir caused by the history text, the society's civics textbook has received hardly any attention. The only substantial discussions so far have been Oguma Eiji's article in the journal *Sekai*, reprinted in Oguma and Ueno 2003 (chapter 2), and Irie 2004.

[45] For an overview of the contents of prewar Japanese textbooks, see Irie 2001.

military service (Nishibe et al. 2001: 7), the Japanese political system is portrayed in the brightest colours (chapter 2), glossing over the numerous corruption scandals and embarrassing episodes of recent years. Although coming four years after the book's publication, the May 2004 revelation that many (probably most) members of the Japanese Diet failed (at least temporarily) to pay their contributions to the National Pension Insurance Fund (*kokumin nenkin hoken*) is surely a blunt violation of the lofty principle of contributing to the "public good".[46]

Far from offering a balanced introduction to the social, political and constitutional structures of contemporary Japan, the civics textbook lays the groundwork to recruit support for a change to the present system along the lines envisaged by historical revisionism.[47] This becomes obvious in the veiled criticism directed at the status quo throughout the book. For example, a paragraph on "gender equality" (*danjo byōdō*) in chapter 2 states:

> Nowadays, as seen in the stipulations of the Equal Employment Opportunity Law or in the Basic Law for a Gender-equal Society, there is a tendency to set aside assigned roles based on sex and to strive for self-fulfillment through one's personal capabilities. However (*shikashi*), at the same time, consideration must be given to the separation of roles based on the physiological and physical differences between men and women. (Nishibe et al. 2001: 64)

A few pages later we find the following statement concerning "freedom of expression" (*hyōgen no jiyū*):

> [Among the civil rights stipulated in the Constitution], freedom of expression is particularly important. This includes speech, publication, music, the internet and demonstrations. Freedom of expression is essential for a democratic polity in which the people decide the character of the political system. [...] However (*shikashi*), on the other hand, there is always the danger that the privacy or the feelings of others might be impaired or that *the order or morals of society* might be undermined, and it is important to acknowledge this. (Nishibe et al. 2001: 68; italics added)

---

[46] For a discussion of similar inconsistencies in wartime Japan, such as the discovery of stockpiled goods in the bombed-out home of General Araki Sadao at a time of severe food shortages, see Oguma 2002: 37f.

[47] See Irie 2004: chapter 1 for a detailed analysis of the civic textbook's critique of the present system.

Such remarks reflect less a concern for the privacy of citizens as for the privacy of *politicians*, who in 2003 pushed a law through the Diet restricting the rights of journalists to investigate the affairs of politicians where private issues are involved—which are, of course, a matter of definition. In another passage, again by subtle deployment of the adverb "however" (*shikashi*), the Tsukuru-kai reveals its inclination to curb the individual's right to privacy:

> Today, many rights are considered as deriving from the Constitution even though some of them are not stipulated in it but rather guaranteed through [national] laws and [the edicts of] regional administrative bodies. [...] The people's right to know is guaranteed in the Access to Information Law (1999). Further, to protect the individual against [unwarranted] freedom of expression, a guarantee of the right to privacy is also being strongly advocated [based on the Constitution]. [...] However, against the recent trend to derive new rights from the Constitution, critics claim that the rights actually defined in it are being devalued as a result of these developments, and new rights are being advocated purely for the sake of legitimizing *personal desires and profits*. (Nishibe et al. 2001: 74; italics added)

Throughout, the book follows the line taken by its main author Nishibe Susumu in portraying the Japanese as selfish, egoistical and uninterested in the common good. Continually stressing the negative aspects of "individualism" and demanding more weight be given to the family, the local community and ultimately the state, the textbook offers no insights into resolving conflicting loyalties to the family and the local community on the one hand, and loyalty to the state on the other (Oguma and Ueno 2003: 45, 55f)—conflicts embedded in Japanese history and culture (Shimazu 2001; Irie 2001: 148). Further, throughout the civics textbook, no mention is made of NPOs and NGOs, the many citizens' movements (*shimin undō*) and the citizen ballots (*shimin tōhyō*) on urgent political questions characteristic of contemporary Japan.[48] The pictorial introduction to the book shows members of the Self-Defense Forces carrying out rescue missions after the Great Hanshin Earthquake in 1995, but ignores the important work of citizens' groups organized to support victims of the earthquake. Disturbingly, however, these pictures also conjure up a Japan of the future—a "superpower" (*taikoku Nihon*) in which the military plays a primary role (Nishibe et al. 2001: 9). The selection of graphics throughout the book also makes its political affiliations clear, as Irie Yōko

---

[48] Indeed, citizen ballots are rejected as a legitimate means of "direct politics" (Nishibe et al. 2001: 79).

(2004: 44f) has shown. Newspaper graphics used to illustrate ongoing national debates such as the controversy over the revision of Japan's defense strategy are all taken from the three conservative papers, *Yomiuri Shinbun* (five times), *Nihon Keizai Shinbun* (twice) and *Sankei Shinbun* (twelve times). None are drawn from major liberal newspapers such as *Asahi Shinbun* and *Mainichi Shinbun*, with circulations of nine million and four million respectively.

In sum, the society portrayed in the Tsukuru-kai civic studies textbook places little emphasis on the citizen as independent agent, on citizens' rights or citizens' participation in the political process, but rather presents a picture of obedient citizens acquiescing in the will of the political elite. A more detailed analysis of the Tsukuru-kai's aims and agenda lies outside the scope of this study and must await future research. However, sufficient evidence has been presented here to verify the *political implications* of the claims of historical revisionism and its vision of state and society as revealed in the civic studies textbook in particular. The next question to be asked is: how much influence do such views wield in Japanese society? The first test of the popularity of the Tsukuru-kai and its backers came with the examination and adoption processes applied to its proposed textbooks in late 2000 and spring/summer 2001.

1.4 TEXTBOOK APPROVAL AND SELECTION 2000/2001

When in fall 2000 the Tsukuru-kai submitted its textbooks for junior high school classes in history (*rekishi*) and civic education (*kōmin*) to the Ministry of Education for examination (*kentei*),[49] few expected these "pedestrian texts" to pass. Their revisionist character along with many disturbing details and errors of fact (Tawara 2001; Richter 2001; Kimijima 2001) made it unlikely that the Monbushō examiners would give their approval. Obviously, the officials in the Monbushō were also quite sceptical, since the examination results showed that the textbooks submitted by the Tsukuru-kai, to be published by Fusōsha were not suitable for classroom use. Although both texts established a new record[50] for the number of

---

[49] For details of the examination process cf. Petersen 2001: 60f; *Kyōkasho Repōto* 2002: 56–60.

[50] Only a single case in the past exceeded the number of revisions required by the Monbushō from Fusōsha—a high school history textbook produced by revisionist authors in the early 1980s. Entitled *Shinpen Nihonshi*, it was first published by Hara Shobō and later by Kokusho Kankōkai. Drawn up by the rightist association Nihon o Mamoru Kokumin Kaigi (Peoples' Conference to

revisions demanded by the Monbushō, the ministry surprised observers by announcing that, after the revisions had been made, the textbook would receive its approval.

Table 1: Number of revisions demanded by the Monbushō for the first drafts (*shiro byōshibon*) of history and civic textbooks for junior high schools produced by 8 publishers.

Publisher	Fusōsha	Teikoku Shoin	Shimizu Shoin	Kyōiku Shuppan	Tōkyō Shoseki	Nihon Bunkyō Shuppan	Nihon Shoseki	Ōsaka Shoseki	Average (omitting Fusōsha)
History	137	29	22	23	18	35	35	13	25
Civic	99	35	22	16	17	34	60	24	30

The figures collated in Table 1 above speak for themselves. While the average number of revisions requested for history texts in 2000 for the other seven textbook publishers was 25, in Fusōsha's case the figure was 137; and the same figures for the civic textbooks were 30 and 99 respectively. Although the results of the Monbushō examination process are not made public, details were soon leaked to academia and a version of the draft history text with notes by the examiners was circulated.[51] It soon became clear that the question was more than one of numbers: while for most publishers only minor revisions—spellings of names and places, errors involving dates or faulty sentence structure—are required, in the case of the Fusōsha/Tsukuru-kai textbook, particularly the section on modern history, whole paragraphs were marked for revision. Even the conservative Monbushō examiners had to acknowledge fundamental flaws in the way the Tsukuru-kai text sought to communicate Japanese history to schoolchildren.

However, the Tsukuru-kai textbook eventually received approval from the ministry in April 2001. This came as a shock not only to Japan's neighbors, but also to large sectors of Japanese society and academia. As numerous commentators observed, even after the revisions had been made the history text still remained unsuitable for use in the classroom. Shortly after the decision was made, the Historical Science Society of Japan (Rekishigaku Kenkyūkai) published a booklet listing dozens of mistakes that had been overlooked in the Monbushō examination process, in addition to clear distortions of historical fact (Rekishigaku Kenkyūkai 2001).

Protect Japan), it had to be revised in more than 500 places and was hardly ever used in the classroom—no more than 9,000 copies were ever in print at any one time. The success of *Shinpen Nihonshi* was further hindered because—unlike the practice in junior high schools—senior high school textbooks are selected by individual schools (see further below).

[51] A detailed list of notes by the Monbushō examiners is available at http:// www.h2.dion.ne.jp/~kyokasho/kentei/huso-reki.htm (last accessed on 25 October 2003).

The uproar incited by the unexpected approval of the Tsukuru-kai textbooks led to organized resistance against their use in schools. This resistance developed into a citizens' movement that has exerted a decisive influence on the textbook issue. While the choice of textbooks for senior high school classes (years 10 to 12) is left to individual schools after approval (*kentei*) by the Ministry for Education and Science, responsibility for the selection (*saitaku*) of textbooks for junior high schools (years 7 to 9) and elementary schools lies in the hands of regional selection boards (*saitaku kyōgikai* or *saitaku shingikai*). These boards are established as advisory bodies by the education committees of local municipalities[52] (*shichōzon kyōiku iinkai*). In the case of senior high schools, the direct participation of teachers and parents in the selection procedure for textbooks is guaranteed. Elementary and junior high schools, on the other hand, are subject to a mixture of bureaucratic decision-making and selection through citizen participation, with the composition of regional selection boards being heavily influenced by the administrative structure and political flavour of the prefecture involved. Discussions over the interpretation and practice of the selection procedure for junior high schools revealed a new facet of the textbook dispute and became a focus of contention between the bureaucracy and the Tsukuru-kai on the one hand—who already shared numerous links—and diverse groups of concerned citizens such as teachers, parents and even students.

The textbook selection procedure adopted for elementary and junior high schools had important implications (cf. ill. 5). In early 2001, 544 regional selection districts (*saitaku chiku*) existed in Japan. In a conurbation this means that each local municipality—e.g., in the Tōkyō prefecture every city district (*ku*) and every city (*shi*)—represents one selection district, while in rural areas several municipalities are amalgamated into a single district (for more details, cf. *Kyōkasho Repōto* 2002: 62–63). For instance, in the Shimo-tsuga selection district in Tochigi prefecture two cities (*shi*) and eight localities (*machi*) have been grouped together. In those selection districts that coincide with a local authority, the education committee of the local municipality (*shichōzon kyōiku iinkai*) decides which textbooks will be used, while in the other selection districts this task is handled by temporary regional selection boards (*saitaku shingikai, saitaku*

---

[52] Within the space of only a few months each year (from April to July) each committee must choose one textbook for each of the 11 subjects taught at elementary school and for the 14 subjects taught at junior high; during this period they may assess more than 400 textbooks. Exceptions to this system include private junior high schools that select their own textbooks, as well as schools governed by the education committees of individual prefectures, e.g., special schools (*yōgo gakkō*).

kyōgikai). These boards evaluate textbook drafts for elementary and junior high schools, and then forward "recommendations" to the education committees of the local municipalities before being dissolved. With around a dozen members (their size depends on the number of local authorities they are advising), the selection boards consist mainly of teachers and members of the education committees or the local administrative bodies.[53] In contrast to senior high schools, where discussions about teaching materials are held in individual schools each year, textbook selection for elementary and junior high schools is carried out only once every four years by the selection boards and municipal education committees.

Ill. 5: Selection Process (*saitaku seido*) for textbooks in Japanese junior high schools (simplified diagram) (Source: Author).

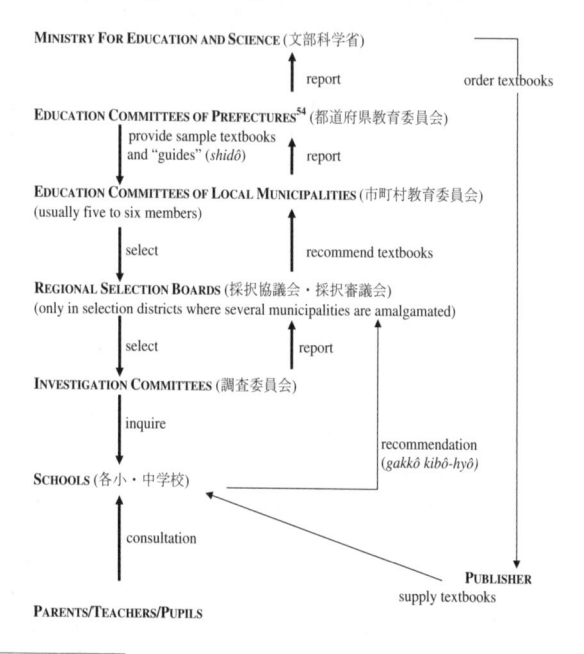

MINISTRY FOR EDUCATION AND SCIENCE (文部科学省)
↑ report   order textbooks

EDUCATION COMMITTEES OF PREFECTURES[54] (都道府県教育委員会)
↓ provide sample textbooks and "guides" (*shidô*)   ↑ report

EDUCATION COMMITTEES OF LOCAL MUNICIPALITIES (市町村教育委員会)
(usually five to six members)
↓ select   ↑ recommend textbooks

REGIONAL SELECTION BOARDS (採択協議会・採択審議会)
(only in selection districts where several municipalities are amalgamated)
↓ select   ↑ report

INVESTIGATION COMMITTEES (調査委員会)
↓ inquire

recommendation (*gakkô kibô-hyô*)

SCHOOLS (各小・中学校)
↑ consultation

PUBLISHER
supply textbooks

PARENTS/TEACHERS/PUPILS

---

[53] Regulations concerning terminology (*saitaku kyōgikai, saitaku shingikai, sentei shingikai*) as well as the size and composition of the selection committees and other details of the selection procedure differ greatly in each prefecture.

[54] The position of the education boards appointed in each prefecture differs from place to place. With the aid of guidelines and administrative "leadership", an individual prefecture can strongly influence the selection procedure, resulting in a unified selection of textbooks for all districts and communities in some prefectures. However, in general, the education committees of the municipalities as well as the regional selection boards exert a greater influence in the choice of textbooks.

The procedure for choosing junior high school textbooks is a complex one. In most cases each member of the regional selection board is allocated one or two of the subject-areas taught in the curriculum. The members view all the textbooks submitted, and convene research sub-committees (*chōsa iinkai*) to consider the recommendations put forward by the schools in the process known as *gakkō kibō-hyō* (whereby each school in the selection district concerned proposes its favored textbooks), as well as other expert opinion. The research committees consult with school principals and teachers and sometimes make a preselection from the textbooks submitted for approval, which is a process known as *shibori-komi*; in most cases two or three textbooks in each subject-area are recommended to the selection boards (Tawara 2001: 84–88; Net 2000: 92–93, 99; Yoshizawa 2001: 123). On the basis of this information and the expert opinion collated, the responsible member of the selection board recommends one to three books in his or her area. The board then either chooses a single textbook from these recommendations or confirms the recommendation put forward by the committee member responsible.

The selection boards then submit their recommendations to the education committees of the local municipalities (*shichōson kyōiku iinkai*). These committees must submit a written report to the education committee of their prefecture (*todōfuken kyōiku iinkai*) before August 15 of the same year. The prefecture administration summarizes all recommendations received from the entire prefecture, calculates the number of textbooks required for the following year, and informs the Ministry for Education and Science in Tōkyō. The textbooks selected will then be used in all elementary and junior high schools in the district concerned. They are delivered to the schools by the publisher based on orders submitted to the Ministry. In Japan, teaching materials for lower-level education are distributed free of charge in accordance with the Law on the Free Provision of Textbooks for Schools in the Level of Compulsory Education (Gimu Kyōiku Shogakkō no Kyōka-yō Tosho no Mushō ni kan-suru Hōritsu) passed in 1963 (Tawara 2001: 100; Net 2000: 100; Monbu Kagakushō 1999). The Ministry for Education and Science remunerates the publishing houses at a fixed price per textbook—a history textbook used in a junior high school costs around 703 Yen (approx. 5.20 Euro) per copy (Murai 2001: 123).

Until the summer of 2001 the passing of textbook recommendations along the chain from the regional selection boards to the Ministry in Tōkyō was regarded as a pure formality, because previously nobody had ever questioned a "recommendation" put forward by a selection board. The recommendations of the boards, which had been established solely for the purpose of choosing textbooks, were understood as binding. However, following recent developments at the lowest level of the selection procedure, that summer controversy erupted over the decisions made by the selection boards and the role of the education committees in the selection procedure.

It had been obvious for some years that political pressure groups—not least the Tsukuru-kai—had been working to undermine the influence of parents and teachers—supported by the teachers' union Nihon Kyōshokuin Kumiai (Nikkyōso for short)—on selection boards and to restrict such practices as *gakkō kibō-hyō* and *shiborikomi* (see above).[55] The increasing lack of transparency in appointments to selection boards (Net 2000: 105–106; Murai 2001: 121–122) as well as blatant attempts to influence committee members by the Tsukuru-kai—through the distribution of publications such as Nishio's *Kokumin no rekishi* (Tawara 2001: 66–70) or the publication of the society's "new textbooks" on the open book market (*shihanbon*)—was met with resistance by various citizen groups. As a result the Tsukuru-kai, which had aimed for a "market share" of 10%, failed to influence the selection procedure in their favor (Yamada 2002: 8; Ōuchi 2003: 264).

The turning point can be identified in events that took place in the selection district of Shimo-tsuga in Tochigi prefecture mentioned above. The Tsukuru-kai had many opportunities to influence textbook procedures in this prefecture where the left-leaning teachers union Nikkyōso had little influence. Indeed, the Shimo-tsuga selection board was the first to choose both Tsukuru-kai textbooks and submit their decision to the education committees of the municipalities.[56] While the presentation of recommendations from the local education committees to the prefecture administration was previously regarded as a mere formality, the education committee of the Fujioka municipality stunned the public by an-

---

[55] According to the *Asahi Shinbun*, the selection procedure for members of selection boards had been altered in at least 29 prefectures by the beginning of May 2001. Moreover, it was made more difficult for teachers to become members. Fifteen prefectures, including Tōkyō, Tochigi and Kanagawa, had completely abolished the practice of *shiborikomi*. *Asahi Shinbun* 2 May 2001: 1 and 34; cf. also *Kyōkasho Repōto* 2002: 65; Yamada 2002: 5; Yoshizawa 2001.

[56] This decision was heavily debated among the 23 members of the selection board itself. The responsible board member had recommended, as required, three books for history and social science classes; the history books were published by Nihon Bunkyō Shuppan, Tōkyō Shoseki and Kyōiku Shuppan. While the board's final vote should have followed the recommendations put

nouncing in July 2001 that it would disregard the recommendation of the regional selection board and vote against adoption of the Tsukuru-kai textbooks (*Asahi Shinbun* 17.07.2001: 38). The five members of the Fujioka committee unanimously agreed that the history textbook presented "distorted interpretations of history"; that it had already led to considerable "international tensions"; and that its "contents were beyond junior high school teaching levels." (*Asahi Shinbun* 7 July 2001: 38) Moreover, board members alleged that the Tsukuru-kai had tried to influence their decision by sending informational material to the board in violation of regulations (*Asahi Shinbun* 18 July 2001: 3).

In taking this unprecedented step, the Fujioka education committee was responding to a series of protests received from across the country by telephone, fax, and e-mail. These protests were organized and coordinated by networks of citizens' groups such as the Kodomo to Kyōkasho Zenkoku Net 21 (Children and Textbooks Japan Network 21), an activist organization that developed out of the support movement for historian and textbook author Ienaga Saburō during a series of widely-publicized legal actions he fought against the Japanese state from the 1960s to the 1980s.[57] Other organizations that lobbied the committees in Shimo-tsuga included the Center for Documentation of School Textbooks (Kyōkasho Jōhō Shiryō Sentā) and the Printers' Union (Shuppan Rōren) (Uesugi 2002). As a result of this vociferous protest movement, coordinated primarily over the internet (Ducke 2003: 209–210), and in response to heavy media interest, the Shimo-tsuga selection board eventually backed down and recommended the textbook produced by the Tōkyō Shoseki publishing house, which had been picked by most committees. This decision made Shimo-tsuga a precedent for the whole of Japan and after this no selection board was to choose the Tsukuru-kai textbooks. Since April 2002 only nine private schools, along with "special schools" (*yōgo gakkō*) for the disabled in the prefectures of Tōkyō and Ehime (where selection is decided by prefecture administrations), have been using the Tsukuru-kai textbooks. In April 2002, precisely 521 copies of their texts were delivered to

---

forward by the member responsible, in these two subjects 11 members surprisingly ("suddenly") voted for the Tsukuru-kai textbooks, despite their omission from the list of recommendations. Since no one text had received an "absolute majority", a second vote was held in which the Tsukuru-kai textbooks received 12 votes and thus were recommended for use by the board. Cf. *Asahi Shinbun* 18 July 2001: 3.

[57] For further information on the Ienaga procedures, see Petersen 2001: 77–78; and Foljanty-Jost 1979: passim; Nozaki 2002; for more on the support movement for Ienaga Saburō, cf. Foljanty-Jost 1979: 52–55, 133–134.

Japanese junior high schools—amounting to a market share of 0.039%. A year later, in April 2003, following a directive from the prefectural governor issued on 15 August 2002, three newly established junior high schools in Ehime prefecture also adopted the Tsukuru-kai textbooks—a decision that was harshly criticized in Japan as an autocratic step that bypassed the established selection procedures (Asahi Shinbun 16 August 2002: 1, 2).

Table 2: Market share of the eight publishers of history textbooks for Japanese junior high schools 2002–2006 in comparison with the period 1998–2002 (*Kyōkasho Repōto* 2002: 66; *Asahi Shinbun* 12 September 2001: 37).

Publisher	Share 2002–2006	Share 1998–2002	Change
Tōkyō Shoseki	51.3%	41.1%	+10.2%
Ōsaka Shoin	14.0%	19.3%	+5.3%
Kyōiku Shuppan	13.0%	17.8%	−4.8%
Teikoku Shoin	10.9%	1.9%	+9.0%
Nihon Shoseki	5.9%	12.9%	−7.0%
Shimizu Shoin	2.5%	3.4%	−0.9%
Nihon Kyōiku Shuppan	2.3%	3.5%	−1.2%
Fusōsha	0.039%	-	+0.039%

Although the protests of summer 2001 prevented widespread use of the Tsukuru-kai textbooks in junior high schools, the release of new textbooks onto the market did not pass without consequences. It was no secret in Japan that, over a number of years and influenced by their new competitor, the mainstream publishing houses were increasingly tending to delete from their textbooks the so-called "dark" chapters of Japanese wartime atrocities. According to Tawara Yoshifumi of Children and Textbooks Japan Network 21, in their latest editions most of the seven mainstream publishers had omitted detailed reference to issues such as the "military comfort women" (*jūgun ianfu*) or the Nanjing massacre, thus reverting to the kind of coverage common in school textbooks some 20 years previously (Tawara 2001: 35–40, 178–183; Net 2000: 109f; Tawara 2000). While, for example, in 1997 the textbooks of all seven publishers accorded the "comfort women" at least a brief mention, among the 2001 editions (intended for use until March 2006) only three textbooks make *any* mention of this issue, albeit extremely brief. It is significant that the market share of these three publishers amounts only to about 20% of the total. As for the Nanjing massacre, while four of the 1997 textbooks mentioned it, only two of the 2001 editions retain short references to the massacre. And while five of the earlier editions mentioned the biological warfare experiments conducted in Manchuria by Unit 731, in 2001 only one textbook did so. Lastly, the term "aggression" (*shinryaku*), established in the 1980s for describing

Japanese warfare on the Asian continent and used in all the 1997 versions of junior high school textbooks, was replaced in 2001 by the expression "advance" (*shinshutsu*) or simply dropped altogether along with the relevant passages (Tawara 2001: 35–40, 178–183; Net 2000: 109f).

The 2001 selection procedure also revealed that those textbooks which had been previously considered "progressive"—i.e., those which gave reasonably detailed treatment of the "darker chapters" of Japan's modern history—were losing ground, above all those published by Nihon Shoseki, but also Ōsaka Shoseki and Kyōiku Shuppan. In contrast, the textbook published by Tōkyō Shoseki, which dealt only briefly with controversial topics, increased its market share to over 50% of the total. This reinforced the existing trend toward concentration of the textbook market into a few hands—a tendency which in the long term will produce a smaller number of textbooks for schools to choose from. Indeed, in 1998 only seven textbooks were available for teaching history in junior high schools, a marked decline from the 19 on offer in 1960. This tendency is also observable in other subjects, as well as in elementary schools where there is a noticeable trend toward fewer textbooks and a growing concentration of market share in the hands of a few publishing houses.[58]

Table 3: **Numbers of textbooks available in selected subjects in elementary and junior high schools, 1960 and 1999 (Source: Net 2000: 102).**

Elementary School	1960	1999
Japanese	12	6
Social Science	11	5
Geography	12	2
Mathematics	10	6
Natural Science	11	6
Geometry	16	3
Junior High School		
Japanese	17	5
History	19	7
Geography	9	2
Mathematics	19	6
Natural Science	15	5

---

[58] For further information on the more recent developments of 2001/2002, cf. *Kyōkasho Repōto* 2003: 62–71, 77, 83.

Table 4: Concentration (in %) of the market share of elementary and junior high school textbooks by subject held by the three leading publishers in 1997 (Source: Net 2000: 102).

Elementary School	%
Japanese	94
Social Science	96
Mathematics	96
Natural Science	85
Junior High School	
Japanese	88
Geography	81
History	78
Social Science	79
Mathematics	78
Natural Science	91
English	83

Until 1963, individual schools chose the textbooks used in elementary and junior high school classes. German researcher Gesine Foljanty-Jost regards the present system of regional selection districts, introduced in 1964, as part of a series of measures designed to reverse the previously valid democratic and citizen-oriented textbook legislation step by step (Foljanty-Jost 1979: 33–35). According to critics of the bureaucratization of the selection procedure, the increasing concentration of Japan's textbook market can be countered only by reforming the current system and returning to textbook selection at the level of the individual school.

However, such a reform is unlikely to be carried out in the near future. Public attention will again focus on the selection process carried out at municipality level when the textbook debate enters its next round in late 2004 and spring/summer 2005. As of April 2004, the Tsukuru-kai is preparing revised versions of its textbooks for submission to the MOE. The forthcoming debates over the examination and selection process are likely to be even more heated those of 2000/2001. The consequences of the growing influence of historical revisionism for the future course of Japanese politics will be "unpredictable but inevitably disturbing" (McCormack 2000: 69f)—not to mention the implications for Japan's relations with Korea and China, as Prime Minister Koizumi Jun'ichirō's visits to the Yasukuni Shrine have recently underlined (see chapter 2).

The Tsukuru-kai is recouping its forces, promising "revenge" for its defeat in the selection process in 2001. Tanaka Hidemichi, the association's president since late 2001, has reaffirmed the society's objective of fighting against "Marxist and anti-Japanese masochistic historians who distort Japanese history and history education" (Tanaka 2004: Internet). There is little doubt that the Tsukuru-kai can back up its words with strong financial backing as well as the considerable political support it enjoys.[59] The restructuring of the society's leadership under Tanaka, and a vigorous membership drive launched in the second half of 2001 to counter recent losses[60]—among the most prominent defectors were Kobayashi Yoshinori and Nishibe Susumu (Uesugi 2003a: Internet)—were undertaken as preparatory steps for the society's promised "revenge", and its political connections will again be a central issue of the next round of the textbook debate in 2005. The Tsukuru-kai's links with politics and politicians, which will be crucial to the future development of the issue, are explored in detail in the next section.

1.5 THE TSUKURU-KAI AND POLITICS

1.5.1 Historical Background: The Debates of the mid-1990s

When the textbook controversy first erupted in East Asia as an *international* conflict in 1982, Japanese politicians reacted by introducing the "paragraph regarding neighbouring countries" (*kinrin shokoku jōkō*) into the official rules for the examination of textbooks. This was done to improve bilateral relations with South Korea and China (cf. Tawara 2001: 143; Watanabe 2002: 5; Kondō 2001: 86; Tawara 2002: 24). As we have seen, this innovation led in turn to the inclusion in school texts of passages critical of Japan's wartime past—at least until the 1990s (Chung 1998; 2003a; 2003b). Despite media coverage in Asia and America that focused intensely on "historical denial" on the Japanese side, this development undoubtedly fostered reconciliation with East Asia and strengthened Japan's international reputation. Foreign media coverage also drew atten-

---

[59] However, after making a large profit with the "bookmarket version" of the Tsukuru-kai textbook in 2001, Fusōsha ended the 2002 financial year with a deficit. Fusōsha has also rescinded plans to publish the Tsukuru-kai history text as supplementary teaching material and to publish an elementary textbook authored by the Tsukuru-kai (Uesugi 2003a: Internet).

[60] In July 2003, Tsukuru-kai membership had dropped to under 8,500 (*Kyōkasho Repōto* 2004: 25). Some observers have stressed recent efforts by the Tsukuru-kai to cooperate with religious organizations such as a number of Shintō shrines, the central organization of Shintō shrines (Jinja Honchō), and smaller sects such as Makuya (Kirisuto no Makuya), as well as outspoken right-wing organizations such as the Nippon Kaigi in recruiting new members (Uesugi 2003b: Internet).

tion to the "undue remarks" (*bōgen*) of politicians who opposed changes in history education and ridiculed efforts to teach Japanese children the "dark chapters" of Japan's wartime past and present the Asia-Pacific War as a war of aggression. Such *bōgen* were deliberately designed to relativize Japan's war responsibility or simply deny wartime atrocities (see below).

Over the last few decades, the balance between a critical view of Japan's wartime past and the revisionist perspective on the war has been shifting back and forth, with the rise of historical revisionism since the 1990s prompting a shift towards the apologetic view—above all in the public sphere, but also in history education. In most countries, history education is, to a certain degree, also the product of calculations based on *Realpolitik*. In the case of Germany, which in Japan and other countries is often considered the shining example of "successful" *Vergangenheitsbewältigung* (coming to terms with the past), such calculations played a central role in postwar Germany's push to re-enter the community of nations and to win back the trust of her neighbors.

> Germans are still divided over how to remember the war, but they have greater incentive than their Japanese counterparts to satisfy neighboring countries. This is not because [...] Germans [are] more remorseful by nature than Japanese. Some Germans feel guilt, shame, and remorse for their wartime actions as do some Japanese. Others in both countries do not. Rather, larger numbers of Germans than Japanese currently believe that teaching their children positive accounts of Nazism and the war will cost them too much in the future. Germans, notably political leaders, recognize that they have more to lose by clinging to their wartime claims than do Japanese. Their consensus is that the problems created by officially repudiating the Nazi war are less serious than those created by continuing to defend it. (Hein and Selden 2000b: 10; cf. also Ishida 2002 for a balanced Japanese view of German *Vergangenheitsbewältigung*)

While affirmative views of the Nazi past and efforts to deny the Holocaust have been marginalized in German politics, academia and society, in Japan apologetic views rather *dominate* the political establishment, at least the conservative parties, and are also present in the public sphere where public memory is preserved (see chapter 2). Politicians who advocate apologetic and affirmative views of their countries' wartime past clearly believe that they have more to win than to lose. While at least as many ordinary Japanese feel remorse about World War II as do their German counterparts, as I show in chapter 3, Japan's political leaders largely subscribe to affirmative views of Japan's wars and openly promote these views. It is precisely this connection between historical revisionism as an academic and media-driven movement on the one side and politics on the other, and the contrast of these politicized views of history with the views of the majority of the population, which underlines the significance and the explosive potential of the ongoing textbook debate.

In this section I am chiefly concerned to demonstrate the mutual influences of conservative politics and neonationalist historical revisionism and to show that historical revisionism has its origins within politics. As we saw in chapter 1.1, apologetic views of war and colonialism have been a constant feature of postwar Japanese politics. However, revisionism reached new heights on the eve of the 50th anniversary of the end of World War II in summer 1995, triggering intense discussions about Japan's past (Seraphim 1996). Already in 1993, Prime Minister Hosokawa Morihiro had caused uproar within the conservative camp by admitting that he "considers the previous war to have been a war of aggression and a wrong war." (cited in Rekishi Kentō Iinkai 1995: 443) While liberal critics applauded the fact that "the Japanese government finally has chosen to clearly accept responsibility for Japanese warfare and colonial rule" (Yoshida 1994: 23), several organizations such as the Japan Bereaved Families' Association (Nihon Izoku-kai) (Arai 2001: 38) and the Yasukuni Shrine (Yoshida 1995: 205) issued "counter-statements" praising the "Greater East Asian War" as a "war of self-defense to secure the life and property of the [Japanese] people." The Association to Respond to the Heroic Souls (Eirei ni Kotaeru kai) launched a full-page protest advertisment in the daily Sankei Shinbun under the desparate heading "Japan is not a country of aggression" (*Nihon wa shinryaku-kuni de wa arimasen*) (Yoshida 1995: 210). Within the LDP, a "History Examination Committee" (Rekishi Kentō Iinkai) was established which in 1995 issued a publication (Rekishi Kentō Iinkai 1995) summarizing the opposition to Hosokawa's views. Individual politicians-turned-historians further undermined the prime minister's statement through the deliberate use of "undue remarks" (*bōgen*) such as the comments made by Nagano Shigeto in 1994:

> I still think the interpretation of [the Greater East Asian War] as a war of aggression is wrong. [...] Japan stood at the brink of extinction, stood up and fought for its existence. At the same time, Japan seriously thought about liberating colonies and establishing the East Asian Co-Prosperity Sphere. [...] Its war objectives as such were, at the time, basically within justifiable limits. (cited in Wakamiya 1995: 10)

Commenting on Japanese war atrocities, Nagano added that he believed that "the Nanjing incident is a fabrication." (cited in Wakamiya 1995: 10) And in opposing plans to adopt an "apology resolution" in the Diet (see below), Minister for Environmental Issues [!] Sakurai Shin reconfirmed that

> Japan did not mean to conduct a war of aggression. […] As a result of the Japanese wars, Asia was liberated from European colonial rule and almost all countries won independence. As a consequence of this independence, education was disseminated and economic growth began to occur all over Asia. (cited in Wakamiya 1995: 11)

That such views are still very prominent among Japan's political class has been confirmed by more recent statements. In July 2003, for example, LDP faction leader Etō Takami called the Nanjing massacre a fabrication and told reporters that Japan's annexation of Korea in 1910 was "not a colonial conquest, but, due to the fact that both sides signed a treaty of annexation, a legally correct step approved unconditionally by the United Nations."[61] (cited in *Asahi Shinbun* 13 July 2003: 1) Similar remarks have also been made by Asō Tarō of the LDP (*Asahi Shinbun* 3 June 2003: 2) and Tōkyō governor Ishihara Shintarō (*Asahi Shinbun* 29 October 2003: 38). In contrast to the 1990s, however, politicians who make such statements have not been relieved of their posts, despite protests both from within Japan and from its neighbors.

The controversy ignited by the 50th anniversary of the war escalated in 1995 when the cabinet of Prime Minister Murayama Tomiichi of the Socialist Party of Japan (SPJ) promoted the adoption of an "anti-war resolution" or an "apology resolution" in the Diet—notwithstanding the fact that the SPJ was very much the junior party in the coalition cabinet headed by Murayama, and in the face of strong resistance from the LDP, the dominant coalition partner, against any official apology for Japan's wars. Although Murayama eventually pushed through the resolution in the Diet, his success was a Pyrrhic victory. The "Resolution to Renew the Determination for Peace on the Basis of Lessons Learned from History", adopted on 9 June 1995 (see appendix 2), was not the decisive statement Murayama and others had hoped for. The prime minister was forced to accept a compromise statement as a result of strong pressure from conservative groups within the LDP. The resolution finally adopted expressed "condolences to those who fell in action and victims of wars and similar actions *all over the world*" (italics added), thereby relativizing Japanese aggression in Asia as a "normal action", comparable to warfare conducted by the European imperial powers. Moreover, the resolution did not make clear the identity of the victims it referred to: the passage cited above could be interpreted as a message of support for Japanese families

---

[61] The United Nations, of course, was founded only after the end of World War II.

bereaved by the war. The second paragraph of the resolution was similarly ambiguous:

> Solemnly reflecting (*hansei*) upon *many instances of colonial rule and acts of aggression in the modern history of the world*, and recognizing that Japan carried out those acts in the past, inflicting pain and suffering upon the peoples of other countries, especially in Asia, the Members of this House express a sense of deep remorse. (italics added)

Again, Japan's wars are placed in the larger framework of imperialism and warfare "in the modern history of the world" and thus relativized as a "normal" event in history. This kind of formulation is reminiscent of ultraconservative German historiography of the 1980s which aimed at relativizing German war atrocities, e.g. depicting the Holocaust as a "conventional genocide" similar to the purges of Stalin in the Soviet Union or Pol Pot in Cambodia—efforts that were fiercely opposed in German society and academia. (The cynical comparison of numbers and methods of killing in some studies seems a highly inappropriate way of approaching history on the part of former aggressors, not to mention the *political* implications of such theories.) This pressure from within the LDP, where many lawmakers-turned-historians insisted that Japan had nothing to apologize for since the "Greater East Asian" war had been a purely defensive war, made it impossible for Murayama to proceed with his original plan of a more outspoken apology. He rather had to accept a compromise solution to avoid the danger of ending up with no resolution at all. It is hardly surprising that the resolution found little acceptance outside Japan while arousing considerable criticism within the country.

A few months after the passing of the resolution, Prime Minister Murayama made a personal attempt to make up for the failure to make a true apology. On 15 August 1995, the 50th anniversary of the ending of the war, he made a statement (*Murayama danwa*) in which he unambiguously acknowledged that "during a certain period in the not-too-distant past, Japan, following a mistaken national policy, advanced along the road to war, only to ensnare the Japanese people in a fateful crisis, and, through its colonial rule and aggression, caused tremendous damage and suffering to the people of many countries, particularly to those of Asian nations." (MOFA 1995: Internet; see also appendix 2) He also expressed his "sense of profound remorse" and added that he felt "feelings of deep remorse and state my heartfelt apology". The statement was endorsed as a cabinet decision (*kakugi kettei*) and remains the official position of the Japanese government regarding Japan's wartime past. Murayama's successor, Hashimoto Ryūtarō, despite being known to support affirmative views of the war, was the first member to endorse the Murayama statement in the House of Councillors on 26 January 1996. Subsequently, every Japanese head of cabinet, including the present Prime Minister Koizumi Jun'ichirō, has followed this course.

Why did the series of declarations made in summer 1995, in addition to Hosokawa's statement in 1993, not satisfy Japan's neighbors and lead to a consensus in Japanese society? What were the reasons for continuing doubts over the sincerity of Japan's "apologies"? No one could ignore the fact that fewer than half the 511 members of the House of Representatives had attended the Diet session of June 1995 in which the apology resolution was adopted, despite its compromise character. Many conservative members of the LDP, which opposed the adoption of *any* resolution, stayed away from the Diet rather than be forced to either vote against the resolution—and so provoke a political crisis—or vote against their conscience. As a result, the resolution was not even tabled in Japan's upper house, the House of Councillors. Organizations founded to oppose the resolution ridiculed the "House of Representatives' resolution that has no authority and was shelved in the House of Councillors" (Shūsen Gojūshūnen Kokumin Iinkai 1995: 11). The fate of the resolution was seen as "equivalent to having been rejected" (Shūsen Gojūshūnen Kokumin Iinkai 1995: 22). The resolution was no doubt perceived in exactly this way by Japan's neighbors, the former victims of Japanese aggression. Openly obstructed within the national parliament, the Diet resolution lost much of its credibility as well as its envisaged symbolic meaning.

To add insult to injury, politicians opposing the resolution formed a variety of lobby groups, giving evidence of the strength of apologetic views of the war in Japanese politics and the paucity of "genuine" remorse. Already by the end of 1994, approximately half the LDP Diet membership had formed an organization known as the Parliamentarians' League on the Fiftieth Anniversary of the End of World War II led by ultra-conservative Okuno Seisuke (former Minister at the National Land Agency), and including Mori Yoshirō (then LDP secretary-general) and Hashimoto Ryūtarō (former MITI minister). The League's "sole purpose was to torpedo Murayama's attempt to adopt a *fusen ketsugi*" (Mukae 1996: 1014). In its guidelines, the organization stated:

> We cannot approve of a resolution containing words of remorse, apology, and the renunciation of war because it would be tantamount to reconfirming biased post-war interpretations of our history, thereby creating difficulties for our nation's future. (cited in Mukae 1996: 1015)

Similarly, in the opposition New Frontier Party (Shinshintō, NFP), the Parliamentarians' League to Bequeath Correct History was founded, including well-known political figures such as Nagano Shigeto and Ozawa Tatsuo—although Shinshintō head Ozawa Ichirō declined to join the League (Mukae 1996: 1016).

Backed by conservative organizations, these various associations also seemed to have a basis in the wider society. A variety of conservative nationalist groups opposing a war apology, including the Shintō Shrine Headquarters (Jinja Honchō), the Military Pensioners' Association (Gun'on Renmei) and the Japan Bereaved Families' Association (Nihon Izoku-kai), had founded the National Committee for the 50th Anniversary of the War (Shūsen Gojū-shūnen Kokumin Iinkai) which included influential members such as former Prime Minister Fukuda Takeo; active politicians Okuno Seisuke and Nagano Shigeto; influential financial figures such as Inaba Kosaku, chairman of the Japanese Chamber of Commerce and Industry; and Nagano Takeshi, chairman of the Japanese Federation of Employers (Nikkeiren). The chairman of the National Committee was the composer Kase Toshikazu who linked the committee to older political organizations of the extreme right, especially the Citizens' Association for the Defense of Japan (Nippon o Mamoru Kokumin Kaigi), now renamed the Japan Conference (Nippon Kaigi).

Just before the adoption of the Diet resolution, at the end of May, the National Committee held a large-scale rally in Tōkyō. Going under the title "Festival of Asians Living Together" (*Ajia kyōsei no saiten*),[62] it was co-sponsored by the committees from the LDP and the NFP mentioned above. The event was held in the concert and sporting venue Budōkan, where the official state ceremony to commemorate the end of the war is held each year on 15 August. The stated purpose of the event was "to commemorate *all war victims in Asia* who dedicated their lives during World War II to liberate Asian nations" (Shūsen Gojūshūnen Kokumin Iinkai 1995; National Committee 1995; italics added), and the organizers were cynical enough to invite representatives from 20 Asian nations including South Korean president Kim Young Sam, Jiang Zemin of the People's Republic of China, Lee Teng-hui of Taiwan and Suharto of Indonesia. In the end, some 15 Asian countries including Thailand, Indonesia and Malaysia sent official representatives, although most—such as Thanat Khoman, a former Minister of Foreign Affairs from Thailand and Syed Hussein Alatas, then Vice-Chancellor of the National University of Malaya—did not hold government positions at the time.[63] From Japan,

---

[62] The official English title was "A Tribute, Appreciation and Friendship. A Celebration of Asian Nations' Symbiosis".

[63] For a complete list of participants, see National Committee 1995: 36 (Asia), 37–39 (Japan).

some 39 conservative Members of the Diet participated in person, while a further 110 sent official representatives. Additionally, some 10,000 participants attended the event, making up an impressive audience. For several months, the National Committee had been active in collecting signatures aiming at preventing an apology resolution by the Diet. It succeeded in collecting more than five million signatures by 8 May 1995,[64] and during the rally in May issued a "statement of opposition against a Diet resolution" (*Kokkai ketsugi hantai no ketsugi*):

> On the occasion of the 50th anniversary of the war, the masochistic and servile historical consciousness [of the Japanese], which has been distorted by the policies of the postwar occupation, has to be reconsidered. On the basis of a fair and true historical account, we have to recover [our] history and restore the honor and pride of the Japanese. (Shūsen Gojūshūnen Kokumin Iinkai 1995: 58)[65]

In the same statement, the Committee reaffirmed the neonationalist view of Japan's wars as wars of Asian liberation, while the suggestion that Japan had conducted wars of aggression was dismissed as "absurd" and "arbitrary" (National Committee 1995: 13). With its forceful campaign[66] to prevent a "Diet resolution of remorse and apology unilaterally incriminating our nation in the war", the National Committee influenced a number of politicians, particularly within the LDP. It was largely due to pressure from this source that Prime Minister Murayama was forced to agree to a revision of the resolution which effectively diluted it. For the LDP, it was important to placate the conservative lobby groups, some of whom play a key role in securing organized votes (*soshiki-hyō*) in support of the LDP. They knew that members of the Izoku-kai (Japan Bereaved Families' Association), for example, which is particularly strong in rural areas, could never support a resolution that would brand Japan as an aggressor and render their beloved husbands, fathers and brothers killed in the war as murderers of civilians across Asia. With a claimed membership of more than one million households, the LDP chose not to ignore the Izoku-kai (Hata 2002a: 13; Arai 2001: 39). At the same time, to avoid the

---

[64] Shūsen Gojūshūnen Kokumin Iinkai 1995: 9; for the distribution amongst the prefectures cf. ibid., 53.
[65] The English version, titled "Tōkyō Declaration for 'Asian Nations' Symbiosis'", lacks similar wording but rather evokes the image of a united Asia that has faced "unbearable humiliation" and only recently has found "harmony" (National Committee 1995: 11).
[66] The committee also organized events in all the major Japanese cities (Shūsen Gojūshūnen Kokumin Iinkai 1995: 16–19).

1. Historical Revisionism in Contemporary Japan

dangers inherent in abandoning the idea of a Diet resolution altogether, Murayama himself agreed to a compromise solution.

In the end, the resolution was adopted only because of the three coalition parties' shared desire to stay in power. This was the fundamental driving force behind an agreement that fell well short of expressing a unanimous Japanese apology for the war. The resolution that was finally adopted did not satisfy anybody: for Japan's neighbors, it lacked a clear statement of guilt and apology; for the Japanese Left, the circumstances in which it was adopted were "embarrassing" (*hazukashii*) (*Asahi Shinbun* 10 June 1995); and for the opponents of an apology, any resolution was too much. One observer drew the conclusion that the resolution was a lost opportunity for Japan:

> [The 9 June Diet resolution] could have demonstrated Japan's strong commitment to a new globally oriented pacifism that, unlike its postwar isolationist pacifism, is anchored firmly in an honest appraisal of Japan's own past history, as well as a true effort at reconciliation with its Asian neighbors. In that sense, unfortunately, the Japanese government failed not only other nations but also its own. (Mukae 1996: 1030)

Although the National Committee could not prevent the revised resolution from being adopted, successful lobbying by conservative activists had robbed it much of its envisaged symbolic meaning. The events organized by the National Committee and the flow of publications that followed[67] were only the start of a series of "counter-declarations" that further undermined the Diet resolution.

The most important of these "counter-declarations"—apart from the continuing "undue remarks" of conservative politicians[68]—was a publication produced by a committee of the dominant political party, the LDP. The ambiguously named History Examination Committee (Rekishi Kentō Iinkai) had been founded after the statement of apology by Prime Minister Hosokawa in 1993 and had organized a series of lectures by academics, journalists and other conservative "opinion leaders" or "critics" (*hyōronka*) between October 1993 and February 1995. These lectures, along with the committee's own deliberations, were published in late 1995 as the *Summary of the Greater East Asia War* (*Daitō-A sensō sōkatsu*) (Rekishi Kentō Iinkai 1995). This publication constitutes the most comprehensive

---

[67] The National Committee also sponsored two movies, *The Light of Independent Asia* (*Dokuritsu Ajia no hikari*) and *The Glory of Free Asia* (*Jiyū Ajia no eikō*); Shūsen Gojūshūnen Kokumin Iinkai 1995: 14f.

[68] Cf. McCormack 2001: 226–229; Wakamiya 1995: 9–16.

77

"counter-statement" against the apologies of Hosokawa and Murayama and the 1995 Diet resolution. Among the members of the History Examination Committee who authorized this publication was a stellar cast of political notables (Rekishi Kentō Iinkai 1995: 446; Tawara 2001: 154): the then president of the Izoku-kai, Hashimoto Ryūtarō (Prime Minister 1996–1998); the then LDP secretary-general Mori Yoshirō (Prime Minister April 2000-April 2001); the chairman of the Lower House Investigation Committee on Constitutional Questions (*Shūgiin kenpō chōsakai iinchō*) Nakayama Tarō; former chairman of the House of Councillors Investigation Committee on Constitutional Questions (*Sangiin kenpō chōsakai iinchō*) Murakami Masakuni;[69] Itagaki Masashi, son of Itagaki Seishirō, an army general considered responsible for the outbreak of the Manchurian Incident (1931) and convicted as a class A war criminal by the IMTFE; later LDP faction leader Etō Takami; and present LDP secretary-general, Abe Shinzō, tipped to be a future leader of the party—and the country (cf. Maeno 2003: 275).

The lectures published by the committee in 1995 were given by well-known war-apologists and historical revisionists such as Nishio Kanji, Tanaka Masaaki, Takahashi Shirō, Kobori Keiichirō, Okazaki Hisahiko, Nishibe Susumu and Etō Jun. Most contain harsh criticism of the Hosokawa statement (Rekishi Kentō Iinkai 1995: 11, 443) and repeatedly affirm that "the Greater East Asian War (Asia-Pacific War)[70] was not a war of aggression, but rather a war [undertaken] for self-defense (*jison jiei*) and [...] the liberation of Asia (*Ajia kaihō no sensō*)." (Rekishi Kentō Iinkai 1995: 11, 308 etc.) This statement is almost identical with the description of the war found in the Tsukuru-kai textbook (Nishio et al. 2001: 277), to which many of the lecturers sponsored by the History Examination Committee had contributed. Japan's responsibility for the war is consistently denied throughout the publication. Some contributors go further and attribute part of the responsibility to China and Korea, since "their weakness invited [!] Russian aggression" in Asia (Rekishi Kentō Iinkai 1995: 13). The book aroused a great deal of attention in China due to its direct denial of the Nanjing massacre, particularly in the contribution by Tanaka Masaaki (Rekishi Kentō Iinkai 1995: 252–261; cf. also 304f; regarding Tanaka cf. Yang 2001: 64f).

---

[69] Murakami was convicted of bribery in the so-called KSD scandal in 2000; see Mainichi Interactive 2001.
[70] The terms "Greater East Asian War" (1941–1945) and "Asia-Pacific War" (nowadays usually defined as the war conducted from 1931–1945) are here used synonymously.

The LDP-sponsored book makes many claims about the war that were later to become standard revisionist dogma. Alongside the blaming of the IMTFE prosecutors for the view of history considered predominant in contemporary Japan (Rekishi Kentō Iinkai 1995: 272–295, 329 and passim), throughout the book we find the repeated claim that the war was fought as an unselfish act to liberate Asia from European imperialism and aggression:

> The Manchurian Incident, the China Incident and the Greater East Asian War [...] were a fight for survival between the colored races and the white race. Since the Russo-Japanese War [1905], the colored races had all depended on Japan to be liberated from colonial rule. Since this would be a terrible blow, the whites united in order to suppress Japan. (Rekishi Kentō Iinkai 1995: 62f)

And further:

> The Greater East Asian War was a glorious and international contribution, a sacrifice without precedent in the history of mankind. [...] The Japanese are a righteous people. (Rekishi Kentō Iinkai 1995: 67)

In this kind of argument, some conflict is apparent in interpreting a war that contained elements of an anticolonial conflict—Japanese resistance to the Western colonial drive into East Asia—but at the same time contained imperialist elements, aiming at establishing Japanese hegemony over Asia. In conservative circles in Japan, however, it is remembered as an exclusively anticolonial war, while Japanese imperialist and colonial ambition is denied. In Asian countries that were victims of Japanese expansionism, the war is rather remembered as an imperialist Japanese conflict—although a minority in those countries nonetheless acknowledge a Japanese contribution to the anticolonial independence fight. But it is, above all, the re-emergence of a crude Social Darwinist "law of the jungle" that is particularly disturbing in this context. While this notion has increasingly disappeared from international politics since World War II, it has made a strong comeback in the writings of Japanese historical revisionists:

> Although people [from countries] that have been victims of aggression don't like to hear this, in the fight for the survival of mankind it is legitimate to be an aggressor as long as you win (*katte shinryaku suru no ga tadashii no desu*). (Rekishi Kentō Iinkai 1995: 65)

While not all its authors were members of the LDP, this publication by the party's History Examination Committee—containing the signatures of 105 LDP lawmakers (Rekishi Kentō Iinkai 1995: 446)—reflects the views of a large and influential section of the LDP—a group that is still very much in control today as the names listed above demonstrate. Some observers (Tawara 2001: 139f; Kang 2001a; Takahashi 2002: 42) consider this apologetic manifesto as the start of the movement for historical revisionism that developed in Japan in the late 1990s. The Tsukuru-kai, which was represented among the authors of the LDP publication, was founded in 1996, and its first publication repeats many of the claims made in the *Summary of the Greater East Asia War* (see chapter 1.1). The same can be said of its school history textbook which was issued in 2000. As a result of these parallels, commentators have argued that the Tsukuru-kai textbook was in some respects written *for the LDP* as a response to the desire in conservative circles for a stronger statement of the affirmative view of the war to influence Japanese society at large (Watanabe 2002: 4; Kang 2001a; Takahashi 2002: 42).

1.5.2 Contemporary Political Debates

Since its foundation in 1996, the Tsukuru-kai has been working to fulfill its principal objective of disseminating an affirmative view of the war in Japanese society. Since the setback the society received in 2001 with the limited adoption of its school textbook (see chapter 1.4), the mass media have become its main field of engagement (see chapters 1.1 and 1.2). Through these activities conservative views of history are spreading in Japanese society, although, as I show in chapter 3, they have not yet become predominant. Some observers stress that it is only a question of time before the alliance between conservative politics and the historical revisionism coalescing around the Tsukuru-kai will reach fruition. It is true that, as a result of the formation of the Tsukuru-kai and its growing media profile, the "affirmative" view of Japanese history has emerged from its isolated position in right-wing circles and conservative politics and gained some attention in the wider society.

In its present and future campaigns, the Tsukuru-kai can be sure of continuing political support. Recent developments have demonstrated the society's close connection with politics and cooperation in concrete political issues. Their most obvious political links are the membership of a number of politicians in the society, mostly those with a special interest in questions of history and national pride. One notorious example is former Minister of Education Machimura Nobutaka, who in 1998 publicly aligned himself with the Tsukuru-kai by complaining that Japanese history textbooks "are lacking in balance" and over-emphasize Japan's responsibility for the war (cited in Tawara 2001: 41, 141; cf. also Uesugi

2001: 17; Net 2000: 114). Machimura—who in September 2004 became Foreign Minister—is one of a number of national and local politicians, many of them affiliated with the LDP, who are members of the Tsukuru-kai (Tawara 2001: 171–177). To cite another example, in July 2000 the LDP members of Chiba prefectural assembly issued a statement whose title clearly reflects Tsukuru-kai views: *Memorandum demanding appropriate measures to produce a history textbook that allows [one] to have pride and love for the Japanese state* (Nippon-koku e no aijō to hokori o motsu koto ga dekiru rekishi kyōkasho sakusei ni mukete tekisetsu na taiō o motomeru ikensho) (Tawara 2001: 123). The reference here to the Japanese state (*Nippon-koku*) supports the assumption often made by critics that neonationalists fail to make a distinction between state and nation, and indeed support a particularly strong statist variant of neonationalism directed at strengthening citizens' loyalty to the state and state authorities.

In addition to LDP politicians who belong to the Tsukuru-kai and support the society's activities, there are many more politicians who hold revisionist views and express them publicly. In May 2000, Prime Minister Mori Yoshirō told the Shintō Association of Spiritual Leadership (the official English name of the Shintō Seiji Renmei): "I have promoted ideas which the government has tended to avoid, and have continued to affirm to the Japanese people that Japan is a country of the gods, with the emperor at its center."[71] Mori's pronouncement became known as the "Country of the Gods" statement (*kami no kuni hatsugen*) and is considered by a leading Australian scholar as an expression of the "precise racist and exclusionary formula of Japanese identity promoted in the official ideology of 1930s and 1940s fascist Japan." (McCormack 2001a: xvi) However, such views are of central importance to the historical narrative promoted by the Tsukuru-kai, which has been called an "historical view of the Imperial Country" (*kōkoku shikan*) (Kimijima 2001: 57).

The close links between conservative politics and the Tsukuru-kai are also reflected in contemporary political discussion and controversy. For example, in the debate over the revision of the Japanese Constitution, Tsukuru-kai members are cooperating closely with the political proponents of a revised Constitution which would include the revision (or deletion) of the war-renouncing Article 9 in order to allow Japan to use its military forces as an instrument of foreign policy. In conservative circles, such a move is linked closely with national prestige and national power. Since Article 9 of the Constitution restricts Japan's ability to deploy

---

[71] Cited in McCormack 2001: xvi; cf. also Tawara 2001: 111–113 and the homepage of the Shinto Online Network Association (http://www.jinja.or.jp/jikyoku/kaminokuni/kaminokuni2.html).

military power—notwithstanding the recent "revision [of Article 9] by reinterpretation" (McCormack 2001b; Takahashi 2003: 151)—the abolition of it and other restraints on Japanese political and military engagement are a major objective of the conservative political camp and the Tsukuru-kai members who support them.

Ill. 6: Cover of the bi-weekly magazine *Sapio* criticizing the excessive restrictions binding Japan's power (used by permission of Shōgakukan).

However, moves such as these by the right wing do not go unchallenged. Any criticism of the prevailing pacifist attitudes in Japanese society are still considered as a "direct challenge to the collective identity of Japan as a peaceful country" (Katzenstein 1996: 151), and any constitutional changes that might promote a "war-capable Japan" (*sensō dekiru kuni*) are met with vigorous opposition in Japanese society, particularly among academics, NGO members, lawyers and teachers (Tawara 2001: 157; Tawara 2002: 36; Takahashi and Miyake 2003: 46; Takahashi 2003: 128f, 170f; Ōuchi 2003: 89–93; Tanaka 2002a: 211–214; Ōe Kenzaburō in *Asahi Shinbun* 11 June 2004: 37). This opposition to military expansionism should be seen in the context of Japan's military budget: with an annual expenditure of more than US$ 40 billion, it has the third-largest military budget in the world, by far the largest in East Asia.

Table 5: **Military budgets of major countries in 2003 (Source: IISS 2004).**

		Annual Defense budget (in billion US$)
1	USA	382.6
2	Russia	50.8 (2002)[73]
3	Japan	41.4
4	United Kingdom	41.3
5	France	34.9
6	Germany	27.4
7	China[74]	22.4
8	Italy	22.3
9	Saudi-Arabia	18.4
10	India	16.2
	South Korea	14.8
	Australia	9.9
	Brazil	9.7
	Canada	9.1
	Spain	8.5
	North Korea	1.6

And in response to continuing U.S. pressure, Japan is increasing its military activities as a part of its foreign policy, a fact noted not only by domestic opponents of military expansion, but also by East Asian nations.[74] Having the ability to project military power as a part of foreign policy—whether within the framework of UN missions or as a partner of the U.S.—has long been advocated by conservative politicians and lobbyists who present it as an essential part of becoming "a normal country" (*futsū no kuni*). Despite the imprecision of this slogan, its proponents claim that "a normal country" is one that "possesses normal armaments (*gunbi*) and can conduct war in a normal way (*futsū ni sensō dekiru*)" (former General Director for Foreign Relations of the Defense Agency, Okazaki Hisahiko cited in Rekishi Kentō Iinkai 1995: 362). Less polemical commentators argue that a revision of Article 9—particularly part 2 of Article 9—is necessary as a *symbolic act*, to legalize the existence of Japan's SDF

---

[72] *Military Balance* ignores the Russian official budget, which amounts to only US$ 23 billion, but rather estimates "actual defence expenditure in Russia using purchasing power parity (PPP) rates", giving an estimate of "total military-related expenditure […] [as] the equivalent of $50.8bn." (IISS 2004: 271)

[73] The Chinese defense budget is a hotly debated topic, as official figures are considered to be much lower than actual expenditures. See Carpenter 2004; IISS 2004: 294f.

[74] "Pacifism is slowly fading" was the warning cover title of the *Far Eastern Economic Review* (FEER 1 November 2001) after the so-called anti-terrorism law passed in Japan in October 2001.

within the constitutional framework and form the basis for participation in UN missions. Kitaoka Shin'ichi, former Tōkyō University professor and now Japan's Deputy Permanent Representative to the UN argues: "Although I do not favor an increase in the military arms buildup, it is hard to deny that Article 9 [...] imposes restrictions on the development of a healthy security policy (*kenzen na anzen hoshō seisaku*)." (Kitaoka 2000: 258; cf. also 262–272, 302; Heginbotham and Samuels 2003)

As a result of strong domestic opposition to the further militarization of Japan's foreign policy and the revision of Article 9,[75] the conservative lobby has increased its efforts at weakening this opposition. Opposition to the revision of Article 9, they argue, derives from the pacifism and lack of patriotism characteristic of contemporary Japanese. By entrenching a "bright" historical narrative and strengthening patriotism and love of country, the argument goes, opposition to the revision of Article 9 of the Constitution will be eroded. In order to achieve these aims, history education in schools must be revised as the first priority—although recently the whole education system has come under attack (Ōuchi 2003; Takahashi 2003). Although the raising of national consciousness and patriotism (*aikokushin, aikokushugi*) have long been included as official objectives in the guidelines for history lessons in Japanese schools,[76] in the eyes

---

[75] In an opinion poll conducted by Asahi Shinbun in 2001, 74% opposed a revision of Article 9, with only 17% favoring it; in 2004 the respective figures were 60% and 31% (Asahi Shinbun 1 May 2004: 1), probably reflecting a recent increase in Japanese military participation worldwide which is considered by many as incompatible with the present constitution. In hearings on a revision of the Constitution organized by the Lower House Investigation Committee on Constitutional Questions (Shūgiin Kenpō Chōsakai) between 2001 and 2004, a majority of participants opposed revision of Article 9 (*Asahi Shinbun* 14 May 2004: 4). At the hearings, Oguma Eiji, a liberal who favors the preservation of Article 9 and who has received considerable attention with his critical writings on nationalism and patriotism (Oguma 1998; Oguma 2002; Oguma and Ueno 2003), argued that Article 9 restricts U.S. demands for increasing Japanese participation in U.S. military activities. Such pressures would inevitably lead to an escalation of Japanese military activity following any revision of Article 9 (*Asahi Shinbun* 14 May 2004: 4).

[76] When the Monbushō "Curriculum for Study in Junior High Schools" (*Chūgakkō gakushū shidō yōryō*) were revised in 1989, the very first sentence in the history section stated that the study of the subject should "foster the consciousness of being a [Japanese] national" through making students "think about the peculiarities of the culture and traditions of our country from a broad perspective." (Monbu Kagakushō 1989: Internet) In the 2002 revision, the further aims of "nurturing feelings of love for the country" and of "raising our awareness (*jikaku*) as Japanese" are included in the guidelines for civic studies for elementary schools (Takahashi 2003: 43).

of conservative politicians such as Nakasone Yasuhiro, Mori Yoshirō, Ishihara Shintarō and Asō Tarō, the primary goal of education should be love of country (*kuni o ai suru kokoro*) rather than the "formation of the character of the individual" as currently stated in the Basic Law of Education (Kyōiku Kihonhō) (cited in Ōuchi 2003: 34) adopted during the U.S. occupation. A number of conservative politicians advocate a revision of the Basic Law of Education along these lines.[77] Several proposals for a revised law have been drafted, the best-known being that of the Central Commission of Inquiry for Questions on Education (Chūō Kyōku Shingikai) of the Ministry of Education which delivered a final report on 20 March 2003 stating that "patriotism" and "respect for history and tradition" should be included as an objective of education in a revised Basic Law of Education (Takahashi 2003: 64). Although these proposals have all met with strong resistance (Takahashi 2003; Ōuchi 2003; Nichibenren 2002), the LDP seems poised to push through a revision in the near future.

Conservative politicians advocating such measures have gained support from a number of groups connected with the movement for historical revisionism, above all the Japan Conference (Nippon Kaigi) mentioned above. In order to cement official communications with this avowedly right-wing association, the LDP in 1997 established a platform called the Exchange Forum of Nippon Kaigi and Parliamentarians (Nippon Kaigi Kokkai Giin Kondankai) headed by LDP heavyweight Asō Tarō, present Minister for Public Management, Home Affairs, Posts and Telecommunications in the cabinet of Koizumi Jun'ichirō and tipped as a future prime minister. He was seconded by Nakagawa Shōichi (Minister of Economy, Trade and Industry), with Hiranuma Takeo (former Minister of Economy, Trade and Industry) serving as secretary-general (Tawara 2004; Takahashi 2003: 81f).

Another recently formed pressure group which also supports the demand for a reform of the Education Law is known as the Society for the Demand for a New Basic Law of Education (Atarashii Kyōiku Kihonhō o Motomeru Kai). The resonance of the name with that of the Tsukuru-kai is not incidental, since the membership of the two societies is almost identical.[78] The secretary-general of the Motomeru-kai is historian Taka-

---

[77] Cf. Saaler 2003b; Ōuchi 2003 (particularly chapter 3) for concrete proposals on revision of the law.

[78] See Tawara 2004; Ōuchi 2003: 97f. In January 2003, the Motomeru-kai reorganized itself into the Exchange Forum for Influential Office Holders Concerned with the Reform of Japanese Education (Nihon no kyōiku kaikaku yūshokushoa kondankai); see Tawara 2004 for details and ibid.: 120f for a list of the forum's members.

hashi Shirō, an early member of the revisionist movement, who already in 1995 claimed that postwar education had not only been stripped of its prewar militarist character, but that "patriotism as such had been eliminated from history education." (Rekishi Kentō Iinkai 1995: 310) Takahashi is well known in Japan for his low estimation of the contemporary education system in general, and also of contemporary Japanese youth and their attitudes (or lack of them)—all of which he blames on "faulty" (i.e. unpatriotic) history education:

> [As the result of] bullying (*ijime*), truancy (*futōkō*), the destruction of class discipline (*gakkyū hōkai*), the dyeing of hair (*chapatsu*), and youth prostitution (*enjo kōsai*), the situation in schools has become serious (*taihen*). The reason for this destruction of education is history textbooks. (cited in Tawara 2001: 124)

In September 2000 the Motomeru-kai submitted its "Request for a New Basic Law of Eduction" to Prime Minister Mori. It contained six points that it demanded be included in any revised Basic Law of Education (cited in Takahashi 2003: 91f):

1. The promotion of respect for tradition and for patriotism
2. An emphasis on education in the family
3. The strengthening of religious sentiment and moral education (*dōtoku kyōiku*)
4. Service to one's country and local area
5. International cooperation in countering "the current crisis of civilization"
6. Clarifying administrative responsibilities in education

These points form a concise summary of the Motomeru-kai's aims of developing patriotism through education and introducing moral education combined with a strong religious (read: Emperor-centered Shintō) component. The society hopes that these innovations will eventually alter social attitudes and produce a generation of citizens oriented to the demands of state. To enhance the group's chances of achieving these aims, point 6 hints at the growing pressure on regional administrative bodies and municipalities to change the selection system for textbooks, a system which, as we saw in chapter 1.4, was the main reason that the Tsukuru-kai texts were rejected by Japanese schools in 2002.

Not content with reform of the education system, history textbooks and the Basic Law of Education, conservative politicians and activists are vigorously pressing their claims for an increased emphasis on patriotism in a revised Constitution. This claim is frequently aired in the Investigation Committees on Constitutional Questions (Kenpō Chōsakai) in both Houses of the Diet. "In the Constitution, there are many provisions about the rights of citizens, but extremely few about their duties, and balance is lacking", LDP member Ono Shin'ya lamented in April 2004 (*Asahi Shinbun* 29 April 2004: 1; cf. also *Asahi Shinbun* 14 May 2003: 3; Ōuchi 2003: 35f). While representatives of the opposition Democratic Party insisted that "it is the most important task of a constitution to *limit* the powers of state authority and guarantee the rights of the people (*hitobito*)", the LDP stresses that "the public good (*ōyake*) is taken only lightly these days and this is the negation of the spirit of the Japanese people (*Nihonjin no tamashi no hitei*)." (*Asahi Shinbun* 29 April 2004: 1) According to the LDP members of the Research Committee on Constitutional Questions, this trend should be countered by including the concepts of "Japanese pride and identity" in the Constitution, which in concrete terms means honoring such traditional institutions as "Shintō, Bushidō, the Imperial House, and the tradition of a rice-growing society [sic]." (*Asahi Shinbun* 29 April 2004: 1) In a recent draft summarizing the LDP's ideas about a revised Constitution, terms like "state", "patriotism", and "national character" can be found "almost innumerable times." (*Asahi Shinbun* 17 June 2004: 1; cf. also *Asahi Shinbun* 20 February 2004: 4).

The direct links between discussion of the Constitution and contemporary politics have been recently demonstrated in the controversy over Japan's participation in the US-led war in Iraq. Although the Koizumi cabinet met with little active opposition to its decision to send troops to Iraq in 2004, widespread public disapproval of this policy triggered the suggestion that the government use the education system to promote its views among Japanese youth. As Koizumi reportedly stated to a Diet commission: "Teachers should not be saying that the SDF is going to war and that dispatching troops is against the Constitution. This kind of teaching causes problems. Teachers should also be telling their pupils that the SDF is making a contribution to peace." (cited in *Asahi Shinbun* 6 February 2004: 37)

The views of the general population on these issues are very different. According to a survey conducted by *Asahi Shinbun* in May 2004, 54% of Japanese oppose the inclusion of new civic *duties* in a revised Constitution. The newspaper reported that supporters of a revised Constitution list as their chief concern the inclusion of "new *rights*", such as the rights to privacy and information (26% in the survey), but rarely cite the need to include new duties (*Asahi Shinbun* 1 May 2004: 1, 16f). In addition, the push by the Right to include patriotism as an educational objective in any revised Basic Law of Education has raised popular suspicions: in August 2003, 264 municipalities drew up a joint protest against such a revision which they submitted to the Ministry of Education and Science (*Asahi Shinbun* 13 August 2003: 1, 27).

However, other municipalities and prefectures have taken the first steps to enforce patriotic education in practice. Since the adoption in 1999 of the "National Flag and National Anthem Law" (Kokka Kokki-hō), which declared the *Hinomaru* flag the national flag and the *Kimigayo* anthem the official national anthem (Tawara 2001: 106–110; Hook and McCormack 2001; McCormack 2001a), pressure has been increasing throughout Japan to make use of the *Hinomaru* flag and the *Kimigayo* anthem compulsory in all school ceremonies. The issue is particularly controversial in Tōkyō, where the prefectural government is headed by right-wing populist and former novelist Ishihara Shintarō; here teachers not participating in the singing of the *Kimigayo* have been suspended (Nishihara 2004; Ikezoe 2004; *Asahi Shinbun* 1 April 2004: 37; 6 April 2004: 34; 7 April 2004: 2).[79] The city of Fukuoka has introduced a system of assessing an individual pupil's "achievements" in reaching "awareness as a Japanese" (*Nihonjin toshite no jikaku*) and making "efforts" in terms of patriotism (*aikokushin tsūchihyō*); such assessments have been made part of the half-yearly reports on pupils' progress (Takahashi 2003: 57, 75f). The problems—practical and moral—faced by students who are not Japanese nationals when confronted with "patriotic education" have aroused much criticism, but solutions have not been forthcoming either from politicians, administrators or the municipalities concerned (Ōuchi 2003: 126–128; Takahashi 2003: 57–59).

Since any definitive revision of the Basic Law of Education is still some time away, the Ministry of Education and Science has taken steps to introduce basic education in the principles of patriotism. Through its controversial "notebook of the mind" (*kokoro no nōto*), used in elementary and junior high schools all over Japan, pupils are being confronted with questions such as "What actually is freedom?" (*Jiyū-tte nan darō*), and encouraged to learn how to "transmit and receive Japaneseness" (*kataritsugi, uketsugu Nihon-rashisa*) and to "love our country and promote its development" (*waga kuni o ai-shi, sono hatten o negau*) (Ōuchi 2003: 132–

---

[79] In all, 150 public school teachers who boycotted the singing of the national anthem at commencement ceremonies were punished by the Tōkyō Board of Education between the end of March and beginning of April 2004. The Board stressed that its decision conformed with the new policy requiring that the flag be "hung facing the front of the stage" and that "teachers and school staff stand and face the national flag and sing the national anthem". Other municipalities, such as the city of Kitakyūshū, went even further and demanded that staff and students must sing "sincerely" (*tadashiku kokoro o komete*) (cited in Hook and McCormack 2001: 11).

135; Takahashi and Miyake 2003; Takahashi 2003: chapter 1; Irie 2004: chapter 3). Because this "notebook" is treated as supplementary course material, it is not subject to any examination or selection process, and critics have labeled its introduction a "return to state-issued textbooks" (*kokutei kyōkasho*) in the manner of prewar Japan (Irie 2004: 128). In terms of content, the text is reminiscent, as its critics have stressed, of prewar "moral education" (*dōtoku kyōiku*) which aimed at producing "good children"—the title of a 1940 textbook (*yoi kodomo*)—and pliant Imperial subjects (*shinmin*) (Takahashi and Miyake 2003; Takahashi 2003: 19; Irie 2004: chapter 3).

Considering the heat generated by the ongoing "patriotism debate" (*aikokushin ronsō*) in Japan (Oguma 2002; Kang 2003; Tahara, Nishibe and Kang 2003), the strong emphasis in the "notebook of the mind" on "love for our country", respect for "the traditions of our country" (*waga kuni no dentō*) and the need to "preserve Japaneseness" (*Nihonrashisa*) is indeed a daring step. The importance of the issue for the bureaucrats in the Ministry of Education, however, is demonstrated by the fact that a budget of more than 730 million Yen was authorized (Takahashi 2003: 19) to produce and distribute the notebook—free of charge—in elementary and junior high schools throughout Japan.

It is in the framework of these contemporary debates that the increasing affinity of historical revisionism with politics and politicians has become clear—and it is also clear that this cooperation aims to secure popular support for certain political objectives, support that is manifestly lacking at present. While Japanese public opinion still strongly rejects the idea of a revision of Article 9 of the Constitution and the Basic Law of Education, the manifold activities of the Tsukuru-kai and the Motomeru-kai are contributing to a slow change of attitudes in society. We might postulate a similar situation with regard to popular views of history. In recent times, the affinity of historical revisionism and conservative politics has become most obvious in the ways history is being interpreted in the *public sphere* in Japan—in historical monuments and memorials, in statements about history emanating from politicians, and in historical museums run or sanctioned by state authorities. In the next chapter, I discuss the historical associations of some of these public monuments and institutions, and in chapter 3 I ask whether these historical statements located in the public sphere are based in a broader social consensus.

2. Historical Revisionism and the Politics of Memory

In addition to history education and the much-contested contents of history textbooks, history in the public sphere—the historical interpretations underlying the national "realms of memory" embodied in monuments, memorials, museums, and public ceremonies—has been credited with an important role in shaping historical consciousness and collective identity.

In discussions about Japan, the allegation is frequently made of the strongly selective character of the memory manifested in the public sphere, of a striving to (actively) forget or suppress certain facets of Japan's past and to brush aside the different emphases made by others. This is sometimes called the politics of oblivion. Selection, however, is a basic mechanism when constructing an historical narrative or as part of the development of historical memory intended to provide a basis for collective identity. Historical facts that are considered essential are selected to be remembered, while others are forgotten, sometimes deliberately. Although the ways in which history is interpreted for the purpose of constructing identities are always strongly influenced by political factors, as Jan Assmann has demonstrated in analyzing the "cultural memory" of ancient high cultures such as Egypt or the Hethitians (Assmann 1997: 70 and passim), in modern states the selection criteria for the creation of a collective historical memory need to be based on a social consensus. They must also be acceptable within the framework of international relations since, in an era of increasing globalization and transnationalization, historical perspectives and "historical consciousness" have become a basis for bilateral trust and reconciliation.

Here, of course, lies a huge potential for conflict, both within a society and in its relations with other states. Some historians have predicted a gradual fading away of concern with a national past that inexorably recedes with the passage of time. Reinhard Koselleck, for example, claims to observe "increasing unemotionality regarding research criteria, [...] less moral dismay, accusations and blaming of others through the means of history writing. All these methods of coming to terms with the past lose their political-existential reference, they fade away and scientific research or hypothesis-led analysis takes their place." (Reinhard Koselleck, cited in Assmann 1999: 14; cf. Koselleck 2002: 327f) However, as Aleida Assmann and others have stressed, this "scientification of the recent past", which in theory should increasingly give way to an academic "science of history", has not happened in the case of Germany with the history of the

2. Historical Revisionism and the Politics of Memory

Third Reich and German wartime atrocities. "One could even say that the exact opposite of what Koselleck has predicted is happening at present. The Holocaust, despite increasing temporal distance from the actual events, is not losing its topical character and fading out of awareness, but is paradoxically moving closer and becoming more vital." (Assmann 1999: 14) As we saw in chapter 1, the same can be said of Japan where, far from lessening or becoming more scientific and dispassionate, discussions about the wartime past are escalating and gaining in importance in both society and politics.

This phenomenon is to be explained—as Aleida Assmann has proposed for the German case—as the working of the general mechanisms that contribute to the formation of historical memory, which enter a particularly crucial phase when what she calls "communicative memory" evolves into "cultural memory" (Assmann 1999: 15 and passim). At the beginning of the 21st century, the development of historical memory regarding the Second World War has entered the stage where "the past experiences of contemporaries,[80] if they are not to be lost, have to be translated into a cultural memory for posterity. Living memory thus gives way to a memory based on [communications] media, with carriers such as monuments, memorials, museums and archives." (Assmann 1999: 15) It hardly needs saying that these processes of "translation" involve much potential for debate and friction between involved parties, and it is exactly this conflict over translating communicative memory into a permanent cultural memory that has caused so much stress to the fabric of Japanese society in recent times. As we shall see in what follows, politicians have taken a leading role in defining cultural memory as far as the public sphere is concerned. This, again, is not a particularly Japanese phenomenon: "Since there is no such thing as the self-organization of cultural memory, it has to rely on the media and politics. However, the transition from the living individual memory to the artificial cultural memory is problematic, since it involves the danger of distortion, reduction and instrumentalization." (Assmann 1999: 15) The creation of memory within the framework of these processes is subject to the exigencies of identity politics, which are important to modern societies and especially to their ability to come to terms with past wars. In Japan, as we will see in this chapter, it is the attempt to impose a certain historical narrative in the public sphere (i.e., in monuments, memorials, museums and public cere-

---

[80] Assmann calls these experiences and the memories based on them "communicative memory", which she defines as "orally transmitted memories that usually connect three generations." (Assmann 1999: 13)

monies)—a narrative which is not based on a social consensus—that lies at the root of the fiery debates over how to memorialize the national story.

In this process of memorializing history, wars have always played a particularly important role and have been the source of much heated debate (Fujiwara 2001). It is therefore not surprising, as we saw in chapter 1, that in Japan the current debate is focusing on the history of "the last war" (*saki no sensō*)—over which there is no consensus, even on naming the conflict. The importance of war in constructing the framework of historical memory reflects the observation that the creation of memory in general is much affected by the factor of pain. Nietzsche, one of the pioneers of research on memory, argued this point:

> Whenever man has thought it necessary to create a memory for himself, his effort has been attended with torture, blood, sacrifice. The ghastliest sacrifices and pledges, including the sacrifice of the first-born; the most repulsive mutilations, such as castration; the cruelest rituals in every religious cult (and all religions are at bottom systems of cruelty)—all these have their origin in the instinct which divined *pain to be the strongest aid to mnemonics.* (Nietzsche 1887, cited in White 1973: 361; emphasis added)

Nietzsche's observations are confirmed when considering the role wars have played—and still play—in the historical memory of national states (Fujiwara 2001; Fujitani et al. 2001: 2). The modern wars conducted by nation-states were bloodier than earlier conflicts and costlier in terms both of material and human life. This, of course, is explained by the tendency of modern warfare to pit not so much army against army, but rather nation against nation, leading eventually to the mobilization of an entire country including its population, its national economy, its material resources, and its science. The devastation brought about by the "total wars" waged on behalf of the modern nation-state led to serious questioning of the fitness of the nation-state as the ideal form of political existence. As one historian put it: "The connection between the nation and mass death disturbed [..] optimism [about the future]." (Bodnar 2000: 954) As a result, as part of the task of nation-building, wars had to be remembered in a way that re-affirmed the integration and integrity of the (postwar) nation and the nation-state, and thereby generated optimism about the future—an integral part of national identity in every modern nation-state. Re-affirming national identity and optimism about the future also presupposed a strong connection between historical memory and mourning for the war dead—another universal facet of historical memory. As Aleida Assmann puts it: "The anthropological core of cultural memory lies in the memory of the war dead." (Assmann 1999: 33; see

2. Historical Revisionism and the Politics of Memory

also Reichel 1999: 17f) In Japan, too, discussions about how best to mourn the dead of "the last war" are closely interlinked with the construction of historical memory, as I explain in detail below.

In this chapter, I assess the uses (and abuses) of history in the political arena and demonstrate that the dominant historical narrative to be found in the public sphere in Japan closely resembles that of historical revisionism, particularly at the level of national politics. However, in order to pursue the question raised in 1.5.2 why Japan's apologies for its wartime past are considered insincere by Japan's Asian neighbors, here I want to stress the influence of historical revisionism in the public sphere by analyzing historical interpretations underlying memorials, monuments and historical museums. In doing so, I will concentrate on those "realms of memory" that are supported, utilized or sanctioned by representatives of the Japanese state and therefore, in one way or another, have to be considered as official versions of recent Japanese history. While all prime ministers since Hashimoto Ryūtarō have endorsed the official view of Japan's past as set out in the self-critical Murayama statement of 1995 (see chapter 1.5.2 and appendix 2), the historical perspectives underlying many memorials, monuments and museums in the public sphere are quite different.

To illustrate this point, I analyze the version of history promulgated by the Yasukuni Shrine, frequently visited by postwar Japanese prime ministers (see appendix 4) as the "most important" institution for the mourning of the war dead. In response to international sensitivities, since the mid 1980s heads of government refrained from visits to the shrine, but as a result of the renewed regular visits of Prime Minister Koizumi since 2000, the debate has resurfaced.[81] While Japan still lacks a central national war-memorial, several projects have been discussed and realized in recent years, and these more recent expressions of the self-understanding of

---

[81] A search of the contents database of *MagazinePlus* (Nichigai Associates, http://web.nichigai.co.jp/) resulted in 753 hits (i.e. articles) for the search string "Yasukuni jinja" between 1982 and May 2003. Debate about the Shrine climaxed in 1985 (65 articles), as a result of the visit of Prime Minister Nakasone in that year, and again in 1986 (73 articles), 2001 (257 articles) and 2002 (107 articles). An examination of the publications involved shows how the issue has polarized the political media. Most articles were published in the conservative to right-wing journals that support the Yasukuni Shrine, such as *Shokun!* (64 articles), *Seiron* (50 articles), *Voice* (37), *Jurisuto* (24), *Bungei Shunjū* (17) and *Sapio* (14), or in the liberal to left-wing journals that oppose it, such as *Sekai* (42 articles), *Shūkan Kin'yōbi* (28), *Sunday Mainichi* (20), *Asahi Journal* (16) and *Ronza* (14). Apart from these journals, only *Shūkan Shinchō* (20), *Ushio* (16), *Chūō Kōron* (12) and *Economist* (12) had significant hits. All the other magazines listed published fewer than ten articles on the subject between 1982 and 2003.

the Japanese state are also treated here. While the official standpoint embodied in the Murayama statement is still considered valid, the historical views underlying these institutions should be considered an alternative or semi-official reading of the recent history of the Japanese state.

2.1 THE YASUKUNI PROBLEM

The "Yasukuni problem," or the ongoing controversy over the Yasukuni Shrine (Yasukuni jinja 靖国神社) in Tōkyō, symbolizes the disputes surrounding the commemoration of the war dead and the display of historical views in the public sphere.[82] The shrine has become a focal point for the politics of memory in Japan. Originally established as the Tōkyō Shōkonsha, the Yasukuni Shrine was given its present name in 1879 (Antoni 1998: 341; Pye 2003: 52; Kobori 1998: 30). The memorial was originally dedicated to those killed in action during the period of turmoil leading up to the Meiji Restoration (1853–1868), as well as government troops who died during the civil wars of the 1870s. Later soldiers, sailors and airmen who fell "in defense of the nation in Japan's wars with other countries" were included. Today, "the divine spirits" of all members of the Japanese military and individuals affiliated with the military who died for "the Emperor and the nation" between 1853 and 1945 are "worshipped"[83] at the Shrine. This commemoration and worship as "gods" (*kami* 神) and "heroic souls" (*eirei* 英霊) includes individuals sentenced for committing war crimes by the International Military Tribunal for the Far East (IMTFE), such as wartime Prime Minister Tōjō Hideki (Tanaka 2002a: 39; see below), but generally excludes civilian victims of war—Japanese as well as Asian.[84]

---

[82] While previous studies have focused on the religious aspects of the Yasukuni problem (Antoni 1998; Nelson 2003) or juristic-political issues (Muramatsu 1987: 315; Lokowandt 1981), the problem of the view of history presented by the Yasukuni Shrine and the implications of the political sanctioning of this view through official visits by prime ministers, cabinet members and parliamentarians have received little discussion. See Cornelißen, Klinkhammer and Schwentker 2003 for various aspects of the culture of memory in Germany, Italy and Japan.
[83] The term "worship" is used by the Yasukuni Shrine in its English-language publications.
[84] The criteria for an individual to be honored at the Shrine are somewhat flexible. One absolute condition is "death in battle" (or as a result of battle) in military units that went to war to defend the emperor and the country (*kangun*). The classification of military forces into "government units" or "rebels" was often established only decades after the death of the combatants concerned (Akaza-

2. Historical Revisionism and the Politics of Memory

In view of the Shrine's past as a central institution of the state-sponsored Shintō religion before the war and as a symbol of militarism[85] and the Japanese wars in general, as well as its more recent role as a representation of revisionism, it remains a controversial site. Time and again, highly-publicized visits by conservative politicians highlight the contentiousness of the issue in the spheres of politics, society, and the media. The regular visits by prime minister Koizumi Jun'ichirō in particular (see cover photo), the first prime minister since Nakasone Yasuhiro in the early 1980s[86] to visit the Shrine annually (2000–2004) (see appendix 4), have added flames to the Yasukuni fire. The heated contemporary debate over the "Yasukuni problem" is focused on the following issues:

- The relationship of state and religion and the related issue of whether an official visit[87] by the prime minister is in conflict with the separation of state and religion as set out in article 20 of the Constitution (cf. Yokota 2004).
- The relationship of state and citizen, reflecting the fact that all service personnel who died during the war are compulsorily commemorated at the Shrine and included in the list of those worshipped there ("soul registers"). The Shrine determines those who are to be "worshipped" in accordance with the registers of fallen soldiers compiled by the Ministry of Welfare (Kōseishō, now the Ministry of Health, Labor and

---

wa 2002: 5). Included among those worshipped in the Yasukuni, and in addition to combat soldiers, are persons affiliated with the military (*gunzoku*) and a number of civilians—primarily nurses in war zones, but also schoolchildren who volunteered toward the end of the war (1945) to work in armaments factories. For exact numbers of individuals enshrined, see appendix 3.

[85] Tanaka 2002a: 17f. From the beginning, the Yasukuni Shrine was governed directly by military institutions, i.e., the army and navy ministries, or their predecessors, and was guarded by military police (Kenpeitai). The Shrine soon took on an important role in the system of ideology designed to stabilize the Japanese nation state through the construction of state Shintō. In conjunction with the Ise Shrine (Ise Jingū 伊勢神宮) and the Meiji Shrine (Meiji Jingū 明治神宮) built in 1915–1920, the Yasukuni Shrine became one of the three major holy sites of state Shintō. The approximate 150 *Shōkonsha* in other cities were renamed "national defense shrines" (Gokoku Jinja 護国神社) in 1939, limited to one institution per prefecture, and placed below the Yasukuni Shrine in the hierarchical structure of Shintō shrines. However, in contrast to the Yasukuni Shrine, they remained under the administration of the Home Ministry. See Tanaka 2002a: ch. 1.

[86] On the Nakasone visits, see Tanaka 2002a: chapter 5.4.

[87] On the distinction between official visits and visits of politicians as private individuals, see Hata 2002a: 12; Tanaka 2002a: 142–144.

Welfare, Kōsei Rōdōshō) (Tanaka 2003: 62). Naturally this has become a problem in the case of Japanese Christians and Buddhists, as well as for the descendants of servicemen from Taiwan (27,863 people) and Korea (21,181) in particular, whose fathers and grandfathers were often forced into the Japanese military and who continue to resist their veneration in a Japanese shrine (cf. Tanaka 2002a: chapter 7.2). And while some Japanese nationals ask themselves whether "forced commemoration" violates the right guaranteed in the Constitution for the freedom of religion of each citizen,[88] the Shrine maintains that once someone joins the "heroic souls" worshipped at Yasukuni, he cannot be separated from the union of souls acknowledged there (Tanaka 2002a: 224).

- The international implications of official visits made by the prime minister, primarily in view of the fact that since 1978, 13 military personnel and one civilian who were tried (and eventually executed or died in prison) as Class A war criminals[89] (*A-kyū senpan* A 級戦犯) by the IMTFE are honored in the Yasukuni Shrine. These include not only the wartime prime minister, Tōjō Hideki, but also the Commander-in-Chief of Japanese troops in Nanjing in 1937, Matsui Iwane.[90] This aspect of the "Yasukuni problem" highlights the frequently cited significance of the Yasukuni Shrine as a "symbol of Japanese militarism" during the prewar era, and it is also a fundamental aspect of the understanding of history embodied in the Shrine.
- Another aspect of the Yasukuni problem that is rarely discussed directly is the interpretation of history expressed in official statements emanating from the Shrine and documented in its museum, the

---

[88] See in particular the work of Tanaka Nobumasa (Tanaka 2002a; 2002b; 2003). The worship of people as gods is generally rare in Shintō. The best-known example is Sugawara Michizane, who is enshrined in Kitano-Tenmangu in Kyōto. In addition, there are a number of shrines in which famous historical figures are commemorated, e.g., the medieval generals Uesugi Kenshin, Toyotomi Hideyoshi and Tokugawa Ieyasu, and several military figures of the Meiji era who were not accepted into the circle of "Yasukuni Gods", e.g., Nogi Maresuke, Saigō Takamori and Tōgō Heihachirō. See in general Inoue 1999, especially 147; see also Kobori 1998: 57–60; Hardacre 1989: 90f.

[89] Class A: crimes against peace; Class B: conventional war crimes; Class C: crimes against humanity.

[90] Those honored at the Shrine include of course all war criminals of Classes B and C who were either sentenced to death or died in custody. For the official reason for the inclusion of 14 Class A war criminals, see Yasukuni Jinja Shamusho 1992: 32–35. See also Kobori 1998: 144; Etō and Kobori 1986: passim, especially 102–123; and Tanaka 2002a: chapter 5.2.

Yūshūkan. To be sure, the religious issues connected with the Shrine are too complex to outline here (cf. Antoni 1998; Nelson 2003). Nevertheless, in view of the historical message communicated by the exhibitions in the Yūshūkan Museum, the "Yasukuni problem" might be redefined as the "Yūshūkan problem". The worship of the war dead, and the now mitigated demand for nationalization of the Yasukuni Shrine (cf. Lokowandt 1981: chapter 4.2), have become lesser issues in the ongoing public debate. Instead, the interpretation of history validated by the Shrine, and the Yūshūkan Museum in particular, has become the focus of controversy. From the Shrine's perspective, presenting an affirmative interpretation of the war is necessary in order to commemorate the nation's fallen soldiers without "soiling" their reputation (cf. Wakabayashi 2000: 338ff; Fujiwara 2001: 167f; Maeno 2003: 15). But this interpretation is viewed with great mistrust both within Japan and by Japan's neighbors, China and the two Koreas, since it corresponds so fundamentally with the revisionist representation of history sketched in chapter 1.

2.2 The Historical Narrative of the Yūshūkan

In the words of the Shrine's own publicity material, the Yūshūkan Museum (遊就館)[91] aims to "communicate to its visitors a more accurate truth about modern Japanese history" (*Nihon kingendaishi no shinjitsu o yori tadashiku rikai shite itadaku tame*) (Yasukuni Jinja Shamusho 2002). Justification of the wars pursued by modern Japan is provided by presenting them as defensive wars or wars of Asian liberation (*Ajia kaihō sensō*). The museum seeks to confirm the belief that the soldiers commemorated fought a fair and just war and gave their lives in fulfilment of a just mission for the Emperor, the nation, and their families. Hence, the Yūshūkan exhibition fosters not only a justification of Japan's wars but also the refusal to assume responsibility for war.

The museum presents an affirmative interpretation of the war from the display on the (First) Sino-Japanese War 1894/95 to depictions of the end of the war in 1945. A line of blue neon light extends throughout the entire exhibition as a way of underlining historical continuity. Moreover, the Japanese wars are presented as a centuries-long struggle against Western

---

[91] The museum was founded in 1876 (for more about the founding of the museum, see Kobori 1998: 240–250). In 1932, it transferred to a new building which is still used today as the main exhibition hall. Between 2001 and July 2002 the museum was renovated, refurbished and expanded.

colonialism and imperialism, as is clearly shown right at the start of the exhibition. The main exhibition begins (in room number 6) with the Battle of Plassey of 1757 [!] and the "penetration of European imperialism" into East Asia. (While England's victory at the Battle of Plassey indeed established its hegemony in East Bangalore, this development had little immediate impact on Japan as it was fighting its own "home-grown" economic crisis at this period.) Following a presentation of the "heroic battles" of the anti-Tokugawa (and anti-foreigner) movement of the late Edo period (*bakumatsu*, 1853–1868) as well as of the civil war of the Meiji-Restoration in 1868/69, the founding of the Shrine itself and its relationship to the imperial household is depicted in a special exhibition (room number 9). The continuity of Japanese history is emphasized by tracing an unbroken line from the legendary first emperor Jimmu—represented in the form of a statue—up to the "Rescript on Education" (Kyōiku Chokugo) of 1890, one of the founding documents of the modern nation-state.[92]

The historical narrative that unfolds in later displays presents the Japanese wars waged between 1894 and 1945 as a constant struggle for independence, or for the liberation of Asian "brother nations" from Western colonial rule. The Russo-Japanese War of 1904/05 is depicted in a multimedia display in a special exhibition room (*Nichiro sensō panorama-kan*) and is given an extremely militaristic slant. Details about the consequences of this war, the dark side of Japan's colonial rule in Korea beginning in 1910, or the problematic issues surrounding the "Greater East Asian War" (*DaitōA sensō*) waged between 1937 and 1945 (exhibition rooms 16–20)—such as the Nanjing incident of 1937—are either omitted or are depicted in distorted fashion. Thus, the treatment of Nanjing is limited to a depiction of the city's capture by Japanese forces; no mention is made of the massacre of the civilian population—the real "Nanjing incident"—that *followed* the city's fall. The explanatory text, in the exhibition room labeled "China Incident", reads as follows:

> Nanking Incident
> After the Japanese surrounded Nanking in December 1937, Gen. Matsui Iwane distributed maps to his men with foreign settlements and the Safety Zone marked in red ink. Matsui told them that they were to observe military rules to the letter and that anyone committing unlawful acts would be severely punished. He also warned Chinese troops to surrender, but Commander-in-Chief Tang Shengzhi ignored the warning. Instead, he ordered his men to defend Nanking to the death, and then abandoned them. The Chinese were

---

[92] For the significance of the Rescript on Education see Antoni 1998: 214–217.

2. Historical Revisionism and the Politics of Memory

soundly defeated, suffering heavy casualties. Inside the city, residents were once again able to live their lives in peace.[93]

Following a detailed depiction of the "Greater East Asian War" spanning five exhibition rooms, the conclusion is presented that the war was fought to secure Japan's independence and livelihood and that it was a war of liberation for Asia from the Western colonial powers. Moreover, the war attained these goals indirectly since after 1945 a significant number of Asian nations achieved independence or at least a degree of autonomy.

After viewing the historical exhibition, visitors are ushered into the "large exhibition hall" where they are confronted with weapons, helmets pierced with bullet holes, and other pieces of equipment used by the Imperial Army and Navy. There is a puzzling contradiction between the putative role of the Yasukuni Shrine as a "memorial for peace" (*heiwa kinenkan*) (cf. Shintō Seiji Renmei 2003: 9f; Yaskukuni jinja shamusho 2002) and the displays and their accompanying texts—including military fighter aircraft from the Pacific War, artillery, tanks, and one-man submarines used for suicide missions (*gyorai*).[94]

Ill. 7: The Yūshūkan Museum in the precincts of the Yasukuni Shrine, Tōkyō (Photo: Sven Saaler).

---

[93] This is the original English version of the exhibition text. The Japanese version closes with the sentence "Nankin ippan shimin ni wa heiwa ga yomigaeta" (peace returns for the common citizens of Nanjing)—borrowing the title of an article printed in a popular Japanese daily newspaper in December 1937.

[94] Also, the homepage of the Yūshūkan, updated in 2002, displays a heavily martial character (www.yasukuni.or.jp/yusyukan/).

The reasons for the political explosiveness of the Yasukuni Shrine, and the visits made to it by conservative politicians, should by now be clear enough: the resistance to the visits, both within Japan and from abroad, is not directed against the commemoration of war dead (although the way soldiers are "worshipped" here seems more than atavistic), but is rather a protest against the distorted presentation of history in the Shrine, which is *sanctioned by the state* and receives official recognition through visits by national leaders. While the official position of the Japanese government toward the war in East Asia still accords with the Murayama Declaration of 1995, the historical interpretation presented at Yūshūkan is slowly becoming the semi-official reading of history adopted by the Japanese *state*, a reading echoed in many other memorial sites that either receive funding from the government or are in some way recognized by it (see below, chapter 2.3).

The reading of Japan's military past reflected by the Yūshūkan Museum is not, however, supported by the majority of Japanese, as I discuss further in chapter 3. Thus, it is met with fierce criticism not only from abroad, but also in Japan itself. Despite such opposition, the Shrine continues to promote its version of history and justifies this by the strengthening of Japanese patriotic sentiment that will follow from the dissemination of a "bright" version of the nation's past. In his justification of the enshrinement of the 14 individuals classified as war criminals by the IMTFE, Matsudaira Nagayoshi, a former high priest of the Shrine, blamed many of the problems facing modern Japan on the view of history that evolved as a consequence of the Tōkyō trials (*Tōkyō saiban shikan*). "As long as the ideology of the Tōkyō trials is accepted, there will be no restoration of the Japanese spirit (*Nihon seishin*)."[95]

During Nakasone's incumbency, the commotion created over the past few decades by politicians visiting the Yasukuni Shrine has incited discussion about establishing an alternative institution that would serve as an undisputed national memorial for the victims of war—and, in contrast to the Yasukuni Shrine, not be limited to members of the military forces. Even today there exists no central national memorial for the victims of war in Japan (Arai 1994: 5). However, as a quasi-national memorial, the Yasukuni Shrine receives by far the greatest attention as the main repository for Japan's politics of memory, not only in Japan itself but also abroad (Tanaka 2003: 63; Jinja Honchō Kyōgaku Kenkyūjo 2000). Although other major commemorative sites have been established over the years, none has been able to emerge from the shadow cast by the Yasukuni Shrine.

---

[95] Cited in Hata 2002b: 26; for similar statements by Nakasone, see Arai 1994: 16; see also Kobori 1998: 6, 177, 187–190, 224 and passim.

The main reason for this is that these memorials do not represent an historical consensus either; indeed, some are as controversial in their historical readings as the Yasukuni Shrine, and none of them includes the victims of Japanese warfare in Asia in the circle of those memorialized, as critics of the Yasukuni Shrine repeatedly emphasize (Obinata 2004: 85; Arai 2001).

2.3 Historical Interpretations Underlying Other Memorials

2.3.1 Chidorigafuchi

Since only members of the military are venerated at the Yasukuni Shrine, demands were voiced quite early for a national war memorial that would also include civilian victims, especially the victims of Allied bombings including the atomic bombs dropped on Hiroshima and Nagasaki. As early as 1959, a memorial for Japan's war victims was established in the vicinity of the Yasukuni—the Chidorigafuchi Cemetery for the War Dead (Chidorigafuchi Senbotsusha Boen 千鳥ヶ淵戦没者墓苑).[96] A broad consensus emerged in politics and society over the concept for the memorial, and even the Socialist Party (SPJ) expressed its consent (Zaidan Hōjin Chidorigafuchi Senbotsusha Boen Hōshakai 1989: 2). Initially conceived as a hybrid between a collective cemetery and a "tomb of the unknown soldier" (*mumei senshi no haka*), Chidorigafuchi became a site where the remains of fallen soldiers who remained unidentified (more than 350,000 at present) found their final resting place.[97] Since 1963, 800,000 Japanese civilians who died during the war have been commemorated here as well (Chidorigafuchi Senbotsusha Boen 2003). Each year in the first half of August a memorial ceremony is held at Chidorigafuchi attended by representatives from the government; Buddhist, Christian and other religious organizations (cf. Zaidan Hōjin Chidorigafuchi Senbotsusha Boen Hōshakai 1989: 69); and members of the Self Defense Forces (SDF) (cf. Zaidan Hōjin Chidorigafuchi Senbotsusha Boen Hōshakai 1989: 60–61) as well as members of the Imperial family. Nonetheless, the memorial re-

---

[96] The institution's official title in English is the "Chidorigafuchi Unknown Soldier's Tomb" (Zaidan Hōjin Chidorigafuchi Senbotsusha Boen Hōshakai 1989: 9). However, the entrance to the tomb is marked with a sign reading "Chidorigafuchi National Cemetery".

[97] A cabinet meeting held on 10 December 1953, decided that a "cemetery for the unknown war dead" (*mumei senbotsusha no haka*) should be erected in which "the remains of those who died, and which could not be returned to their families, shall be enshrined." See Tanaka 2002a: 74–78.

ceives little attention in Japan; the name "Chidorigafuchi" has instead become synonymous with cherry blossom and the *hanami* festival—evoking the obligatory picnic party under cherry trees held in late March or early April. While more than six million people visit the Yasukuni Shrine each year, Chidorigafuchi could count only around 180,000 visitors in 2001.

Ill. 8: Chidorigafuchi Senbotsusha Boen in Tōkyō (Photo: Sven Saaler).

The two main reasons for Chidorigafuchi's lack of prominence and acceptance are the imprecise nature of the institution itself and the obstructionist policies pursued by supporters of the Yasukuni Shrine. In contrast to the latter, the Chidorigafuchi memorial—despite its designation as a cemetery (*boen*)—is not considered a religious site but rather, according to the official definition, simply as a "park" (*kōen shikichi*) (Shushō Kantei 2002). This definition was devised to help resolve one aspect of the "Yasukuni problem", the division of religion and state. However, in the eyes of proponents of the Yasukuni Shrine, the missing religious dimension at Chidorigafuchi is a distinct disadvantage for an insititution that purportedly serves to commemorate the war dead. Classifying Chidorigafuchi as a mere "park" ensured that a location was created where important foreign visitors could pay their respects to the victims of war during state visits. However, as a result of the many problems evaded—rather than addressed—by the foundation of the Chidorigafuchi memorial, its legal, religious and political status remains unclear. On its homepage and in its brochures the site describes itself evasively as "to a certain extent [!] a memorial for unknown soldiers" (Chidorigafuchi Senbotsusha Boen 2003). Moreover, the question of Japan's responsibility for the war is avoided at Chidorigafuchi, too, and so for critics of Yasukuni it fails to represent an acceptable alternative as a national memorial. The Yasukuni Shrine and the organizations that support it (cf. Yagyū 2003: 246–249) have obstructed the establishment of Chidorigafuchi as a national memorial from the planning stages (Sen'yūren 2002: Internet). The Yasukuni Shrine has repeatedly insisted on its role as the main memorial for Japan's victims of war—and insisted that it must remain so. In its view, Chidorigafuchi can at best fulfill a complementary role, but can never diminish the central significance of Yasukuni. This point was firmly made in an official declaration by the Shrine's administrative body:

> The remains of those enshrined at Chidorigafuchi are limited to victims of the battles that took place after the China Incident (*Shina-jihen*); the significance of this constraint should not be underestimated. The souls of martyrs from the Bakumatsu and Restoration periods up to the last Great War (*konji taisen*) with its 2.46 million fallen soldiers are commemorated in the Yasukuni Shrine. Thus the Chidorigafuchi memorial is not a substitute for the Yasukuni Shrine. (Yasukuni Jinja 2002)

When legislation was approved for the founding of the Chidorigafuchi Memorial the government officially had to declare that "in contrast to the Yasukuni Shrine, where the souls (*rei*) of all the victims of war are commemorated, it is only in special cases that human remains are kept in the [Chidorigafuchi] 'tomb'. […] Thus, the character of the memorial and the Yasukuni Shrine are essentially different." (Sen'yūren 2002) Chidorigafuchi has not been able to anchor itself firmly in the minds of the people. Since 1963, the official memorial ceremony of the Japanese government held each year on the anniversary of the end of the war (August 15) has no longer been staged at Chidorigafuchi, but in the concert and sporting venue known as the Budōkan (武道館) adjoining it.[98] This development

---

[98] This ceremony is attended by the Emperor and his wife or palace representatives, the head of the government, the presidents of both houses of parliament, and the president of the Supreme Court. Foreign dignitaries are usually not invited to attend (see Pye 2003: 51–54, Zaidan Hōjin Chidorigafuchi Senbotsusha Boen Hōshakai 1989: 54).

has further decreased Chidorigafuchi's importance, and has in turn reinforced the significance of the Yasukuni Shrine as the "most important religious site of the Japanese people".[99]

2.3.2 Shōwakan and Heiwa Kinen Tenji Shiryōkan

Following growing criticism of the "existence of the Yasukuni Shrine" (*Yasukuni jinja no arikata*) from the mid 1980s, when the history textbook debate reached its first international climax, politicians began considering the creation of a "new institution" (*atarashii shisetsu*) which would be an undisputed memorial with an historical basis acceptable to broad sections of society, and which would receive greater recognition than Chidorigafuchi. The issue crystalized new developments in the early 1980s in Japan's "politics of memory" that ran parallel to the history textbook issue. However, as in the past the Yasukuni Shrine categorically rejected all plans to create a new memorial and asserted its own position as the traditional commemorative site for those who died for the Japanese nation. Yet, by the early 1980s, many politicians were no longer willing to accept the burden for Japan's foreign policy that holding fast to the Yasukuni Shrine entailed.

In the mid 1980s the Ministry of Welfare (Kōseishō) began considering plans for another memorial that would be opened on the 50th anniversary of the end of the war. This new memorial would exist alongside the Yasukuni Shrine and would also commemorate the civilian victims of war. Above all, the new institution would overcome the—continuing—lack of a national *peace* memorial in Japan, which explains the lengthy project title: "Memorial for the Victims of War and a Memorial for Peace" (*Senbotsusha tsuitō heiwa kinen-kan* 戦没者追悼平和祈念館) (Hosoya and Ide 1995: 23; Itō 2002: 26).

Since even the *planning* of a new memorial would irritate supporters of the Yasukuni Shrine, it was decided in the Kōseishō that the Japan Bereaved Families Association (Nihon Izoku-kai) would be included in the planning. The support of this association was (and is) essential to the LDP in mobilizing voters in rural areas—a factor which may also explain why conservative circles within the LDP still insist on official visits to the Yasukuni Shrine (Hata 2002a: 13; Hata 2002b: 16f; Arai 2001: 39). In a way similar to the discussions outlined in chapter 1.5.1 over the Diet resolution admitting Japan's responsibility for the war, strong resistance

---

[99] This claim was made in a call by the Shrine's main administrative body (Jinja honchō) to nationalize the Shrine, quoted in Lokowandt 1981: 193.

emerged against any memorial or associated exhibition that would openly admit Japan's war guilt. While politicians, intellectuals and representatives of the media from all parts of the political spectrum were involved in the initial stages of planning for the new memorial, it soon became clear that the views of the Japan Bereaved Families Association would hold sway. Other participants on the planning committee then withdrew, including one of the spokespersons for the liberal camp, the historian Hosoya Chihiro. Hosoya left the commission in 1994 in protest against the historical interpretation to be embodied in the exhibition envisaged as part of the planned memorial and which he saw as legitimizing and glorifying Japan's war of aggression (Fujiwara 2001: 115; Hosoya and Ide 1995: 31). Moreover, according to critics of the project, the large budget allocated for the memorial stood in stark contrast to the Japanese government's refusal to pay reparations to the victims of Japanese aggression in Asia—who, moreover, are not included in commemorations at any of the Japanese memorial institutions (Hosoya and Ide 1995: 31; cf. also Arai 1994: 3f).

Plans to establish the memorial in 1995 finally failed. It was only in March 1999 that, as an ancillary product of these plans, the so-called "Shōwa Hall" (Shōwakan 昭和館) was established in the vicinity of the Yasukuni Shrine. The official English name of this institution is the National Showa Memorial Museum and its management (*un'ei*) has been delegated by the Ministry of Welfare to the Izoku-kai.The Shōwakan is less a memorial than an "exhibition centre and central archive", where, in accordance with its guidelines, the "suffering of the [Japanese] population during wartime" (*sensō no rōku*) are to be conveyed to the younger generation.[100] The institution seeks to present "the life of the people during and after the war" and to collect materials (documents and objects) connected with this topic. However, the fact that the museum subsumes the wartime and postwar periods (1935–1955) without distinction serves to emphasize Japan's role as a victim of war, which is also a central aspect of the revisionist interpretation of history. In its exhibition, therefore, the consequences of war for the Japanese population only are presented, while neither the reasons for war nor the issue of Japan's

---

[100] Shōwakan 2002. The museum's English-language brochure states its rationale thus: "We convey the life of Japanese during and after World War II". Its objective is "to collect, store and exhibit historical data and information that is related to the hardships of citizens' life, including the bereaved families of those who died, during and after the World War II, and provide an opportunity for future generations to know about these hardships."

responsibility for initiating the war are mentioned at all (Fujiwara 2001: 114f; Itō 2002: 29, 34; Arai 1994:).

Of the Shōwakan's seven levels, the fourth floor of the building houses a library, the fifth floor contains a multimedia gallery, while the permanent exhibition takes up the sixth (the postwar period) and seventh floors (wartime conditions). The exhibition is divided into the following sections:[101]

Seventh Floor (Wartime conditions, 1935–1945)
- Parting with family (in Japanese: *sennin-bari*, i.e., "good-luck belts for soldiers, made with a thousand stitches embroidered by a thousand different women")
- Longing for family
- Family life around 1935
- Life under governmental control
- Hardship of school children and students
- Preparation on the home front and air raids
- August 15th, 1945—Declaration of the end of the war

Sixth Floor (Post war period, 1945–1955)
- Overcoming the war disasters—appearance before the war and present state
- Starting afresh from the ruins
- Bereft family (in Japanese: *hahaoya no sengo*, i.e., "the postwar of mothers")
- Postwar years for children
- Towards revival
- Body experience zone (in Japanese: *taiken hiroba*; here objects such as clothing, books and personal effects from the wartime and postwar period can be seen and touched)
- The changing times—1935 to 1955

Initially, the Shōwakan also contained the following displays:
- *Kataritsutaetai senchū, sengo no kioku*, i.e., "what I want to communicate of my wartime and postwar memories"; this area featured testimonies of war participants recorded on video.
- "Bright stories (*akarui wadai*) to inspire people's dreams"
- A plea made by 100 million (people) (*100 man-nin no negai*)

The keyword of the entire exhibition is "suffering" (*rōku*), i.e., the suffering endured by Japanese civilians—children, mothers, women, fami-

---

[101] The following descriptions are drawn from the museum's English-language brochure.

2. Historical Revisionism and the Politics of Memory

lies—during the war. The rationale seems to be that, by remembering this "suffering", a contribution will be made toward peace in the future. Yet, while wartime suffering is limited to Japanese soil, the war itself remains a vague event on the horizon, distant and anonymous. With the exception of the bombings, only the indirect consequences of war are presented in the displays—and then only those that affected the Japanese population: poverty, hunger, and the black market. Visitors learn nothing about Japanese soldiers and military forces—their very existence is barely acknowledged—and they learn no more about the events that led up to the war, which is not mentioned directly anywhere

Certainly, it was precisely this kind of exhibition—avoiding any clear statements on responsibility for the war and its causes—that was planned for the Shōwakan from the beginning by the Ministry of Welfare. In the words of a statement issued by the Ministry in 1997: "Because there are differences in the understanding of history, a positive presentation of the truth about the war is immensely difficult" (*sensō no jijitsu o kyakkan-teki ni teiji suru koto wa konnan*). Thus, "creating an exhibition that would facilitate an historical judgment" (*rekishi-teki hyōka o fukumu kanōsei no aru tenji*) should be avoided (cited in Itō 2002: 28). The result is a "memorial" that tries to reconstruct a "neutral" version of the war from the perspective of a Japanese victim. In this one-dimensional presentation of history there are neither causes nor perpetrators, because only in this way could the goal of creating an exhibition that does not permit an historical judgment—or even historical reflection—be achieved.

The same can be said for another institution, the Heiwa Kinen Tenji Shiryōkan (The Exhibition Centre and Reference Library for Peace and Consolation). This institution opened in November 2000 and is located on the 31st floor of the Sumitomo Building (Sumitomo-biru) in Tōkyō's Shinjuku district. The organization responsible for the museum is Heiwa Kinen Jigyō Tokubetsu Kikin (The Public Foundation for Peace and Consolation), founded in 1988. The Foundation is a legal body (Dokuritsu gyōsei hōjin) approved by the Ministry of Public Management, Home Affairs, and Post and Telecommunications (Sōmushō). The creation of this institution reveals the Japanese government's efforts to make up for the lack of a national "peace memorial", since the word "peace" is used here for the first time in the official designation of a memorial institution. The mission of the Heiwa Kinen Tenji Shiryōkan is "to communicate suffering [by soldiers and the civilian population] to ensure that the truth (*shinjitsu*) of this horrific war is not forgotten, and that subsequent generations learn about it" (Heiwa Kinen Jigyō Tokubetsu Kikin 2002: 1). In its English-language brochure, the museum states as its mission:

Remembrance and consolation for those Japanese—non-pensioned veterans, post-war internees, and repatriates—who suffered indescribably as a result of the last war, and as a symbol of the desire for lasting peace. In many cases, their sufferings were beyond description. [...] The main purpose of this reference library lies in providing Japanese people today with a better understanding of the hardships endured by those who suffered in the war, repatriates and others. (PFFPC 2002: 1)

Throughout the exhibition in the Heiwa Kinen Tenji Shiryōkan, no mention is made of the sufferings of war victims in other Asian countries. This is reinforced by the structure of the exhibition itself, which covers the following subjects:[102]

- Vestibule (From Peace to War)
- Call-up notification
- The war dead and the bereaved
- Life in Siberian POW camps (*rāgeri*)
- POWs after the war
- Repatriates from the former colonies (*hikiage*)
- Forum for transmitting recollections (*kataritsugu ba*, area equipped with videotapes, books and computers)

Ill. 9: **The exhibition at the Heiwa Kinen Tenji Shiryōkan in Shinjuku, Tōkyō (Photo: Sven Saaler).**

---

[102] For a detailed description of the exhibition see Heiwa Kinen Jigyō Tokubetsu Kikin 2000.

In contrast to the Shōwakan, this exhibition includes—in addition to displays featuring civilian victims—soldiers and postwar internees (particularly those interned as POWs in Siberia (*Shiberia yokuryū*), as well as repatriates from Japan's former colonies (*hikiage*), predominantly Manchuria. In an English-language brochure issued by the Heiwa Kinen Tenji Shiryōkan, the three main groups featured in the exhibition are depicted as pitiful cartoon figures with accompanying text:

- Japanese mother with small child grasping her hand: "Abandoning everything and even losing my baby, I barely managed to return alive."
- POW digging coal with a shovel: "Forced to perform hard labor in the extreme cold of Siberia, we suffered continually from hunger."
- Army veteran: "Wounded in fierce fighting and with no food, I thought I was done for." (PFFPC 2002: cover)

Ill. 10: A page of the English-language brochure produced by the Heiwa Kinen Tenji Shiryōkan (used by permission).

Exhibition and Reference Library for Peace and Consolation
Remembering the Misery of War

| Abandoning everything and even losing my baby, I barely managed to return alive. | Forced to perform hard labor in the extreme cold of Siberia, we suffered continually from hunger. | Wounded in fierce fighting and with no food, I thought I was done for. |

The Public Foundation for Peace and Consolation, Incorporated Administrative Agency

Here, once again, the keyword is "suffering" (*rōku*): the displays are concerned predominantly with the suffering of the *Japanese* people, while victimized Asian peoples are either not mentioned or simply excluded as a result of the heavy emphasis given to the victim status of Japanese. The war depicted in this exhibition occurs *in Japan*, not in continental Asia where most of the actual combat took place. Neither is the war named unequivocally. The expressions "Asia-Pacific War" and "Greater East Asian War" are avoided; throughout the exhibition only indefinite terms such as "the front" (*senzen*), "this war" (*konji taisen*) and "the last war" (*saki no sensō*) are used. As at the Shōwakan, the exhibition fails to address the background and the reasons for the war; for example, it depicts the hardships experienced by "repatriates" from the colonies and the Japanese puppet state of Manchukuo but fails to ask why they settled on the Asian continent in the first place. Although the exhibition seeks to keep alive the memories of the war, especially among the younger generation, and thus make a contribution toward maintaining peace in the future, a memorial that fails to address Japan's war responsibility or mention the Asian victims of Japanese aggression would receive less than unanimous approval in present-day Japan. Thus, despite an intensive advertising campaign and free entry, the memorial in Shinjuku remains little known five years after its opening, attracting fewer than 50,000 visitors annually.

2.3.3 Daitōa Seisen Taihi

If the exhibitions and memorials discussed so far consciously avoid direct references to the war and Japan's war responsibility, others present an even more direct and affirmative interpretation of the war. The memorial stone dedicated to the IMTFE judge Radhabinod Pal, an Indian national, located in the premises of the Gokoku Shrine in Kyōto, has already been mentioned (see chapter 1.1). The inscription praises Pal for acquitting Japan of the charge laid by the IMTFE that Japan had pursued a war of aggression, and thus implicitly absolves Japanese of responsibility for the outbreak of war. There are several other memorials dedicated to Pal throughout Japan. In the spa resort town of Atami near Tōkyō there is a temple with a Buddhist Kannon statue known as the Raising Asia Kannon (kō-A kannon).[103] The temple is dedicated to the seven Class A war criminals sentenced to death by the IMTFE including Matsui Iwane, founder of the Raising Asia Kannon and, as we saw, commander-in-chief of Japanese forces during the massacre of Nanjing in 1937. The main hall (*hondō*) of the temple houses, in addition to an assortment of war memorabilia, a photo of Pal and calligraphy by Matsui and the six other Class A war criminals. The temple precincts contain a number of memorial

---

[103] The official title of the temple is "Shūkyō hōjin reihaisan kō-A kannon".

cenotaphs, and Matsui and his co-accused are further commemorated in the "Cenotaph of the Seven" (Shichishi no hi). The inscription on the cenotaph was made by Yoshida Shigeru, Japan's prime minister from 1946–1947 and 1948–1956, and carries his signature.

Ill. 11: **Cenotaph of the Seven (Photo: Sven Saaler).**

In addition, a smaller cenotaph dedicated to Class A and Class B war criminals can be found in the temple precincts. In November 1971, members of the leftist Red Army (*sekigun*) faction detonated explosives close to the cenotaphs, splitting the Cenotaph of the Seven in two.

Other memorials are still more forthright in their affirmative view of the war. Quite often it is a single word, such as the term chosen to the designate the war, which makes a memorial site controversial and which can lead to domestic conflict as well as international complications. The exhibitions discussed in section 2.3, for example, use the neutral term "the last war" (*saki no sensō* or *konji taisen*) when referring to the Asian theater in World War II to avoid the dilemma of choosing between the generally accepted alternatives of '15-year war' (*Jūgo-nen sensō*) and 'Asia-Pacific War' (*Ajia Taiheiyō sensō*). The term *Daitō-A sensō* ("Greater East Asian War") was the official name used for the war between 1942 and 1945 in order to emphasize the Japanese struggle against "the West" as a war to liberate Asia. Today, it is mainly favored by the revisionist movement, but can also be found in a number of memorials and exhibitions. The memorials to Judge Pal are one example (Wakamiya 1995: 13; Kimijima 2001; Takahashi 2001: 35). In some cases, "Greater East Asian War" has been replaced by "Holy Greater East Asian War" (*Daitō-A seisen*), a term that for many years was found only in right-wing publications (cf. Takahashi 2001: 54) and internet sites.[104] But in Ishikawa prefecture in 2000 the term achieved a measure of respectability when a twelve-meter-tall commemorative cenotaph was erected in the Gokoku Shrine (Gokoku jinja) with official approval, bearing the inscription *Daitō-A seisen no taihi* (Great Monument to the Holy War in Greater East Asia) (see above, ill. 2).[105] The front of the monument bears the legend:

Daitōa ohomi ikusa wa	The unsullied battle for East Asia
bansei no	is the mirror
rekishi o terasu	of the history of ten thousand generations
kagami nari-keri	held before our eyes

Ill. 12: Inscription on the Great Monument to the Holy War in Greater East Asia (Photo: Sven Saaler).

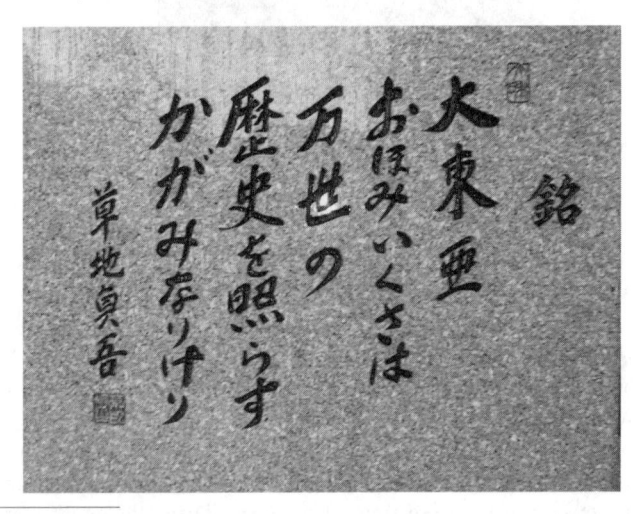

---

[104] A search under the category "Seiji"—"Seiji"—"Dantai" in the Japanese version of the internet search engine Yahoo yields a huge number of sites dealing with the subject, such as "Club Kamikaze", the "Uyoku Kyōwaha" ("right-wing republicans"), the "za. Uyoku" and the "Dai-Nihon aikoku-tō". See http://dir.yahoo.co.jp/Government/Politics/Organizations.

[105] The only other example known to me where the term *seisen* is used in an inscription is a monument erected in Mito in 1986 to commemorate "the Greater East Asian War" (Daitō-A Sensō Kinenhi).

2. Historical Revisionism and the Politics of Memory

While the designation of the war in East Asia and the Pacific as a "holy war" (*seisen*) can be found in sources of the 1930s and 1940s,[106] some politicians such as the prewar Lower House parliamentarian Saitō Takao regarded it as a "euphemism" (*bimei*) and a "ridiculous" expression, even when in widespread use at the height of the war (Kinmonth 1999: 337). During the postwar period, the term[107] became restricted to right-wing circles. Incidents such as the designation of Japan as a "land of gods" (*kami no kuni*) by former Prime Minister Mori Yoshirō (from Ishikawa prefecture [!]) in 2000 (see above, chapter 1.5.2) have until recently been dismissed with a smile.[108]

Planning for the monument in Ishikawa was initiated in 1996—the year in which the Tsukuru-kai was founded—by the right-wing associations Nihon o Mamoru-kai and Sen'yū-kai. The project was privately financed with funds donated by approximately 2,300 private individuals and 400 companies and associations, and a total of almost 100 million Yen was collected. The land where the monument is sited is administered by Ishikawa Prefecture in accordance with legislation governing city parks (Toshi Kōen-hō), but is leased to the Gokoku Shrine. However, the prefecture's administrative body must approve any alterations and construction work in the park, named *Honda no mori kōen* and located in the heart of the tourist area of Kanazawa. Disregarding numerous protests from

---

[106] While the term was used primarily for Asia's struggle (under Japanese "leadership") against the imperialist West, in 1934 a film entitled *Seisen no kagayaki* (*The Brightness of the Holy War*) was produced with the support of the Imperial Army. Between 1937 to 1939 the term Japanese "holy war" was commonly used by Japanese sources to describe the Japanese war *in China*; cf. BBK Mitsudai Nikki, 28 December 1937; BBK Rikushi Kimitsu Dai-nikki, 19 November 1938; BBK Rikuman Kimitsu Dai-nikki, December 1938. The very general use of the expression to legitimize Japanese expansionism is confirmed in a statement made by the army general Minami Jirō, Minister of the Army from 1932 to 1934 and later Commander-in-Chief of the Kwantung Army: "I never thought about it [the use of the term *seisen*] very deeply. I used the word because it was in wide currency at that time among the general public." Cited in Morris 1963: 44.

[107] Today the term "holy war" (*seisen*) is primarily used in Japanese as a synonym for the Islamic term *jihad*. The *Kōjien* dictionary has only a brief entry under "seisen", directing the reader to the entry under "jihad". The CD-ROM edition of the comprehensive reference book "Super Nipponica" (Nihon dai-hyakka zensho), published by Shōgakukan, lacks an entry under "seisen".

[108] The idea of Japan as a "land of gods" reaches back into Japanese antiquity. According to Ronald Toby: "*Shinkoku* thought, as first expressed in the archaic histories compiled in the eighth century, was premised on the notion that the Japanese land and people were uniquely descended from Japanese progenitor deities and 'confirmed' by foreign recognition." Toby 2001: 19.

within the prefecture (including those made by members of the Japan Bereaved Families Association, the Nihon Izoku-kai), but also from Okinawa and Korea (*Asahi.com* 1 May 2001; 2 May 2001; Yamaguchi 2001), the Ishikawa administration gave consent for the monument on 24 April 2000 and it was opened on 4 August in the same year with a ceremony performed in front of more than 1,000 guests. A declaration read out during the event emphasized that the memorial was to be seen as a prayer for eternal peace (*eikyū no heiwa o kinen shi*). Nakata Kiyoyasu, Chair of the Commission for the Erection of the Great Monument (Taihi Konryū Iinkai), added in an interview that the memorial was erected "to enlighten people who are unaware of our real history (*tadashii rekishi*); to reinstate a sense of pride in Japanese; and to rectify the nation's reputation and that of its heroes (*eiyū*)." (Asahi.com 4 May 2001) Once again it was "the truth" of Japanese history that needed communicating to Japanese. Each year on 4 August, the anniversary of the memorial's unveiling, a "Festival of the Holy Greater East Asian War" (*Daitō-A seisen-sai*) is held that is dedicated to propagating the "positive" interpretation of history underlying the concept of the "Holy War".

The completion of the "Great Monument to the Holy War in Greater East Asia" was a dispiriting event for those who reject the sanitized version of Japan's wartime past. Certainly, there are museums that present alternative interpretations of recent Japanese history, but most of them are private institutions or prefectural museums and memorials. The well-known prefectural peace museums in Hiroshima and Nagasaki consider the causes of the war to a limited degree, although they still focus on the wartime damage suffered by Japan, the devastation wreaked by the atomic bombs on Hiroshima and Nagasaki, and the meaning of these terrible events for mankind. This kind of narrative also forms the basis for the strong pacifism characteristic of postwar Japan, which from time to time is reconfirmed by events such as the damage sustained by Japanese fishing boats after the detonation of an experimental H-Bomb on Bikini Atoll in 1954 (cf. Orr 2001: 47–49). Nevertheless, in the exhibitions in Nagasaki and Hiroshima, Japanese responsibility for the war is still somewhat ambigious and is never made explicit.

We must turn to the prefecture of Okinawa for the closest approximation to a truly inclusive war memorial. The history of Okinawa contains a strong streak of independence from Japan which is confirmed in historical displays in museums in the archipelago. Some commentators criticize the fact that aspects of the region's history, such as the massacres of Okinawan civilians by Japanese forces during and after the Battle of Okinawa in 1945, have not yet become a part of the "national memory" but are rather excluded from the national mindset (Yakabi 2002: 88). War memorials in Okinawa, however, are designed to keep these painful memories alive. The exhibitions associated with them often stress the archipelago's long history of independence from the mainland and, regarding the war, present a narrative of double victimization—victimization of Okinawa by Japan and of Japan by the war. The exhibition in the Peace Memorial Park completed in 1999 refers to "massacres" carried out by the Japanese army in Okinawa in the final stages of the fighting in April/May 1945, but also speaks unequivocally of a Japanese "war of aggression" of which the annexation of Ryūkyū and the transformation of the island group into Okinawa prefecture in 1878 was just the beginning. While the exhibition was being set up, strong pressure was exerted by the Prefectural Government Office to omit these aspects and prevent the exhibition from becoming "overly anti-Japanese" (cf. Yakabi 2002: 87). Although such political-administrative resistance was eventually overcome, this quarrel did not lead to any kind of positive debate about Okinawa's history, as critics have noted (Yakabi 2002: 87f). Nevertheless, today the Okinawa Prefectural Peace Memorial Park is considered by many Japanese as exemplary in many respects.

Although this positive reputation is partly based on the multiple perspectives presented in the institution's historical exhibition, it is the so-called Cornerstone of Peace (Heiwa no ishiji), a memorial erected within the precincts of the park to those who died in the Battle of Okinawa, that has received particular attention.

Ill. 13:   **The Cornerstone of Peace (Photo: Sven Saaler).**

While the leftist-liberal camp still harshly criticizes the fact that Japan has erected memorials to the Japanese war dead, but not for the Asian victims of Japanese aggression, the creators of the Cornerstone of Peace at least took a new approach in deciding to include the names of all who died in the battle, irrespective of nationality. The Cornerstone of Peace includes granite tables on which are inscribed the names of 234,183 persons who died, directly or indirectly, as a result of the Battle of Okinawa. These lists include both military personnel and civilians—Okinawans, Japanese, Americans, Koreans, and Taiwanese. The monument thus fulfils the dual role of "creat[ing] a physical reminder of both the immense suffering caused by Japan's misguided ambitions and of Okinawa's enduring commitment to peace." (Weiner 1994: 170)

The existence of the Cornerstone of Peace underlines the absence of such a "physical reminder" on the national level. This failure is still felt as a black spot in Japan's coming to terms with its past and its handling of the politics of memory. The attitude of the political establishment to issues of public memory and the display of national history in the public sphere is still a much-contested issue in present-day Japan, as the renewed discussions over a new national memorial have demonstrated.

2.4 THE DEBATE OVER A NEW NATIONAL MEMORIAL TO COMMEMORATE THE WAR DEAD

While on the one hand Prime Minister Koizumi is the first head of government since the early 1980s to pay regular visits to the Yasukuni Shrine (four times between 2000 and 2004; see appendix 4), the Koizumi administration has taken up the question of a new national institution (*atarashii shisetsu*) to commemorate the war dead. Keen to shrug off criticism both within Japan and from abroad generated by his visits to Yasukuni, in late 2001 Koizumi set up a commission known as the Discussion Group to Consider Memorials and Other Sites for the Commemoration of the War Dead and Praying for Peace (Tsuitō, Heiwa Kinen no tame no Kinenhi-tō Shisetsu no Arikata o Kangaeru Kondankai 追悼・平和祈念のための記念碑等施設の在り方を考える懇談会). The commission convened ten times during 2002 and comprised the following members:

Imai Takashi, chairman (Chairman of Keidanren)
Yamazaki Masakazu, vice chairman (President, Tōa Daigaku [The University of East Asia, Yamaguchi])
Agarie Yasuharu (former President of Ryūkyū University)
Ueshima Kazuyasu (President, Ueshima Coffee & Foods)

Kamisaka Fuyuko (Author)
Kusayanagi Fumie (Author)
Sakamoto Takao (Professor of History, Gakushūin University [died October 2002])
Tanaka Akihiko (Professor of Political Science, The University of Tokyo)
Nishihara Haruo (former President of Waseda University)
Mikuriya Takashi (Professor of History, Seisaku Kenkyū Daigakuin Daigaku [National Graduate Institute for Policy Studies])

The commission's central task is to clarify the question of *whether* a national memorial is necessary for Japan's war victims; and, if yes, in what form, under what designation, and at which location it should be built. The minutes of the meetings (Shushō Kantei 2003a), which allow us to follow the committee's deliberations,[109] indicate that the new memorial is not intended as a "substitute" for the Yasukuni Shrine (2nd and 9th meeting). Some members have argued that the Yasukuni Shrine is too firmly anchored in people's minds and should remain the central site of commemoration. Above all, it is the necessity to improve relations with Japan's neighbors that has led the majority of members to support the foundation of a new memorial—but not, however, the parallel establishment of an "official" interpretation of history in the public sphere. The late Sakamoto Takao, a distinguished historian, expressed his reservations on this score at the commission's 3rd meeting:

> The nationalism of the 19th century is currently decreasing in importance and, as illustrated by the development of the EU, the international community cannot be renewed when we limit ourselves to nationalism. Yet, in commemorating the war dead, even though we may discern everywhere, even in industrialized countries, tendencies to reconsider traditional forms of commemoration [...], we have nevertheless not yet moved into a new phase of internationalization. No attempts have been made, especially by our neighbors, to approach the commemoration of war victims with an international perspective that reaches beyond Korean or Chinese nationalism [...]. On what grounds should Japan embrace a new direction in this regard?

---

[109] Although the minutes of the meetings are available to the public, statements made by individual participants are not linked to names. However, in some cases (e.g., the quotation from Sakamoto Takao given below) is it possible to identify a statement's source.

A key point in the commission's deliberations was the question of *who* should be commemorated in the new memorial. The group eventually suggested a wide definition for those who should be commemorated, justifying this on traditional grounds, since "according to Japan's cultural traditions, we have always had in our country the wonderful custom (*bifū*) of commemorating enemies and friends together" (3rd meeting). As a result, the memorial should incorporate not only Japanese war dead—both military[110] and civilians—from 1868 to 1945, but also those members of the Japanese Self Defense Forces who died during UN missions, and foreigners who died for Japan in the Second World War. Very significantly, it would also commemorate victims from opposing sides, once again both military and civilians, including the victims of the Nanjing Massacre (5th, 6th and 9th meeting). Whether this concurrent commemoration of victims and perpetrators will gain widespread acceptance will likely become a central issue of future discussions, especially since, in many countries, a similar levelling of the distinction between victims and perpetrators has led to considerable upheaval in the national politics of memory.[111]

Opponents of the government and leftist-liberal groups were quick to voice their concerns that the new memorial will be inadequate as a symbol for the acknowledgment of Japanese responsibility for the war. The commission has assiduously avoided making a clear statement on this profoundly sensitive issue, despite numerous meetings, and the subject is also absent from the group's Interim Report presented to the public on 24 December 2003 (Shushō Kantei 2003b). Instead, the minutes record strong opposition to the expression "war of aggression" (*shinryaku sensō*) and urge that the war should instead be referred to as a "war caused by Japan" (*Nihon ga gen'in o ataeta sensō*) (4th meeting). Such statements reveal the conviction held by some members of the commission that, in a democracy, it is "not the duty of the government to provide a one-sided (*ichigiteki*) interpretation of history and the past." Rather the government "has the responsibility of ensuring that various interpreta-

---

[110] A clear statement of whether those accused or sentenced as war criminals are to be included has not been forthcoming. According to the commission's recommendations, such a decision is best left to "the heart of each individual visitor" (6th meeting).

[111] Germany is a case in point. Here, the parallel commemoration in some memorials of victims of German war atrocities and the German victims of Nazi rule—who are still seen as perpetrators in the eyes of victims of other nationalities—has led to some controversial episodes in the German politics of memory and commemoration. See Reichel 1999: 207, 216, 277; Assmann and Frevert 1999: 163f.

2. Historical Revisionism and the Politics of Memory

tions are made available to the people." (8th meeting and Interim Report, chapter 2.3) In the new memorial, therefore, the war dead should be commemorated without reference to a particular historical interpretation—as is the case with the memorial sites discussed above—and without making any kind of politico-historical judgment.

In their Interim Report of 2003, the commission confirmed the "necessity of a non-religious (*mushūkyō*) memorial for the victims of the conflicts (wars and incidents) [sic]," in which Japan had been "involved" since the Meiji Restoration (*Nihon no kakawatta taigai funsō [sensō, jihen]*) (Interim Report, chapter 2.2). However, the report added that it was "too early" to make a decision about the type, name, and location of such a memorial. The project is justified by the progress of "globalization and development toward [the creation of] a new international community" and the fact that, within this framework, "Japan's future development will attract even greater attention on the part of its neighbors and the international community" (chapter 2.1). It is important that "the world should be shown that Japan is actively seeking to promote peace". At the same time, such a memorial would succinctly communicate the meaning "of war and peace" to a younger generation which has not experienced war at first hand. In sum, the report urges the necessity of establishing a *national* memorial within the terms of Japan's self-understanding as a "peaceful nation" (*heiwa kokka*). Following official confirmation that the proposed institution would not compromise the role of either Yasukuni or Chidorigafuchi, the commission made five brief—if not perfunctory—recommendations for the new memorial (Interim Report, chapter 5).[112]

The commission's deliberations suggest that the new memorial was approved above all to reduce foreign policy frictions caused by the Yasukuni problem (10th meeting and Interim Report, chapter 2). Thus, the commission seems more concerned with *political correctness* than with demonstrating the conviction that Japan must assume responsibility for the war (8th meeting in particular). The establishment of yet another memorial site will likely result in a sort of "second Chidorigafuchi", located in the vicinity of Chidorigafuchi, Shōwakan, and the Yasukuni Shrine, and functioning as an institutionalization of the annual commemorative event held in the Budōkan. Thus, in the Kudan district a sort of "memorial mile" would emerge embracing Yasukuni, Chidorigafuchi, the Shōwakan, and the projected new memorial.

---

[112] For example, the commission proposed that it is "desirable to locate the new institution in the centre of Tōkyō", and suggested that its name be decided through a public competition.

But any new memorial is hardly likely to solve the "Yasukuni problem". Opponents of a new memorial are already organizing resistance (cf. Gotōda 2003: 181; Maeno 2003: 263f). A "gathering to protest against a national memorial" was held in June 2002 (Tanaka 2002b: 25), and on 15 August each year activists collect signatures and distribute information opposing the project.[113] The question of whether a "new institution" would solve the "Yasukuni problem" by providing politicians with an alternative venue to pay their respects to the war dead, and thereby establish a new Japanese policy of remembrance, was answered by Prime Minister Koizumi during his second visit to Yasukuni in April 2002. He remarked that he would still wish to make "official visits to Yasukuni, even after a new memorial has been established." Although Koizumi is unlikely to still be in office when (and if) the new memorial is erected, his successors in the LDP (of which Koizumi is regarded as one of the more progressive members) will no doubt continue along the path he has pioneered. Irrespective of whether a new memorial is ever established, this prime ministerial precedent is bound to keep the "Yasukuni problem" alive.

2.5 COMMEMORATION, THE NATION, HISTORY AND MEMORY

Through the commemoration of war dead and the memory that is created of war itself, history and the interpretation of history become of vital interest to the state and, through this process, the national narrative becomes directly connected with politics. It serves as a base for the self-understanding of the state and the legitimization of the political order. In this process, the tendency to connect the commemoration of war dead with affirmative views of war is naturally strong. Difficulties arise when it comes to evaluating wars that were lost, as in the case of Japan:

> Goals and policies that were thought to be guided by destiny are revealed to be little more than resource-grabbing colonization wrought by rapacious military force and terror. Does this now mean the participants' suffering and death was for nothing or […] for a criminal cause? (Nelson 2003: 444)

---

[113] In a brochure entitled "The Cherry Blossoms in Kudan Weep!" the Shintō Association of Spiritual Leadership (the self-chosen English designation of the pressure group Shintō Seiji Renmei, literally: Shintō Political League) complains that the establishment of a "discussion group to advise on worshipping the dead" ignores the feelings of "the Japanese" (Shintō Seiji Renmei 2003: 1). See also Maeno 2003: 262–264 for similar remarks.

In response to this dilemma, an affirmative or apologetic view of "the last war" has gained a strong position in Japanese politics and the public sphere, a process enforced by a strong political agenda as we saw in chapter 1.5. As I showed in this chapter, the resulting similarities between historical revisionism and the historical views displayed in many areas of the public sphere are striking. Most memorials, especially those run or sanctioned by institutions of the government and therefore expressing the self-understanding of the Japanese state, support a strongly affirmative view of the war, which in historical exhibitions is presented as a defensive war, a war waged for the sake of Asian liberation, or a war that victimized the Japanese people. Notwithstanding the ongoing official affirmation of the "Murayama Statement", Prime Minister Koizumi has explained officially that the "welfare of Japan today is due to the sacrifice of those who died in the war."[114] As Michael Pye comments: "Viewed historically and economically, this statement is completely false. The historical effect of the actions of the war dead, in general, was to lead Japan to catastrophe, including complete economic destruction." (Pye 2003: 54) However, it is an affirmative view of the war that dominates public memory in Japan—in memorials and museums run or sanctioned by the state—and, apart from some prefectural museums, Japanese responsibility for war is not raised in them, and the victims of Japanese aggression are nowhere memorialized or even considered.

By commemorating soldiers who have fallen "for the country" (*kuni no tame*), most modern nations, particularly since World War I (Mosse 1990), claim the citizen as a national possession even beyond death, and simultaneously, "the surviving observers are themselves put in a position where they are offered an idenity." (Koselleck 2002: 287) What Mosse has called "the cult of the fallen soldier" became a centerpiece of the "religion of nationalism" (Mosse 1990: 7), and in Japan has remained so right up until the present day (Harootunian 1999). The Yasukuni Shrine plays a particularly important role in this postwar nationalism which in Japan, as elsewhere, has taken the place of "civic religion" (Mosse 1990: 105, 155). In the Shintō Yasukuni Shrine, one of the three pillars of prewar state Shintō, Japan's war dead are commemorated for sacrificing their lives "for the country", regardless of their religion or ethnicity. Resistance against this "enforced worship", an automatic consequence of "dying for the country", was, and remains, futile (Tanaka 2003: 61; cf. also Tanaka 2002a: chapter 4.3; Rekishi Kyōikusha Kyōgikai 2002: 97). The loyalty shown by fallen soldiers to the nation and the Emperor by offering the

---

[114] Cited in Tanaka 2002a: 231. Similar expressions have been used by Japanese prime ministers since Ikeda Hayato in 1963; see Yoshida 1995: 109f.

supreme sacrifice will be rewarded, and their descendents offered consolation.[115] The worship of a soldier as a "'divine noble spirit' [...] irrespective of his former status and way of life" becomes a source of "deeply felt pride" for future generations (Antoni 1998: 342; cf. also Mosse 1990: chapter 3). The violent death of a nation's citizens thus "obliges future generations to honor their memory" (Reichel 1999: 18) and commemorative activities usually assume either "the form of a politico-religious death cult [...] or that of a politico-secular civil theology, as in all autonomously legitimized democratic states." (Reichel 1999: 18) The commemoration of the dead in the Yasukuni Shrine, and the depiction of their heroic deeds in the Yūshūkan museum, relates more obviously to the first of these two forms, which Reichel also identifies with the honoring of the war dead in Germany under National Socialism, characterized by a strong emphasis on their martyr status (Reichel 1999: 18f). At Yasukuni, this ideology finds strong expression in the permanent exhibition in the Yūshūkan museum, particularly in the exhibition of "relics" such as the personal effects and farewell letters of the soldiers enshrined there.

The chief motivation underlying the worship of the war dead in the Yasukuni Shrine—but also the commemoration of soldiers and the memorialization of war in other memorials and museums—is to reaffirm the identity of the Japanese nation beyond defeat in war. As Benedict Anderson puts it: "Dying for one's country, which usually one does not choose, assumes a moral grandeur which dying for the Labor Party, the American Medical Association, or perhaps even Amnesty International can not rival, for these are all bodies one can join or leave at will." (Anderson 1991: 144; cf. also Harada 2001; Reichel 1999: 70) This "moral grandeur" has to be legitimized by a historical narrative—a "national history [that] is one of continuity, antiquity of origins, heroism and past greatness, martyrdom and sacrifice, victimization, and overcoming of traumata." (Suny 2001: 338) These are precisely the themes embodied in public memorials in Japan, as we have seen throughout this chapter. Although religious motives were no doubt paramount when the Shōkonsha was founded in the 1870s,[116] in the postwar period the Yasukuni Shrine came to play a central role in the political, religious and cultural re-affirmation of the nation and the "reconstruction of the collapsed nation-state" (Tana-

---

[115] For the religious concept of the "calming" of the souls of those who have died violent deaths in war see Antoni 1991: 155–189.

[116] The very name Shōkonsha ("shrine to call back the spirits of the dead") reveals an "obvious relation to essential aspects of Japanese religiosity", namely the "periodic invitations, hospitality extended toward, and eventual dismissal of deities and ancestors." (Antoni 1998: 341)

ka 2003: 61). This remains its chief rationale to the present day. It also explains why, in general, Japanese war memorials eschew a self-critical, reflective approach in favor of an affirmative view of history in order to show that, whatever the failings of particular groups or individuals, "the nation" itself remains infallible.

Memorials such as Yasukuni emphasize that, for the sake of the integrity of the nation, but also for the sake of political continuity and legitimacy, Japan's war dead must be considered victims *for* the nation and should in no respect be regarded as victims *of* the nation sacrificed in the course of a war of imperialist aggression. Ultimately, the affirmative view of the war proves "that, however momentarily wrong, Our country is really always Right." (Anderson 1999: 202) It is precisely here that the difference between history as an academic discipline and history as the product of politicized memory becomes most clear, as many contemporary historians have been at pains to stress. Pierre Nora, one of the pioneers of the study of historical memory, characterizes the differences succinctly:

> History, because it is an intellectual and secular production, calls for analysis and criticism. Memory installs remembrance within the sacred; history, always prosaic, releases it again. Memory is blind to all but the group it binds [...]. History, on the other hand, belongs to everyone and to no one, whence its claim to universal authority. (Nora 1989: 8f; cf. also Assmann 1997: 52f)

3. HISTORY AND PUBLIC OPINION

3.1 HISTORICAL CONSCIOUSNESS

In analyzing the movement of historical revisionism, some observers have reached the conclusion that it enjoys a degree of support—if not "a formidable social base"—in the wider Japanese society (McCormack 2000: 65; cf. also Fujitani et al. 2001: 23; Oguma and Ueno 2003: chapter 1) and that the historical views it advocates—particularly the claim that the Asia-Pacific War was a war of Asian liberation—are spreading among the Japanese people (Irie 2001: 221). But is this really the case? On the face of it, there is powerful evidence for such a view. As we saw in chapter 1, the political connections of the Tsukuru-kai are manifold and, as chapter 2 made clear, the revisionist narrative occupies an important place in public memory. In addition, a number of books authored by historical revisionists have become bestsellers, and the media continue to pay considerable attention to the revisionist phenomenon.

However, other aspects of the question have to be considered before sweeping generalizations are made. Some Japanese commentators, for example, have stressed that many of the bestsellers produced by the movement, such as the bookmarket version of the *New History Textbook* of the Tsukuru-kai, are being bought as much by curious critics of the society as by those who endorse it views. Similarly, the patriotic movie *Pride*, discussed in chapter 1.1, probably attracted as many critics of historical revisionism as supporters. More disturbing are the high circulation figures achieved by the manga of Kobayashi Yoshinori, particularly since they are aimed at the youth market. However, although Kobayashi's work undoubtedly has a considerable influence on Japanese youth, it is less clear that young people are absorbing revisionist views through his writings; rather, it seems that his audience is attracted by his critical views of society in general and his pointed critique of Japanese politics—factors which are by no means unique to him.[117]

---

[117] In a recent issue of the magazine *Sapio*, Kobayashi went so far as to support a 16-year-old high school student who advocated a coup d'état in Japan. In one manga illustration, he quotes a letter presumably received from the student: "I am in first grade at high school and plan to join the Defense Academy and become part of the Self-Defense Forces (SDF). The present bosses of the SDF and their government masters are all stupid people and, if they continue doing stupid things, I will take some of my men and mutiny, destroy the present government and make Japan into the real Japan. Then, I want Yoshinori-sensei

Nevertheless, if the Tsukuru-kai was as influential as some observers suggest, then we would expect to see this reflected in significant shifts in historical consciousness or awareness, in views of their recent history and attitudes towards it held by Japanese in general. It seems, therefore, an important task to investigate the understanding of history prevalent within Japanese society—what we might call the "historical consciousness" of the Japanese people, particularly public awareness surrounding the history of the Asian-Pacific War,[118] the relativization and glorification of which stands at the center of the historical narrative promoted by the Tsukuru-kai. Some commentators have recently characterized such a "historical consciousness"—or an alleged lack of awareness of the realities of the nation's past—as the central problem for bilateral relations, rather than the attitudes of conservative politicians (Chung 2002; 2004; Kawamoto 2002: 127; Abe 2004: 11). However, little research has been done on the question of historical consciousness in Japan (NSKK 1971; Matsuyama et al. 1981; Yoshida 1995).

Before continuing, it is important to define the term "historical consciousness", which is increasingly being used in studies of historical memory and collective memory, albeit with a great variety of nuances. German historian Jörn Rüsen, a pioneer in the study of the subject, has noted that

> historical consciousness comprises anything processing experiences of time into orientations for everyday life. [...] Historical consciousness's ability to recall is triggered by the experience and expectations of time of everyday life. [...] Temporal orientation in life and the creation of an historical identity are the two essential functions of historical consciousness. (Ruesen 2001: Internet)

For Rüsen, the concept of historical consciousness is closely related to the study of historical pedagogy—the science of *teaching* history—but also to that of historical memory, of which historical consciousness can be considered a specific facet (Rüsen 2001; cf. also Borries 2001a: 252). The Japanese research has put a strong emphasis on the dimension of histori-

---

to become the Prime Minister of the new government." In the next frame, Kobayashi takes up this invitation and cheerfully replies to the letter: "OK, then let me become the best dictator human history has ever seen." (*Sapio* 24 September 2003: 61)

[118] While investigation of the historical consciousness of the Japanese is limited in this study to the Asia-Pacific War, further investigations of different historical periods, and the relationships between them, from this perspective are desirable. For a fascinating empirical study of the historical consciousness of young Germans, see Borries 2001b and Borries et al. 2001.

cal consciousness as a nexus between history as an academic discipline, on the one hand, and the personal and collective orientations and identities that guide people through the present and into the future, on the other—factors which are determined by the ways in which people approach the past or assimilate history through education in the widest sense, including the media and the politics of memory.

The recently established Center for the Study of Historical Consciousness is careful to discriminate its subject from other forms of historical understanding:

> The term 'historical consciousness' is relatively unfamiliar in North America, though the field is well established in Europe.[119] The study of historical consciousness is distinct from both historical research and historiographic research. The distinction can be seen in this way: when we study history [...], we are looking at the past. When we study historical consciousness, we are studying *how people look at the past*. [...] The study of historical consciousness differs, as well, from historiography, which examines only how *historians* look at the past. Historical consciousness can thus be defined as individual and collective understandings of the past, the cognitive and cultural factors which shape those understandings, as well as the relations of historical understandings to those of the present and the future. (CSHC 2002: Internet; italics added)

My own usage of the term "historical consciousness" follows this set of definitions and does not—as in previous studies (e.g. White 1973)—primarily use it to describe the attitudes of professional historians or philosophers towards history, but rather as the sum of the predominant understandings of history manifested in a given *society*. In his pioneering studies of collective memory, Maurice Halbwachs made a similar distinction between the collective memory of society and the "memory" preserved by academic history, characterizing the first as vitally important as a base for collective identity, while the second lacks such a function (see Assmann 1999: 131; cf. also Nora 1989: 8f; Borries 2001a: 266–269). While the findings of academic historical research of course exert some influence on the formation of historical consciousness in society, historical consciousness is subject to many other factors and influences. And while the predominant views on history in any given society do not necessarily make up a *consensus*, their analysis permits conclusions regarding the role of history within the triad of politics, (civil) society, and education which

---

[119] See for example the publications of Karl-Ernst Jeismann (1988) and Jörn Rüsen (2001).

would be beyond the scope of traditional academic history. An informed understanding of the ongoing debates on history textbooks, the Yasukuni Shrine and historical memory in Japan demands that we come to terms with the historical consciousness of the "common people" (*ippan no shomin*), as one commentator has termed them—all the more since few studies have so far been undertaken in this field (Abe 2004: 11; cf. also Obinata 2004: 15; Takahashi 2002: 3).

While theoretical research on historical consciousness and related issues has been gathering pace, empirical research is still hard to find, particularly on Japan. This probably has its explanation in methodological problems—the difficulties involved in grasping or measuring something as apparently abstract as the historical consciousness manifested by "the people" or "society." These issues can be tackled in a variety of ways including the analysis of opinion polls which ask questions (directly or indirectly) on topics such as war responsibility or historical knowledge; the identification of popular interest in certain historical characters and events through investigating the ratings of television dramas and the sales of books with historical content, especially historical novels; and understanding what attracts visitors to historical museums and exhibitions. All of these investigative methods are utilized in what follows. While gathering such data can be a complex and difficult task, the results obtained allow us to form some idea of what we might call the historical consciousness of the Japanese.

To state my conclusion from the outset, the data so far gathered indicates an important finding: although the Japanese lack consensus about interpreting their recent past, the views promoted by historical revisionists are by no means broadly accepted in Japanese society; notwithstanding their omnipresence in the political arena and the public sphere, they clearly reflect the views of only a minority of the population about the war. Notwithstanding their public prominence, in the historical consciousness exhibited by the majority of ordinary Japanese, revisionist views of history are anything but representative. As the vehemence of the ongoing debate suggests, however, historical revisionism is strongly championed by a variety of vociferous lobby groups with connections to powerful conservative political groups, wealthy business circles, and influential sections of the media, as we saw in chapter 1.4 and 1.5.

3.2 CHANGES IN VIEWS OF HISTORY WITHIN JAPANESE SOCIETY

The views held by contemporary Japanese of the Asia-Pacific War and of Japan's responsibility for that war are the product of developments both within and outside Japan over the last six decades, and have been influenced by controversies such as the textbook issue and the debates over Yasukuni, and the spillover of these debates into the popular media as well as into formal history education and academic history. In Japan, the nation's recent history is never out of the public eye and the "official" interpretation and control of that history is challenged at every turn. While some observers point to the dominant position enjoyed by "the country" (*kuni*), i.e. the government, in these debates—allowing it, for example, to defeat most of the lawsuits initiated by Ienaga Saburō (see chapter 1)—the publicity generated by these very lawsuits and events such as the textbook controversy of 1982 have triggered major changes in the perceptions held by the Japanese of their own history (Obinata 2004: 15–17; Yoshida 2002: 37). In addition, the recent debates over the nature of historical memory, the politics of memory and the mourning of the war dead have all contributed to the present state of historical consciousness in Japan. As Peter Reichel has stressed in connection with *Vergangenheitsbewältigung* (coming to terms with the past) in postwar Germany, it was the large-scale *debacles* within "the politics of memory", such as the debates about the *Neue Wache*, that *raised* consciousness in society over the problematic German past (Reichel 1999: 11f). It is probably not too much to claim that the Yasukuni debates, as well as a number of heavily-publicized lawsuits—not just the Ienaga lawsuits but also the ongoing claims brought against the Japanese state over the "military comfort women" and "forced laborers"—have contributed to a rising awareness among the Japanese over matters of war responsibility and the international implications of the kind of cultural memory preserved about the war. In particular, the role of litigation cannot be underestimated in this context, and one observer goes so far to say that, in postwar Japan, the courts (together with journalists and lawmakers) have replaced historians when it comes to making *judgemens* about controversial historical issues (Abe 2004: 173).

A good example is the case of the infamous "Unit 731" (731 Butai) of the Imperial Japanese Army, which during the war conducted experiments with biological and chemical weapons in Manchuria, and tested them on POWs. Because the U.S. occupation forces took a special interest in the results of these experiments, the issue was not taken up during the IMTFE and has only lately become a subject of inquiry by Japanese historians. Until recently, the Japanese government refused to acknowledge the weapons experiments as historical fact, stressing that "the activities of Unit 731 have not been finally confirmed." (*Asahi Shinbun* 28 August 2002: 1) On 27 August 2002, however, the Tōkyō District Court ruled that the historicity of the human experiments conducted by Unit 731 had to be acknowledged as a consequence of rulings made during the case under review. This came as a result of the appearance before the court of 180 descendents of Chinese nationals murdered by Unit 731 who had initiated a lawsuit against the Japanese state demanding an official apology and payment of 10 million Yen in compensation for each plaintiff. While the court denied compensation, it clearly stated—in the first such admission by an institution of the Japanese state—that Unit 731 had conducted experiments during which more than 10,000 Chinese nationals lost their lives (*Asahi Shinbun* 28 August 2002: 1, 2, 30). For the Chinese plaintiffs, the confirmation of the historical facts was even more important than the compensation sought, and the media emphasized that the verdict would doubtless have implications for the Japanese government's position not only on Unit 731 but also regarding other Japanese wartime atrocities. Similar litigation leading to the confirmation of unpalatable historical facts of Japan's wartime past has also been conducted in the last two decades, for example lawsuits brought by forced laborers. In conducting these cases, Japanese courts have been very critical of the government, more than once openly censuring the official position on controversial historical events.

The historical consciousness exhibited by postwar Japanese has undergone significant changes. Just as in Germany (Reichel 1999), in the immediate postwar period few Japanese were directly concerned with "coming to terms with the past". While Japan did acknowledge its war guilt in the peace treaty of San Francisco (1951), in these early years most Japanese continued to regard the war as unavoidable (Rekishi Kentō Iinkai 1995: 339), as historical revisionists still claim today. Throughout the 1960s and 1970s, Japan upheld what Yoshida Yutaka has called the "double standard": acknowledging war responsibility and the judgement of the IMTFE as confirmed by the San Francisco treaty as the official stance for external consumption,[120] while *within* Japan, responsibility for the war was denied or at best unquestioned (Yoshida 1995: 82).

---

[120] Article 11 of the San Francisco treaty stipulated the following: "Japan accepts the judgments of the International Military Tribunal for the Far East and of other Allied War Crimes Courts both within and outside Japan, and will carry out the sentences imposed thereby upon Japanese nationals imprisoned in Japan. The power to grant clemency, to reduce sentences and to parole with respect to such prisoners may not be exercised except on the decision of the

One expression of this domestic attitude of denial was the movement to release convicted war criminals from Sugamo Prison between 1953 and 1955 (Yoshida 1995: 82f); another manifestation was the flood of "war narratives" (*senkimono*) which offered sanitized and nostalgic views of the war, mostly written by veterans. These stories have been interpreted as the expression of a "subconscious desire to overcome a complex vis-à-vis the U.S. that had resulted from [Japan's] defeat in war." (Yoshida 1995: 85) In these early *senkimono* dating from the 1960s, war responsibility is never addressed, war crimes are not mentioned—they differ in this respect from the memoirs or autobiographies (*jibunshi*) of the 1970s discussed below. A look at the authors helps explain why: the vast majority of *senkimono* were written by mid- or low-ranking naval officers (Yoshida 1995: 92), and none was written by participants in the war in China—the military theater where most of the atrocities occurred (Yoshida 1995: 97). Another aspect of the "double standard" identified by Yoshida related to the ways in which the memory of the war was preserved and its victims mourned. Ceremonies introduced in the 1960s to memorialize the war were strictly for domestic consumption. For example, at the National Memorial Service for the War Dead (*Zenkoku Senbotsusha Tsuitō-shiki*) that has been held on the anniversary of the end of the war (*Shūsen Kinenbi*, 15 August) every year since 1963, only the Japanese war dead were mourned, excluding Asian victims of Japanese aggression (Yoshida 1995: 109f). Within this cultural context, it is hardly surprising that few changes in the historical consciousness of the Japanese could be observed before the 1960s.

While the normalization of relations with South Korea in 1965 and with China in 1972 had necessitated changes in Japan's attitude to its own past, it was globalization and the information revolution of the 1980s that finally brought an end to the "double standard". Japan-watchers in China, South Korea, and the European countries paid increasing attention to statements on history by Japanese politicians, including those made in a domestic context. Statements offering evidence of affirmative views of the war tended to be noticed abroad and carried implications for Japan's reputation in international society, as well as consequences for Japanese traveling abroad or living overseas. Beginning with the textbook controversy of 1982, history became a vital issue in attempts to achieve reconciliation with Japan's neighbors, bringing the "double standard" into jeop-

---

Government or Governments which imposed the sentence in each instance, and on recommendation of Japan. In the case of persons sentenced by the International Military Tribunal for the Far East, such power may not be exercised except on the decision of a majority of the Governments represented on the Tribunal, and on the recommendation of Japan."

ardy. While increasing number of politicians officially stated that they considered the war to have been a "war of aggression" (Yoshida 1995: 169f), conservative politicians continued making "undue remarks" (*bōgen*), glorifying (*bika*) or justifying (*benmei*) the war and colonial rule, stressing the "benevolence" of Japanese rule in Korea, and denying the Nanjing massacre and other wartime atrocities (see chapter 1.5.1). However, even when these errant politicians were forced to resign their offices (Okuno, Sakurai, Nagano), it became clear that their historical views were not necessarily related to unfavorable election results or their chances of being reelected. Most of the offenders *were* indeed reelected in the elections following their "undue remarks" and none suffered a substantial political setback as a consequence. One of the politicians most notorious for his "undue remarks", Okuno Seisuke, remained active and influential in politics until 2003 and was continually returned to office.

However, in the light of increasing international complications, the character of historical consciousness in Japanese society underwent rapid change, particularly as a result of the textbook controversy of 1982. In an opinion poll taken by *Mainichi Shinbun*, an overwhelming majority of participants rejected any attempt to establish history education along neonationalist lines: while only 6% supported the conservative claim that "the darker aspects of Japan's past before and during the war should *not* be taught in class", 92% approved the *necessity to teach all the facts of the wartime past* (cited in Fuhrt 2002: 128; cf. also Obinata 2004: 20 for a similar poll of *Yomiuri Shinbun*). Clearly, the revisionist agenda for history education was in a poor position to make inroads into society at this period.

While the "war of Asian liberation" thesis is strongly established in the public sphere as a result of the powerful influence of conservative political and pressure groups, the "undue remarks" of rightwing politicians, although the object of considerable public attention, should not be overrated or even considered representative of Japanese politics. Before going on to discuss historical consciousness in society, I want to survey the various attitudes to history found in Japanese politics in general. Even accepting that the Japanese Communist Party and the Social Democratic Party (the former Socialist Party) are nowadays hardly forces to be reckoned with in parliament, diverse views on Japan's past and on Japan's responsibility for the war are still represented amongst Japanese lawmakers. Since a statistical investigation of the historical consciousness of the Japanese political classes is yet to be undertaken, I conducted an investigation of my own for this study. I chose three questions from an opinion poll conducted by NHK (Makita 2000) that directly probed the question of historical consciousness:

Do you think the war of 1931–1945 was a war of aggression or not?
Do you think the war of 1931–1945 was an unavoidable war or not?
Do you think Japan still has continuing responsibility for the war?

In early July 2003, shortly before the current session of the National Diet closed,[121] I sent a questionnaire with these three questions to the 722 members of the Lower and Upper Houses of the Japanese Diet. Within a month, I had received 139 replies (a response rate of 19.25%). The low response rate itself indicates that interest in questions relating to history is not particularly high among the Japanese political classes—or that lawmakers are reluctant to answer such surveys. Compared to some other polls, however, a response rate of almost 20% was still high enough to produce some meaningful results.[122]

Ill. 14: Opinion survey among Japanese politicians, July/August 2003. Question 1: "The last war (*saki no sensō*)[123] was a war of aggression conducted by Japan against its Asian neighbors—what do you think about this statement?" By number of responses. Source: survey by author.

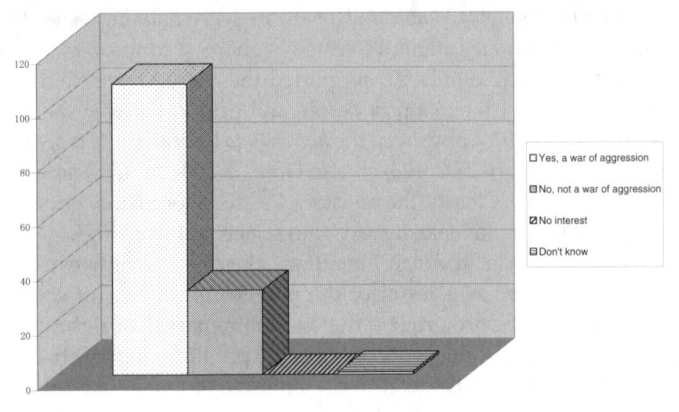

---

[121] To ensure the maximum return, I chose a time when Diet members would still be in Tōkyō and in their offices, but would be less busy than during the period the Diet was in session and when opinion polls were more likely to land on their desks.

[122] When the daily *Asahi Shinbun* (a rather more prestigious organization than a small German research institute in Tōkyō) surveyed LDP lawmakers in the Lower House about the practice whereby husband and wife retain their separate family names (*fūfu bessei*) in April 2004, the response rate was a mere 6.2% (15 answers) (*Asahi Shinbun* 2 April 2004: 4).

[123] Here the last war was defined as "the war that started with the Manchurian Incident of 1931, developed into the war in the Pacific in 1941, and continued until 1945 (the Asia-Pacific War)".

The results reveal above all a range of opinions among Japanese politicians on questions of history, and show that politicians with a critical perspective are as keen to make their views known as those associated with "undue remarks". The low response rate was particularly marked in the case of LDP members: only 32 replies came from the LDP, with the majority (21 replies) denying that Japan had conducted "a war of aggression". Considering that LDP members in particular are notorious for their "undue remarks", this proportion can probably be considered representative of their party. While respondents had the choice of answering either anonymously (via the envelope attached to the survey form) or by fax, some chose to return a fax bearing their name (such as Okuno Seisuke) or their official stamp, sometimes accompanied by comments and explanations. While a high response rate was expected in the case of the Japanese Communist Party (JCP) and the Social Democratic Party (Shamintō, SDP), since of all the parties these are the most opposed to apologetic views of history, the high return of 52 responses from the Democratic Party (Minshutō, DP), which had recently amalgamated with the Liberal Party (Jiyūtō) of Ozawa Ichirō, was quite surprising. Moreover, notwithstanding the fact that the DP is often labeled a second conservative party that differs little in its views from the LDP, the results revealed sharply differing views on history: of the 52 responses fielded from the DP, 44 agreed that the "last war" was indeed "a war of aggression", with only eight disagreeing. Of the other parties surveyed, almost all respondents answered the question in the affirmative: 21 from the JCP, twelve from the SDP, eight from Kōmeitō, and twelve out of 14 lawmakers from other small parties. For question 2, the results followed the same trend: while only 34 participants stated that the war was inevitable, 103 believed that it was not unavoidable, thereby clarifying Japan's responsibility for the outbreak of war.

The responses received for the third question in the survey, which asked about continuing Japanese responsibility for the war, yielded results that were even more surprising.

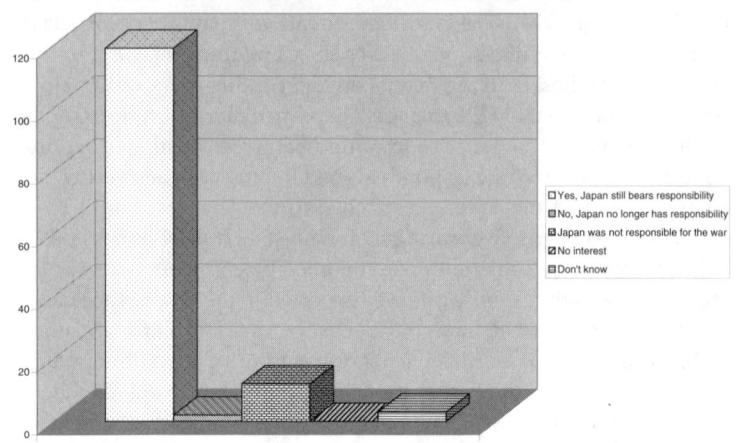

Ill. 15: Opinion survey among Japanese politicians, July/August 2003. Question 3: "Do you think that Japan still has continuing responsibility for the last war?" By number of responses. Source: survey by author.

□ Yes, Japan still bears responsibility
▣ No, Japan no longer has responsibility
▨ Japan was not responsible for the war
▧ No interest
▤ Don't know

While a total of twelve respondents—seven from the LDP, three from the DP and two from the smaller parties—denied that Japan was responsible for the outbreak of the war (one of the options offered), only two respondents denied that Japan still had any responsibility for the war. A total of 119 responses, including 20 from the LDP and 47 from the DP, affirmed Japan's continuing responsibility for the war, and some even added concrete examples such as the removal of the biological weapons which were abandoned by Japanese forces in Manchuria in 1945 and have recently become a political embarrassment and a matter of negotiation with China. Others criticized the questionnaire as "oversimplifying", "binary" and "useless" (despite my statement, in the letter accompanying the questionnaire, that the questions were identical with those asked by NHK in a poll taken in 2000).

In general, the responses to my survey suggest that "even" in Japanese politics, where individual politicians have been making headlines for their "undue remarks" and visits to memorials that advocate affirmative views of the war, perspectives on the nation's recent history cover the full spectrum—and in all parties. One particularly important finding was that even politicians from parties that favor "patriotic" history education and selective, heroic memories of the war, if pressed on the question, do not deny Japanese *responsibility* for the war. Despite such findings, it must be acknowledged that the survey results have been skewed by the low response rate from LDP members, whose views on these matters are reflected in the close links formed with the History Examination Committee in the 1990s (see chapter 1.5.1), among other things.

Conservative politicians, as we have seen, are largely responsible for the affirmative views of the war predominating the public sphere today. The main task of this chapter is thus to inquire whether such views find support in the wider Japanese society. My first task in this inquiry into the historical consciousness of the Japanese, and their views of the war in particular, is to analyze popular opinion polls that pose similar questions to a broad spectrum of Japanese society as those I put to members of the Diet in 2003.

As I mentioned above, we can detect the beginnings of a change in the historical consciousness of the Japanese in 1982 with the escalation of the history textbook problem into an international crisis that damaged Japan's reputation. In response, Japanese politicians emended the rules for textbook examination to include the "paragraph on neighboring countries" (*kinrin shokoku jōkō*), which led in turn to the inclusion in most textbooks of the "darker" chapters of Japan's wartime past, including open treatment of military atrocities, until the early 1990s (Chung 1998; 2003a; 2003b). While these developments undoubtedly fostered reconciliation in East Asia and strengthened Japan's international reputation, they also produced amorphous changes in historical consciousness.

By the mid 1980s, voices critical of Japan's recent past were already in the majority. In an opinion poll conducted by the NHK Broadcasting and Public Opinion Investigation Institute (NHK Hōsō Yoron Chōsa-sho)[124] in 1984, participants were asked: "Do you think the 50 years of Japanese history from the (first) Sino-Japanese War (*Nisshin sensō*, 1894/95) up to the Pacific War constituted a history of aggression against our Asian neighbors?" While 51.4% of respondents[125] agreed, only 21.9% replied in the negative (Yoshida 1994: 27; Yoshida 1995: 12). On the other hand, 44.8% of respondents agreed that "for Japan, which is poor in natural resources, the war was an unavoidable act" (*yamu-o-enai kōi*), while only 38.7% disagreed. Yet despite this result, an overwhelming majority (82.5%) confirmed that "as a Japanese, he/she had to reflect from the bottom of the heart on discrimination against Koreans and Chinese carried on since the Meiji period and on massacres", while only a tiny 5.2% denied the necessity of this. But to turn the tables again, 45.5% agreed that the Pacific War had had *positive* consequences, such as the independence

---

[124] This organization was the predecessor of the present NHK Hōsō Bunka Kenkyūjo (Broadcasting Culture Research Institute). The opinion poll was headed "Views on Peace Held by the Japanese" (*Nihonjin no Heiwakan*).

[125] The survey polled 2623 participants and had a 72.9% response rate.

of Asian nations from Western colonial oppression. Only 25.1% disagreed that Japan could claim credit of this kind (Yoshida 1994: 27; Yoshida 1995: 12). While belief in the positive effects of the war, its inevitability or its character as a war that was forced upon Japan can still be detected in such surveys, war guilt was already strongly acknowledged by the Japanese by the beginning of the 1980s, and it can hardly be said that Japanese society was failing to reflect on issues of war guilt and responsibility.

When questioned in the 1984 NHK survey about the "responsibility of the common people for the war" (*ippan kokumin no sensō sekinin*), 29.5% of respondents considered that most Japanese at the time had cooperated with militarism and bore some responsibility as perpetrators, at least with regard to Asian nations. However, 36.3% answered that the population had been misled by militarists, a response in line with the "military conspiracy" or "single-handed action of the military" (*gunbu dokusō*) theory, a widespread belief in the immediate postwar period which effectively absolved ordinary people of blame and which was also supported by the U.S. occupation authorities. Another 17.6% stressed that, because the war never had a militarist character there was no issue of victims and perpetrators (Yoshida 1994: 27; Yoshida 1995: 12). This latter figure has proved remarkably stable in subsequent polls, as I demonstrate below.

The NHK poll significantly demonstrates that, in the minds of the participants, the responsibility of the state and that of "the Japanese" or the "common people" for the war are two different things. The high proportion of answers stressing that the people were merely betrayed or fooled (*damasareta*) by the military or the political leadership is closely connected to the strong "victim consciousness" (*higaisha ishiki*) of postwar Japanese which has often been emphasized by commentators (Takahashi 2003: 167; Takahashi 2002: 21; Fujiwara 2001: 13–18; Yoshida 1995: 75f, 154–157, 161; Orr 2001). Not only were the "common people" the literal victims of war—through bombing, food shortages, and nuclear attack—they also were the political victims of the misguided or evil policies pursued by a leadership they had not elected.[126]

Postwar Germany has been marked by similar developments. The debate about the "collective guilt" (*Kollektivschuld*) of the German people, and the question whether the Germans were misled by a small group of evil Nazis, has many similarities with the Japanese discussion. However, both in Germany and Japan the debate has taken new directions since the 1980s. Whereas in Germany the increasing discussion of the war guilt of *Wehrmacht* soldiers or the responsibility of "ordinary citizens" for Nazi

---

[126] All Japanese prime ministers from 1932 until the end of the war were military officers.

atrocities and war crimes has been mostly stimulated by the work of foreign scholars (as in the "Goldhagen debate"), in Japan similar issues have been raised on the domestic front. Studies such as *Grassroots Fascism* (*Kusa no ne no fashizumu*) by Yoshimi Yoshiaki (Yoshimi 1987) have played a crucial role in countering the "military conspiracy" thesis by demonstrating, for example, the extent to which ordinary soldiers embraced national policies such as the illusion of a "Greater East Asian Co-Prosperity Sphere" and what they stood to gain by an unswerving loyalty to the military-dominated government.[127]

Thus while changes to the school history syllabus *after* 1982 did not necessarily bring about significant changes in historical consciousness in themselves, they undoubtedly helped solidify an already-existing tendency. In the 1990s, critical views of Japanese wartime history were still in the majority, with the apologetic standpoint undergoing a further decline. In an opinion poll conducted by *Mainichi Shinbun* in 1993 in the Kyūshū region and Yamaguchi prefecture, the 1,000 participants were asked whether they agreed with Prime Minister Hosokawa's statement that "the Pacific War was a war of aggression and a wrong war" (cf. also chapter 1.5.1). To this, 59% replied they agreed or mainly agreed with this statement, while only 16% expressed varying levels of disagreement. In addition, 24% did not know while 1% returned no answer (Yoshida 1994: 23). In another survey by *Asahi Shinbun* taken in the same year, 67% of the participants expressed approval of the Hosokawa statement, while only 15% did not (Yoshida 1994: 23). While the controversy surrounding the Hosokawa statement and the apology resolution of the Japanese Diet (see chapter 1.5.1) triggered an active historical revisionism in the political arena, this was clearly not mirrored in the developing historical consciousness of ordinary Japanese. This conclusion is confirmed by recent opinion polls that show that historical revisionism has found only a narrow foothold in the Japanese population.

One poll offering particularly clear-cut results is the 2000 survey taken by the NHK Broadcasting Culture Research Institute (NHK Hōsō Bunka Kenkyūjo) and published in the monthly journal of the Institute under the heading: "The Views of the Japanese on War and Peace" (Makita 2000). It was conducted in mid-May 2000 and involved 2,143 selected respon-

---

[127] However, already in the immediate postwar period the point was being made that "being deceived (*damasareta*) does not in itself lead to war", but rather there is a need for both "a deceiving party and a deceived party, and both have to come together at a certain point. Therefore responsibility for the war lies on both sides" (Movie director Itami Mansaku, father of Itami Jūzō, in 1946, cited in Yoshida 1995: 58f).

dents, of whom 1,468 (68.5%) replied. In the first place, the survey confirmed that World War II still occupies a central place in the minds of the Japanese and in Japanese historical consciousness. Asked what comes to mind when thinking about war, 73% answered "World War II", 12% "the Vietnam War" and 11% "the Gulf War" (Makita 2000: 3, 16). The level of historical knowledge of World War II was also reasonably high: 91% could identify 15 August as the day the war ended, 55% identified Germany as Japan's ally during the war, and 36% identified 8 December as the day of the attack on Pearl Harbor.[128] However, when asked which of Japan's enemies it had fought against longest during the last war, only 37% gave the correct answer (China), while 41% plumped for the United States (Makita 2000: 18). The next group of questions was directed at eliciting information about the historical consciousness of Japanese and sought to gauge the sense of responsibility felt by Japanese for the wars Japan conducted in Asia and the Pacific in the 1930s and 1940s. To the provocative question "The last war (*saki no sensō*) was a Japanese war of aggression against its Asian neighbors—what do you think about this statement?", 51% agreed while only 15% denied the aggressive character of Japan's wars in Asia (Makita 2000: 19).

Asked whether they considered that "the last war" was unavoidable "for a Japan lacking in raw materials", in contrast to the same question in NHK's 1984 poll, more respondents rejected the notion that the war was inevitable (35%) than supported it (30%) (Makita 2000: 19).

The responses to the question about Japanese war responsibility were even more clear-cut. The results suggest that a clear majority of Japanese believe that Japan still has continuing responsibility for the war, a belief that follows logically from the perception of the war as a war of aggression. Asked whether the postwar generation still had a responsibility for Japan's actions during the last war, 50% agreed that "unresolved problems" required the attention of "later generations", while 27% denied Japan's continuing responsibility and 5% considered that, because Japan lacked any responsibility for the outbreak of war, this question was meaningless (Makita 2000: 19).

---

[128] While no other date offered for the attack on Pearl Harbor (11 February, 3 March, 15 August, 18 September) scored more than 3%, 53% answered that they did not know.

Ill. 16: Opinion survey conducted by NHK in May 2000. Question no. 22a: "The last war (*saki no sensō*[130]) was a war of aggression conducted by Japan against its Asian neighbors—what do you think about this statement?" By percentage of responses. Source: Makita 2000: 19.

- ☐ Yes, a war of aggression
- ☒ No, not a war of aggression
- ▨ No interest
- ☐ Don't know

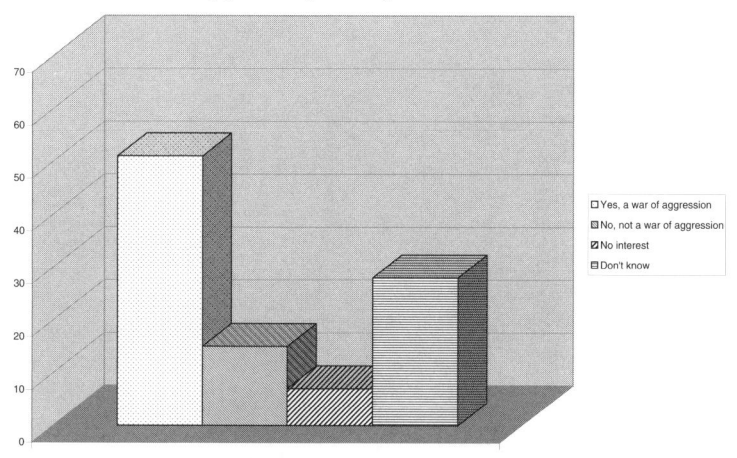

Ill. 17: Opinion survey conducted by NHK in May 2000. Question no. 22b: "Do you think the last war was an unavoidable war of survival for a Japan lacking in raw materials?" By percentage of responses. Source: Makita 2000: 19.

- ☐ No, war was not unavoidable
- ☒ Yes, war was unavoidable
- ▨ No interest
- ☐ Don't know

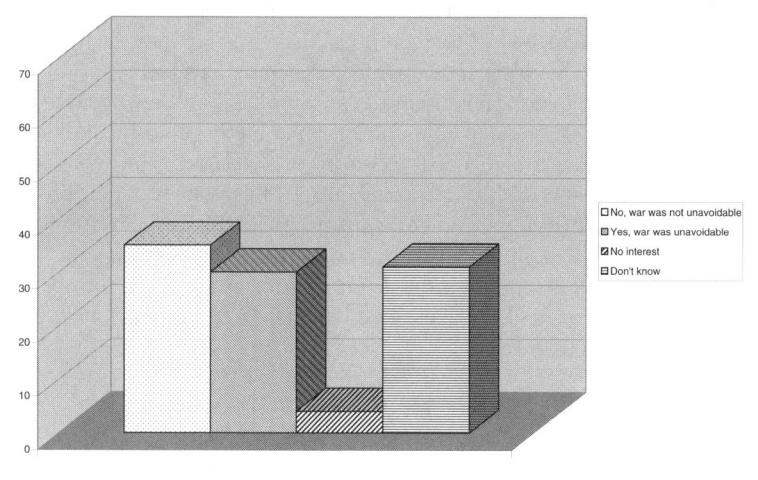

[129] The "last war" in this poll was defined as "the war that started with the Manchurian Incident of 1931, developed into the war in the Pacific in 1941, and continued until 1945 (the Asia-Pacific War)".

Ill. 18: Opinion survey conducted by NHK in May 2000. Question no. 24: "Do you think the postwar generation should still bear responsibility for Japan's actions during the last war?" By percentage of responses. Source: Makita 2000: 19.

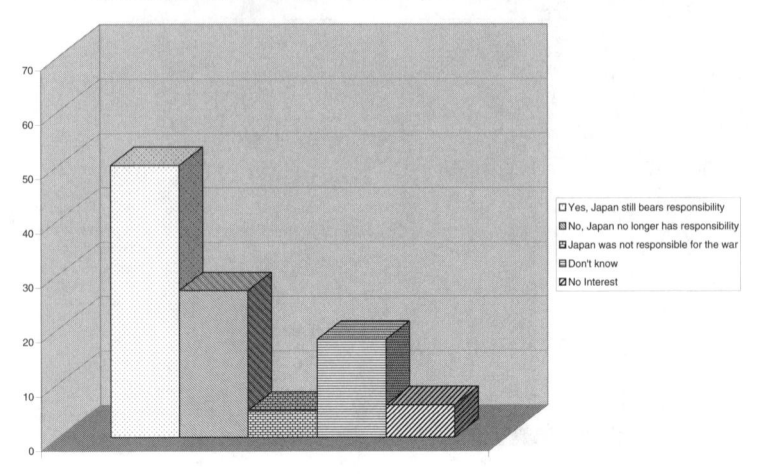

[Bar chart with legend:
☐ Yes, Japan still bears responsibility
▣ No, Japan no longer has responsibility
▣ Japan was not responsible for the war
▣ Don't know
▣ No Interest]

Further proof of a strong sense of responsibility for the war was found in the responses to the question that asked whether Japan could claim credit for the independence achieved by Asian countries in the postwar period. As historian Yoshida Yutaka has pointed out, an emphasis—heavily promoted by revisionists—on the secondary effect of Japanese warfare as stimulating independence movements in Asian nations has been a major facet of postwar historical consciousness. Emphasis on the "positive aspects" of Japanese colonial rule and on Japanese backing for independence movements has regularly been used to relativize Japanese war guilt and war responsibility. However, in 2004 this issue has gone off the boil, and revisionists appear to be losing ground in this area of the debate. In the 2000 NHK poll, only 13% agreed that the last war hastened the independence of Asian countries from colonial rule by the European-American powers, while 45% disagreed that Japan could claim any credit for Asian independence.

Ill. 19: Opinion survey conducted by NHK in May 2000. Question no. 22c: "The last war hastened the independence of Asian countries from Euro-American colonial rule—what do you think about this statement?" By percentage of responses. Source: Makita 2000: 19.

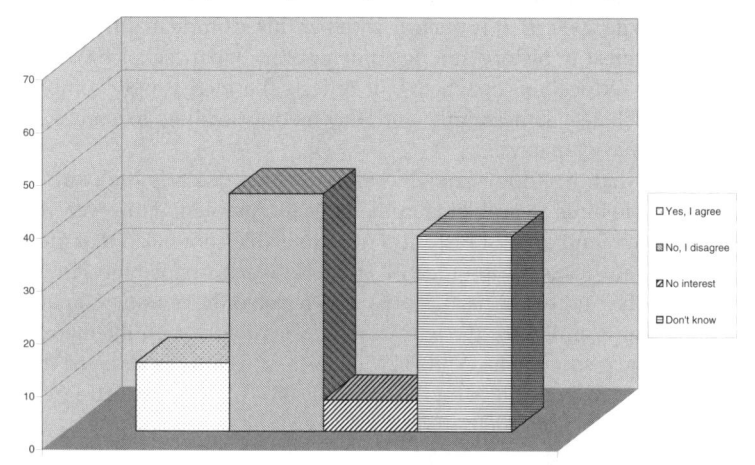

The thesis that the U.S. and Great Britain share the blame with Japan for the outbreak of the war (*Bei-Ei dōzai shikan*) also seems to find little support amongst the Japanese, although the reasons are complex. Participants were confronted with the following statement: "The Euro-American powers exercised colonial rule in Asia as well as Japan, and so Japan alone should not be made to reflect on the past." While 26% agreed, 39% disagreed, probably because they assumed that such an attitude would hinder reconciliation with Asian countries. This is confirmed by a further question which asked which countries Japan should care about (*taisetsu ni suru*) in the future: 60% plumped for the Asian countries, while only 20% named the US and European countries (Makita 2000: 17). As we saw at the beginning of this chapter, the formation of historical consciousness is closely linked to problems in contemporary politics and the Japanese seem to be well aware of such implications.

In general, the Japanese show a great awareness of historical problems that still have implications for Japan, and there is a strong commitment to the necessity of facing the past in the population at large. The 2000 NHK report found that, in comparison with previous polls, the *critical view of the war as a war of aggression*, i.e. the proportion of participants who agreed both that the war was not inevitable *and* that it was a war of aggression, was stable; while the *uncritical view of the war of a war of aggression*, i.e., the combination of answers "war of aggression" and "unavoidable war", is on the wane, as is the *apologetic view of history* that denies the aggressive character of the war and stresses its unavoidability. However, the report also notes a strong increase in the numbers choosing the "don't know" option (Makita 2000: 9). It is unclear whether this attitude mainly reflects a lack of interest in history among contemporary Japanese, or problems with history education, or whether it reflects the increasingly complex historical debates in academia and the media, leading to confusion among ordinary Japanese.

The fact that the "don't know" option rates particularly high among young people hints at problems in the education system. However, this self-professed ignorance of historical questions does not mean that more youngsters are rejecting the idea of Japanese war responsibility. In the NHK poll, the number of participants who rejected the notion of Japan's ongoing responsibility for the war increased markedly with the increasing age of the respondents. While 62% of 16-to-19-year-olds believed that Japan still had responsibility for the war, only 38% of those over 60 agreed with this view (Makita 2000: 10, 19).

Ill. 20: Opinion survey conducted by NHK in May 2000. Question no. 24: "Do you think the postwar generation should still bear responsibility for Japan's actions during the last war?" By percentage of responses, according to age. Source: Makita 2000: 10, 19.

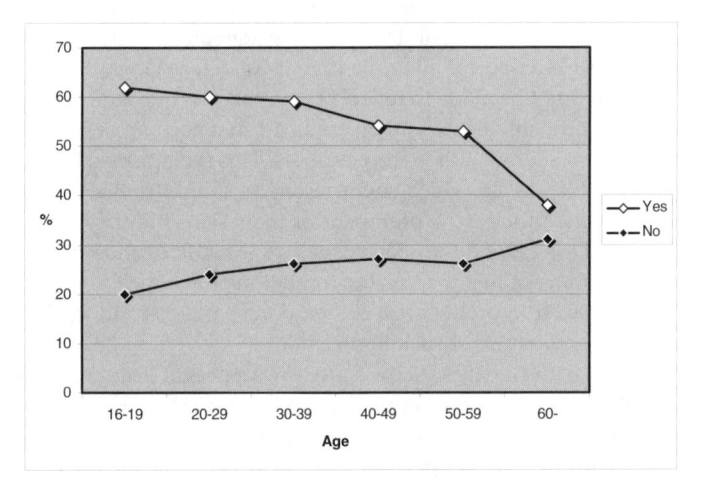

The results show clearly that, while older Japanese tend to deny war responsibility, young people, presumably as a result of the encouragement of a critical approach in history education in Japan during the last decades, do not lack awareness of the problems that stem from Japan's wartime past. Since the history textbook controversy, as noted in the introduction, is above all a debate about Japan's future, what Japan's youth thinks about history is particularly important.

The critical views predominant among Japanese youth picked up by the NHK poll are confirmed by the results of a survey which the author conducted with students at two Tōkyō universities. The results are almost identical with those of the 2000 NHK survey. Over a period of three years (2002 to 2004), I questioned a sample of 816 students at one private and one state university located in the capital.[130] The results were quite similar in every year of the survey and demonstrated a clear tendency to reject revisionist interpretations of Japanese history. They also verified the finding of the NHK survey that revisionist views are particularly unpopular with contemporary Japanese youth. Asked whether they considered "the last war" a war of aggression, 47% agreed, while only 5% disagreed. On the second question of whether the war was unavoidable, only 12% agreed, while 44% denied its inevitability. Almost identical with the NHK survey was the figure of 66% of students who believed that Japan still bore ongoing responsibility for the war; only 8% disagreed, while 3% claimed that Japan did not have any responsibility for the war in the first place.

Ill. 21: Opinion survey of Japanese students, 2002–2004. Question no. 3: "Do you think the postwar generation should still bear responsibility for Japan's actions during the last war?" Source: survey by author.

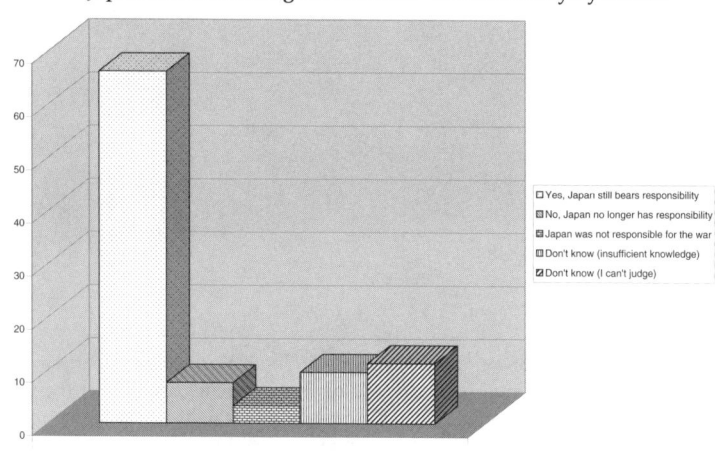

[Bar chart with legend:
☐ Yes, Japan still bears responsibility
☐ No, Japan no longer has responsibility
☐ Japan was not responsible for the war
☐ Don't know (insufficient knowledge)
☐ Don't know (I can't judge)]

---

[130] Participants included 453 female students, 265 male students and 98 students who did not give their sex. See appendix 5 for the full results of the survey.

A minor point of difference from the NHK survey stemmed from a modification made to the student questionnaire: in the latter, the answer "I don't know" (*wakaranai*) was subdivided into two categories, "I don't know, because I lack sufficient knowledge" and "I don't know because I cannot judge such questions". If, as is often claimed, Japanese youth lack interest in historical matters, we would expect most answers falling into the latter category to indicate an inability to judge the issue rather than an admission of ignorance. However, in the survey, the overwhelming majority of those who did "not know" cited lack of knowledge (see appendix 5). This suggests that, rather than lacking *interest* in history, as the truism would have it, Japanese youth are being poorly taught in school and that youngsters are quite aware of their failure to receive an adequate historical education.[131] In the responses to the first question, the proportion of those citing a lack of knowledge was 39%, while the figure claiming deficiency in judgment was only 7%. For question 2, on the inevitability of the war, the respective figures were 34% and 7%. Interestingly, in the third question, the responses among the "don't knows" were almost even, at 10% and 11% respectively. Altogether, this survey confirms the findings of the NHK survey, indicating a fairly high awareness of topical historical questions among Japanese youth,[132] but also revealing the self-perception that current educational methods are failing to equip them with the knowledge necessary to answer important questions on the history of their nation in the depth they desire.

---

[131] In a recent survey of mutual perceptions of South Korean and Japanese students, an overwhelming majority of Japanese students considered that the history of Japanese colonial rule in Korea should be taught in schools in "more detail" or "a little more detail" than at present (46% to 48% among junior high school students in grades one to three, 47% to 58% among high school students in grades one to three, and 82% among university students) (Chung 2004: 45).
[132] See further Yoshimi 1987: 276 and Obinata et al. 1999: 100 for similar results.

Ill. 22: Opinion survey of Japanese students, 2002–2004. Question no. 1: "The last war (*saki no sensō*) was a war of aggression conducted by Japan against its Asian neighbors—what do you think about this statement?" Source: survey by author.

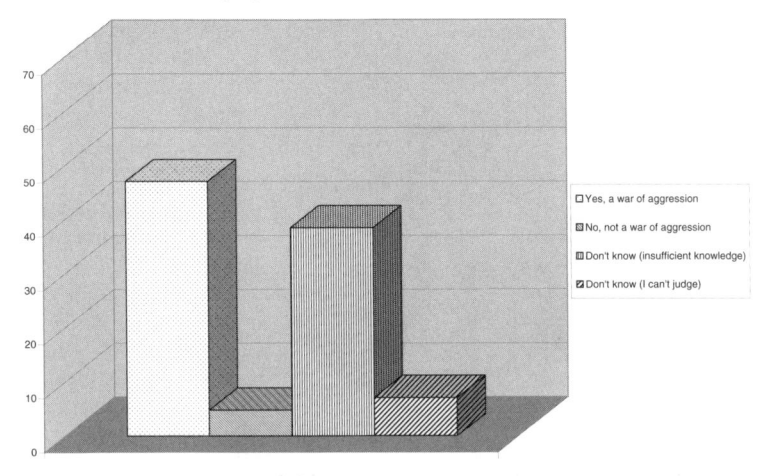

[Bar chart with legend:
- Yes, a war of aggression
- No, not a war of aggression
- Don't know (insufficient knowledge)
- Don't know (I can't judge)]

The survey also revealed quite subtle differences between female and male students: while male students were generally unwilling to admit that they lacked knowledge, the proportion of female students answering the "don't know" option on the grounds of insufficient knowledge was particularly high. In question 1, the proportion of those who chose this option (49%) was higher even than the percentage of students who affirmed that the Asia-Pacific War was a war of aggression (39%).

Ill. 23: Opinion survey with Japanese students 2002–2004. Question no. 1: "The last war (*saki no sensō*) was a war of aggression conducted by Japan against its Asian neighbors—what do you think about this statement?" Source: survey by author.

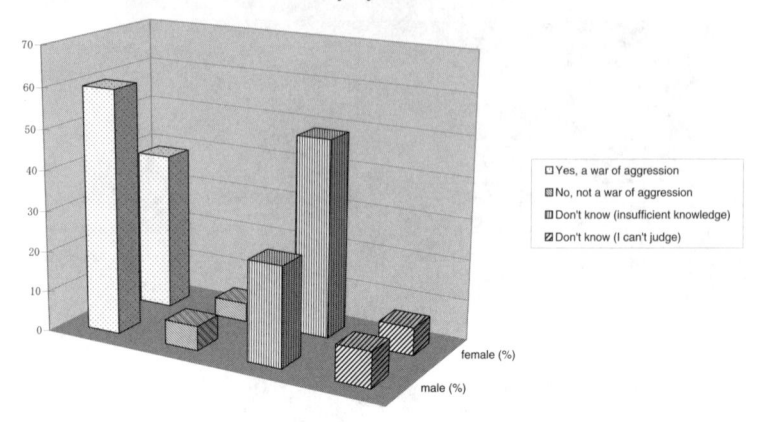

Of course, surveys of this kind are subject to potential distortions—such as responses reflecting "political correctness" or peer pressure (history students would know the kind of responses *expected* of them), or answers that—due to the distinction made by Japanese between *tatemae* (an official position stated to other people) and *honne* (one's real intent or attitude) (Matsuyama et al. 1981: 27)—are made only to satisfy the inquirer, albeit anonymous. However, since the results of all the surveys examined—whether researched or conducted by the author—are conspicuously similar, we are justified in detecting a trend in the recent evolution of historical consciousness among the Japanese, a trend that clearly differs significantly from the apologetic and war-affirmative views held by the Tsukuru-kai and commonplace in Japanese politics. The majority of ordinary Japanese clearly consider the Asia-Pacific War to have been an aggressive act, a war that was *not* unavoidable, and, above all, a war for which Japan still has continuing responsibility. The views of contemporary Japanese youth are particularly clear in this respect, and revisionist thought seems to have made a very limited impact on this group.

3.3 THE QUEST FOR AN HISTORICAL CONSENSUS IN MOVIES, NOVELS AND MUSEUMS

3.3.1 Academic History and the Mass Media

If the historical revisionism described in chapters 1 and 2 is as influential as some observers argue, why then has it failed to find a firmer foothold in Japanese society, given its substantial media presence, political backing and dominance of the public sphere? What are the main factors that have shaped and continue to shape the historical consciousness of the Japanese? And why and how do these factors prevent the revisionist view of history from gaining a greater influence in society and among the population in general?

As the case of Germany illustrates, historical consciousness, as it manifests itself in a given society and culture, is the product of a long evolution and many factors contribute to its shaping. However, as recent studies have shown, influential forces can trigger "changes in historical consciousness in relatively short spans of time, […] i.e. in cases of [historical] phenomena that are marketed in the mass media." (Borries et al. 2001: 336f) Notwithstanding intensive publishing and media activities since the mid-1990s, historical revisionism has hitherto lacked the power to precipitate significant shifts in the historical consciousness of the Japanese. In what follows, I examine other factors that *have* contributed strongly to the long-term shaping of historical consciousness in contemporary Japan and that are working *against* the rapid spread of the ideology of historical revisionism in Japanese society.

First of all, we have to consider the contribution of academic history. Postwar academic history in Japan has been very critical in its approach to wartime history (Conrad 1999). This camp of—self-proclaimed—liberal-progressive intellectuals has become an integral part of what I called in the introduction the "extraparliamentary opposition" in postwar Japan. Strongly Marxist in its methodological orientation, as well as in political coloring, in postwar Japan professional academic history became one of the main pillars of the opposition against the conservative dominance of politics. Through publications in newspapers and magazines, academic historians contributed to the popular spread of critical views of Japan's wartime history; and through a coalition of academic history with historical education and the close cooperation of professional historians with history teachers in schools, critical perspectives were also spread through history education at school level. Notwithstanding conservative attempts to suppress liberal readings through the textbook examination system (*kentei seido*), regarded by many as a form of censorship, critical approaches to the interpretation of Japanese history have largely prevailed in history education.

However, there has recently been increasing discussion of the extent to which academic history contributes to the shaping of historical consciousness in the wider society, with some observers pointing to evidence that their contribution is more limited than most historians would be willing to acknowledge. In recent years, German academic historians have increasingly acknowledged the role of the *mass media* in the shaping of German historical consciousness in the postwar period. While the famous *Historikerstreit* (historians' debate) of the 1980s has achieved a high profile in Germany's dealings with the past and in repulsing a major assault launched by historical revisionism, it is likely that the academic approach to history has had only a limited effect on the historical perceptions of the population in general. Its popular manifestations in the mass media in weekly journals such as *Die Zeit* and a few newspapers such as *Frankfurter Allgemeine Zeitung* did have some effect in shaping public opinion, but with a circulation of only a few hundred thousand their influence was inevitably limited. In the past few decades, the role of television and other mass media has been the focus of historical research in Germany (Steinbach 1999: 40), particularly the role of the TV series *Holocaust*, which was broadcast in the early 1980s and which brought about profound changes in the historical consciousness of ordinary Germans (Zeitgeschichte-online 2004). Similarly, in recent years, the younger generation has been much influenced by the movies in their perception of history, in Germany as elsewhere. As Aleida Assmann has noted of the situation in the U.S., "students form their historical perceptions less from history books and more from Hollywood movies such as *Forrest Gump, Saving Private Ryan* or *Schindler's List*" (Assmann 2001: 114; cf. also Borries et al. 2001: 332f for empirical data on the similar situation in Germany).

Whether the blurring of historical fact and historical fiction characteristic of many recent movies and other media is a positive or a dangerous development is a question that cannot be discussed here. For the moment, however, we have to acknowledge that the mass media exercises a strong influence on the formation of historical consciousness, in Japan as in the US, Germany and elsewhere. Although movies produced in Japan and dealing with the Japanese wartime past are relatively few in number, they convey particular perceptions of the war to Japanese that nevertheless constitute important facets of Japanese historical consciousness. As James Orr (2001) has recently shown, many such movies take up the fate of individual Japanese who are regularly depicted as victims of the war, victims of misgovernment or victims of the brutality of Japan's opponents, above all the atomic bombings of Hiroshima and Nagasaki.[133] However, as Orr also points out, although this consciousness of the Japanese as victims—whether as victims of the atomic bomb, the bombing of Tōkyō, the deportation of soldiers to Siberia by Soviet troops in the last days of the war, or misgovernment by Tōkyō—has been an important facet of historical consciousness in the postwar period,[134] it would be too simple to assume that the kind of victimhood presented in the movies necessarily implies the rejection of war guilt or war responsibility or fosters historical amnesia in itself. There is evidence that, in the immediate postwar period at least, perceiving of oneself as a victim did not preclude acknowledgment of the victim status of Chinese or Koreans (Orr 2001: 13, 23). Even in the case of history texts, as Orr explains, it can be argued that "while victim consciousness in textbooks blunted awareness of a Japanese people's war responsibility, it sharpened awareness of Japanese aggression overall [...]." (Orr 2001: 75, cf. also 105) Orr also credits a number of movies with raising Japanese awareness of their responsibility for the war. Orr selects *The Human Condition* (*Ningen no Jōken*) for special mention, for while

> eventually the forces of war, the army, the system, and ultimately the 'human condition' prove insurmountable [...], this [*Ningen no Jōken*] is the most soul-searching investigation of personal responsibility for Japanese wartime aggression. No one is totally innocent in this tale. (Orr 2001: 108)

Movies such as *The Human Condition* and *Black Rain* (Orr 2001: 129–135) have contributed to firmly establishing "victim consciousness" in Japanese perceptions of the war. According to Orr, the main motive for an emphasis on the role of victim, however, was "a desire to identify with Asian victimhood rather than deny it." (Orr 2001: 175) This attitude, of course, differs radically from the revisionist aim of denying war responsibility, relativizing and affirming Japanese warmaking or reinterpreting

---

[133] The consciousness of being "the only country to have been nuked" (*yuiitsu no hibakukoku*) has played a particularly important role in this regard (cf. Orr 2001: chapter 3).

[134] Although the "German example" of "coming to terms with the past" is often referred to in Japanese writings on history and war responsibility (Yoshimi 1987: 300f), "victim consciousness" is also strongly established in the German postwar mind. Germans share the basic assumption of the Japanese that the German people—even where their role as perpetrators is not denied—were the victims of war, of Nazi tyranny, and of historical circumstance. As Jürgen Straub has recently demonstrated, this attitude is still commonplace in Germany, particularly among the older generation (Straub 2001: passim).

it as undertaken to secure Asian liberation. Indeed, it is likely that, in popular thinking, the victim motif rather functioned (and functions) as a bulwark against revisionist views.

Opinion surveys lend some credence to this assumption. A survey conducted in 26 countries by NHK in cooperation with local research institutions in 1995 revealed a complex picture: the simultaneous existence of a strong victim consciousness along with feelings of remorse on the one hand, but also an awareness that inadequate effort had been put into reconciliation and coming to terms with the past on the other. When respondents in Japan were asked "which country sustained most damage during the war and should therefore receive an apology", 55% answered "Korea", 34% "Japan" and 23% "America" (multiple answers were possible). When asked the question "which country committed acts that it should apologize for", 57% of the Japanese respondents answered "Japan", 49% "America" and 46% "Germany" (NHK 1996: 14f). While the Japanese clearly still feel strongly that Japan suffered during the war and should receive an apology, particularly for the atomic bombings, at the same time most Japanese also consider that their own country still owes apologies for its wartime actions.

These figures are confirmed by the results of more recent surveys; particularly among Japanese youth, there is a strong feeling that Japan still has not done enough to "reflect on the past". In a recent survey conducted among 6,102 Japanese and Korean students from junior high to university level, almost half the university students in the sample (49.2%) considered Japanese reflection on its colonial rule in Korea to be "insufficient" (Chung 2004: 31).[135] While those agreeing that Japan had undertaken "sufficient" reflection never reached more than 15.4% at any level, in the three grades of junior high school the most frequent answer (31% to 36%) was that Japan has "to some degree" reflected on its past as a colonial power, while 26% to 32% stated that its degree of reflection was insufficient (Chung 2004: 31). Asked whether Japan has done enough to compensate for its colonial rule, from the second grade of junior high school to university level the most frequent response (38% from respondents in junior high school, grade two, to 49% in university) was that Japanese compensation is "insufficient" (Chung 2004: 31). These results agree closely with the data presented in the last section (3.2).

In their feeling that Japan should *receive* an apology, the Japanese interestingly are strongly supported by *German* public opinion. In the

---

[135] The author is grateful to Chung Jae-jong from Seoul City University for access to the unpublished Japanese translation of his Korean book *South Korea and Japan*.

1995 international survey discussed above, when German respondents were asked which country should receive an apology, the most frequent response with 38% was "Japan", followed by "England" with 37% and "Germany", with 27% (NHK 1996: 14f), indicating a strong victim consciousness among contemporary Germans, too (cf. also NHK 1996: 20–22). Above all, however, in Germany public opinion strongly condemns the atomic bombing of Hiroshima and Nagasaki. While in countries such as the U.S. and South Korea a large majority replied that it considered the atomic bombing to be "the right decision" (62% and 61% respectively), in Germany only 4% supported this view, while 66% opposed it—a higher figure even than in Japan itself (58%) (NHK 1996: 17). Similar observations can be made by examining media coverage of the "commemoration marathon" in the anniversary year of 1995, marking half a century since the end of the war. While in Germany (as in Japan) none of the documentaries screened to mark this occasion was affirmative of the atomic bombings, in Korea 100% of such programs took a positive stance and in the U.S. 18%; the most frequent figure of 46% balanced affirmative views against disavowal (NHK 1996: 17).

3.3.2 Historical Novels

Indifference rather than outright denial of war responsibility is also a central element in another important cultural medium that has contributed greatly to the formation of the historical consciousness of the Japanese—the historical novel (*rekishi shōsetsu*). The dictionary *Kōjien* defines the historical novel as "a novel that takes a particular era of the past as a stage and aims at drawing a realistic and comprehensive picture of that era. In this respect, it differs from the era novel (*jidai shōsetsu*) that merely uses a certain era as background to the narrative." In presenting a "realistic" picture of a particular historical era or event in its totality, historical novels of course suggest a certain historical reality, although the historical novel itself is of course fiction. Even if it deals, for example, with persons who actually existed, the historical novel is still fundamentally a work of fiction. Nonetheless, in its impact on the reader, the historical novel in a sense replicates historical reality; in practice such novels are not distinguished from historical writing by their audience and their consumption thus contributes to the shaping of popular historical consciousness. As Aleida Assmann claims for Shakespeare's dramas, Japanese historical novels of the postwar period can also be considered as "folkloristic history education inasmuch as they present and strengthen a certain historical basic knowledge regarding genealogy, rulers and battles." (Assmann 1999: 79)

Although historical novels have a long history in Japan, with Mori Ōgai as an important representative of the genre in prewar Japan (Dilworth and Rimer 1977), in the postwar period it is above all the name Shiba Ryōtarō (1923–1996) that stands as a synonym for fiction of this type. His novels are also considered representative of postwar "popular literature" (*kokumin bungaku*), being read by a wide audience (Narita 2003: 6) and sold in large numbers.[136] Since Shiba's novels regularly take up historical themes, many critics consider that his "works of historical fiction and criticism have had an unparalleled influence on the historical consciousness of the Japanese people." (Nakamura 1998: 26; cf. also Narita 2003: 8; Kang 2003: 109) Shiba Ryōtarō's historical novels have not only been long-time bestsellers as books, they have also been recycled as movies and television series and most recently in new media such as websites and CD-ROMs (Furaggushippu 1998; 1999; 2000). Because of Shiba's non-fiction writing, which might be called essayistic treatments of Japanese history, such as *The Shape of This Country* (*Kono kuni no katachi*)—also a bestseller—Shiba has acquired the aura of someone who can accurately communicate the "realities" of Japanese history rather than being regarded primarily as a mere fiction-writer.

The historical picture Shiba presents in his novels, the most important[137] of which are set against the backdrop of the late Edo period (*bakumatsu*) (1840–1868) and the Meiji era (1868–1912), is that of a Japan endangered by foreign enemies and actively rising up, uniting, modernizing and thus defending its national independence and cultural heritage. While Shiba paints a "bright" picture of the Meiji period in his novels, he never touches on the history of the wars after 1931. He considers the wars against China in 1894/95 and Russia in 1904/05 to have been glorious wars that proved the "greatness" of Meiji Japan's political leadership. While the aggressive wars of the 1930s are absent from the novels, Shiba does not deny that the conflicts that followed the Manchurian Incident in 1931 were wars of aggression; rather, in some of his essayistic writings, he presents the picture of a "dark Shōwa era" which is contrasted with the

---

[136] Although virtually unknown in the West and notwithstanding his depicting modern Japanese history in glowing colors, this major Japanese postwar writer has received considerable attention in South Korea and many of his novels have become bestsellers there. Considering the recent quarrels between Korea and Japan over differences of historical interpretation, the popularity of a writer like Shiba in Korea hints at the possibility of reconciliation between the two countries in matters relating to history.

[137] In opinion surveys published in newspapers and magazines, *Ryōma ga yuku*, *Saka no ue no kumo* and *Moe yo ken* always rank as Shiba's most popular works (Narita 2003: 28f).

"bright Meiji". In *The Shape of This Country*, Shiba admits that "the term 'Greater East Asian Co-Prosperity Sphere' was of course a mere glorification" (Shiba 1997: 235) and that the war that started in 1931 "has brought a lot of harm to other nations. [...] It was a war of aggression." (Shiba 1997: 240) He also clearly refutes the revisionist claim that the war was conducted for the sake of Asian liberation: "If there had been a sincere intention to liberate colonies, Korea and Taiwan would have been the first to be liberated." (Shiba 1997: 241)

However, despite such disavowals, Shiba's writings have been a major source of inspiration for historical revisionism. In particular, Fujioka Nobukatsu claims that his own attempts to review modern Japanese history and stress the "bright" stories were very much inspired by Shiba Ryōtarō's reading of history. He had clearly not read *The Shape of This Country*, which first appeared in 1993, carefully enough to grasp Shiba's view of history. As a consequence of such misreadings, the historical narrative created by the revisionists, above all with regards to the interpretation of the Asia-Pacific War, stands in contradiction to the views of Shiba. Rather, it can be argued that his novels and other writings in fact function as a bulwark against the spread of historical revisionism in Japanese society, particularly with Japan's youth, among whom Shiba's popularity remains undiminished.

Nevertheless, as in the case of the movies, while Shiba does not deny Japanese war responsibility and the aggressive character of the war, he "neglects" these chapters of Japanese history. He focuses on the "bright" chapters of the Meiji period and the years leading up to the Meiji Restoration in 1867/68, but fails to address any aspect of Japan's history after 1905 in his novels. Shiba's bestselling novel is *Ryōma ga yuku* (*Ryōma on the Move*), which depicts the historical figure of Tosa samurai Sakamoto Ryōma (1836–1867)[138] as a youthful, agile and far-sighted hero, a political leader with a vision—exactly the kind of figure many Japanese consider to be lacking in recent political life. *Ryōma ga yuku* has been published in numerous editions, in both hardcover and paperback, and is said to have sold almost 20 million copies. It has been adapted for the big screen more than five times since 1974 and more than ten times as television series, including a comedy featuring popular TV star Hamada Kōichi as Sakamoto Ryōma—in this version a fan of modern Western music who aims at bringing change to Japan by spreading jazz. The most recent adaptation of *Ryōma ga yuku* was broadcast as a 10-hour series on TV Tōkyō on New Year 2004 (TV Tōkyō 2004: Internet).

---

[138] For the *historical figure* of Sakamoto Ryōma, see Jansen 1994.

The popularity of "Ryōma" has persisted unbroken until today: every week, hundreds of "Ryōma fans" make the "pilgrimage" to his grave in Kyōto, where the cemetery where he is buried charges a 300 Yen entrance fee—an unusual custom for cemeteries in Japan.

Ill. 24: **Grave of Sakamoto Ryōma and Nakaoka Shintarō in Kyōto (Photo: Sven Saaler).**

Many of the mostly youthful Ryōma fans purchase a granite plate for 1,000 Yen and leave a message at the graveside (see ill. 24) asking "Ryōma-san" or "Ryōma-sensei" for support and guidance in their lives or expressing their admiration "for the way you have lived and the visions you have had." The continuing popularity of the hero Ryōma has also produced an initiative to again make *Ryōma ga yuku* the subject of NHK's *taiga dorama* (Jitsugen suru kai 2004: Internet), the popular annual series discussed further below. In August 2003, Japanese witnessed the current climax of Ryōma's popularity when Kōchi prefecture announced it would rename the prefectural airport as "Kōchi Ryōma Airport" (*Kōchi Ryōma Kūkō*)—the first time that a personal name has been included as part of an airport name in Japan.[139] The governor of the prefecture, Hashimoto Daijirō,

---

[139] See http://www.kochinews.co.jp/senkyo/kihuku8.htm (last accessed on 1 August 2004).

younger brother of former Prime Minister Hashimoto Ryūtarō, took this action in response to a popular campaign that had collected more than 70,000 signatures for a petition to be presented to the governor.

Ill. 25: **Advertisement for "Kōchi Ryōma Airport"** (Source: *Tsubasa no ōkoku* 417, 2004, p. 89; used by permission).

Judged in terms of sales figures, Shiba's other most popular novels are *Clouds over the Hill* (*Saka no ue no kumo*), which portrays the "heroic conduct" of the Japanese military in the 1904/05 war against Czarist Russia (about 12 million copies) and *Tobu ga gotoku* (*Just like Flying*), with close to 10 million copies sold. His more recent novels include *Burn, Sword!* (*Moe yo ken*), with Shinsengumi[140] deputy head Hijikata Toshizō as

---

[140] The Shinsengumi were a group of masterless samurai (*rōnin*) active at the end of the Tokugawa period (1600–1868); acting as a police unit of the Tokugawa Bakufu in Kyōto, they had the task of suppressing the restorationist movement. They are credited with the elimination of anti-government activists such as Sakamoto Ryōma.

protagonist, and *The Days Passing by on Earth* (*Yo ni sumu hibi*), which takes up the youthful Restoration hero Takasugi Shinsaku from Chōshū. Some Shiba novels, such as *The Last Shogun* (*Saigo no Shōgun – Tokugawa Keiki*) and *Drunk as a Lord* (*Yotte sōrō*) have been translated into English, German and other languages, although they do not represent Shiba's most popular writings in Japan. Many of these novels, as with *Ryōma ga yuku*, have been adapted for movies and particularly television series which has led in turn to increased sales of the printed editions. In 2004, the best-selling Shiba novel was *Shinsengumi Keppūroku*, followed by *Moe yo ken*, according to the rankings compiled by online bookseller amazon.co.jp.[141] The reason for the current popularity of these two titles is their subject matter: another novel on the Shinsengumi has been adapted for the NHK's annual historical series (*taiga dorama*) in which Katori Shingo, a member of the popular music group Smap, stars as samurai leader Kondō Isami. Shiba's novels have been adapted five times for this popular series, presently in its 43rd year, including *Ryōma ga yuku*, *Saigo no Shōgun – Tokugawa Keiki* and *Tobu ga gotoku*, some of which are also available on DVD and given repeat showings on satellite television channels.

Analyzing the works chosen for NHK's annual historical series allows us advance some conclusions about the nature of the historical consciousness exhibited by contemporary Japanese. Echoing Shiba's choice of subject matter in his novels, the NHK series deal mostly with themes drawn from the late Tokugawa and the early Meiji period. While material from this period has formed the basis of nine separate series, including the present one, wartime topics are never dealt with and post-Meiji material has featured on only four occasions in 43 years.

Table 6: **Historical periods dealt with in the NHK's annual historical series (Source: NHK 2004: Internet).**

Period	Number of series
Before 1467	8
Period of the Warring States (*Sengoku jidai*), 1467–1573	16
Edo period before 1840	7
Bakumatsu period, 1840–1868	9
After 1868	4

Just as in Shiba's writings, NHK avoids adapting problematic material from Japan's wartime history, but rather focuses on the medieval Period

---

[141] Last accessed on 27 July 2004. Notwithstanding the 100th anniversary of the Russo-Japanese War, *Saka no ue no kumo*, which deals with this war, was ranked only sixth.

of the Warring States and the era leading to the Meiji Restoration, times which many Japanese find fascinating. Of course, in making these selections both Shiba and the NHK are also following sound economic instincts. Even though NHK is a semi-public channel, it pays close attention to its ratings. This must be the explanation for the upsurge in the use of material from the Edo period and the Period of the Warring States after the success of the 1987 and 1988 series, both of which dealt with notable personalities from these periods—Takeda Shingen and Date Masamune. Both series achieved viewer ratings of around 39% and, in subsequent years, more and more themes were drawn from the medieval era and the Edo period. Nonetheless, the record set in the 1987/88 season is yet to be beaten—the 2001 series dealing with Hōjō Tokimune and the Mongol Invasions in the 13th century, for example, attracted an average audience of only 22% of viewers.

In considering this popular fictional material, our conclusion must be that while historical novels, adaptations of such novels for film and television, and historical documentaries such as the recent *Moments When History Moved* (*Sono toki rekishi ga ugoita*) shown on NHK do not actively promote reflection on Japan's wartime past, neither do they promote affirmative views of the war or seek to deny Japanese responsibility for it. Rather, the writings of Shiba Ryōtarō, who achieved popularity with stories set in the "bright" Meiji period, have contributed to the consciousness of contemporary Japanese that Japan's wars of the 1930s and 1940s were certainly wars of aggression, as much through his widely-read historical essays as his historical fiction.

3.3.3 Memoirs and Autobiography

Another kind of writing must be taken into account in our exploration of the factors shaping Japanese historical consciousness: the genre of personal memoirs and autobiographies produced by the wartime generation. In his groundbreaking study *Kusa no ne no Fashizumu* (*Grassroots Fascism*), Yoshimi Yoshiaki (1987) analyzed the recollections of soldiers and sailors of the Japanese Imperial Army and Navy and came to the conclusion that—in contrast to the way in which the war was presented as the object of reflection in the political sphere—"on the level of the people (*minshū*), more than a few had practiced or begun to practice a thoroughgoing examination, verification and reflection on the war […]." (Yoshimi 1987: 297, cf. also 301) A comparative study of reflection about the past and "coming to terms with the past" at a popular level in Germany and Japan has recently been undertaken by Petra Buchholz

(2003). Buchholz came to the conclusion that, while in Germany there is an almost complete absence of critical recollections by perpetrators that describe their participation in wartime atrocities (primarily due to the fact that crimes committed during the Nazi era still can be prosecuted today), Japan has produced a great mass of autobiographical material written by citizens about wartime events, including war crimes (Buchholz 2003: 285f, 358, 362). From the 1970s, amateur authors founded "memorialization groups" (*kioku-kai*) in order to collect testimonies from veterans and survivors, and newspapers as well as magazines published "war series" involving personal recollections of the war and hosted writing contests on wartime themes. At the same time, the "movement for personal history" (*jibunshi undō*)—a term coined by Irokawa Daikichi (cf. Buchholz 2003: chapter I.2.2.2)—was spreading in Japan and resulted in a bumper crop of autobiographies and memoirs of wartime Japan (Buchholz 2003: 132). While the act of writing was itself a step towards "coming to terms with the past" on the part of these authors, their writings, published in considerable numbers, also provided other Japanese with reference material and a strong impulse toward a critical examination of the national past.

These confessional authors, usually in the last third of their lifespan, consider it their "obligation" or "responsibility" to transmit "the truth" about life in the wartime period to the next generation and so prevent the truth of history from "being forgotten". Some also aimed to disclose instances of misgovernment, or their own misconduct during the war (Buchholz 2003: 300–312). While in three-fourths of these cases the authors dealt with events from their childhood and youth, implying some kind of absolution for the actions attributed to themselves (Buchholz 2003: 227), many also touch on controversial issues such as encounters with Chinese and Koreans, in which prewar discrimination is admitted and contrasted with the gracious behavior of Chinese toward Japanese after the Japanese surrender (Buchholz 2003: 279–285). Particularly significant, however, are the testimonies of perpetrators describing their participation in wartime atrocities (Buchholz 2003: 317–325). The many wartime memoirs that appeared differed greatly in perspective and subject matter, and the 1980s boom produced a growing number of works written from the point of view of a perpetrator reflecting on his own participation and war responsibility. The desire to confess personal misconduct or passivity during the war "constituted one of the most frequent motives" for writing one's own personal history (Buchholz 2003: 313). The publication of these memories and recollections of the war in such large numbers doubtlessly contributed to a rising awareness of Japan's responsibility for the war in society at large, and the development of a critical historical consciousness concerning the nation's wartime past.

3.3.4 Museums

Likewise, if we traverse the "realms of memory" as they are preserved in historical museums, we can also find evidence of critical views of Japan's wartime past, an issue touched on in chapter 2. In general, however, notwithstanding the high profile they enjoy in discussions about "the culture of memory", historical museums in Japan do not play a large role in shaping Japanese views of the past, as a number of recent surveys have indicated. In particular, they have no kind of systematic role in history education in Japan (Chung 2004: 63). However, as we have seen, museums and memorials receive much public attention due to their symbolic meaning and their position as bearers of an official version of history that reflects the self-understanding of the state or prefecture that sponsors the institution in question. In prewar Japan, military museums were an integral part of primary and secondary education, particularly from the 1930s. The Yūshūkan in the Yasukuni Shrine (see chapter 2.2), the Defense Museum (Kokubōkan) and the Navy Museum (Kaigunkan) in Tōkyō, each of which attracted up to 750,000 visitors a year in the 1930s and 1940s, and the Memorial Ship Mikasa (Kinenkan Mikasa) in Yokosuka, attracting around 500,000 visitors annually, were all commemorative institutions of national importance. At the local level, institutions such as the General Nogi Memorial Hall (Nogi Kinenkan) in Chōfu, Yamaguchi Prefecture, the Naval Reference Museum (Kaigun Sankōkan) in Shimane, the Naval Memorial (Kaigun Kinenkan) in Maizuru and the Matsuyama City Weapons Exhibition (Matsuyama-shi Buki Chinretsujō) in Matsuyama also played an important role in imbuing the population with "military virtues" (Yamabe 2002).

In recent years, many new history museums have been opened, reflecting a growing interest in history in Japanese society in general (cf. Rekishi Kyōikusha Kyōgikai 2000). However, few of these museums can be considered as potential shapers of historical consciousness or as supplementary forms of historical education, roles considered important by museums in other countries. As a result of the controversy surrounding the Yasukuni Shrine, the Yūshūkan, for example, is rarely visited by school classes; visitor numbers over the last ten years have oscillated between 139,000 (2000) and 231,000 (2003), showing a sharp decline after 1995 and signs of modest recovery more recently—a trend mainly attributable to the renovation and reopening of the museum in 2002.[142] The number of visitors to the

---

[142] Visitor numbers cited in this section have been provided by the museums concerned. I am grateful to the various museum administrations for their cooperation.

Shōwakan (see chapter 2.3.2) has varied between 55,000 and 62,000 annually over the last three years, and visitors to the Heiwa Kinen Tenji Shiryōkan have numbered between 37,000 and 52,000 in the same period—notwithstanding free entrance and massive advertising throughout Tōkyō's train and subway networks. However, all of these exhibitions in the capital region are only rarely used as destinations for school excursions.

In contrast, museums such as the Hiroshima Peace Memorial Museum, which counts many school classes among its more than one million annual visitors, but also the Nagasaki Atomic Bomb Museum and the Okinawa Prefectural Peace Memorial Museum (around 400,000 visitors annually), figure as destinations for the large-scale school trips (*shūgaku ryokō*) undertaken by all pupils once at each level of their schooling. All these institutions actively promote "peace studies" for school classes on excursions and can therefore be ascribed a certain role in shaping political and historical views among the young. In addition, the various peace memorials at prefectural and municipial level are utilized for short school excursions; these include the Ritsumeikan University Peace Museum in Kyōto, and also the Osaka International Peace Center, which attracts between 80,000 and 100,000 visitors a year; the Saitama Prefecture Peace Exhibition (40,000 to 50,000 visitors per year); and the Kawasaki City Peace Memorial (40,000 to 60,000 visitors). While the question of Japanese wartime responsibility is rarely raised directly in any of these exhibitions and memorials, they differ from the institutions described in chapter 2 by avoiding the promotion of affirmative views of war or glorifying war—their primary objective is to promote peace education, and schools are their major audience.

In general, however, Japanese history museums nowadays are less directed to history education and more to serving the tourism industry. While the number of history museums has been growing over the past two decades, as with the mass-media productions analyzed above most do not deal with the history of wartime Japan in the 1930s and 1940s, but rather with other more "glorious" historical periods and famous and popular historical figures. Unlike Germany, for example, no network of national memorials and educational sites relating to the Second World War has been established in Japan.[143] Opened in 1981 as Japan's national

---

[143] Notwithstanding the high reputation of some of these memorials and museums in Germany, observers have pointed out the dangers of transmitting a false or distorted picture of history. "I once visited Dachau, because American friends of mine urged me to. Everything there was clean and orderly, and one needed a lot more imagination than most people have to imagine what had happened here forty years ago. Stones, wood, barracks, the place where the

history museum, the National Museum of Japanese History (Kokuritsu Rekishi Minzoku Hakubutsukan, abbreviated as Rekihaku) in Sakura, Chiba Prefecture, gives a broad overview of the history of Japan, but hardly touches on the modern period. In general, this institution rather functions as a folklore museum, as its Japanese title—*minzoku* means folklore—suggests. Although some schools in the capital region use it as a destination for short school excursions and for history education, the number of visitors has been steadily declining in recent years, from a high of 600,000 in 1983 to around 200,000 per annum in recent years. In the capital region, the history museum that boasts the highest number of visitors is the Edo-Tōkyō Museum (Edo Tōkyō Hakubutsukan) in Ryōgoku; it is geared to attracting tourist visitors and focuses on the local history of Tōkyō, formerly Edo. Between 1.3 (2000) and 1.7 (2003) million visitors visit the museum annually, most of them tourists including many foreign visitors.

Apart from the prefectural history museums (*kenritsu rekishi hakubutsukan*) specializing in local history that are found in almost every prefecture, other historical museums record only a modest number of visitors, mostly tourists for whom history education is not their primary aim. For example, the Reizan History Museum (Reizan Rekishikan) in Kyōto, focusing on the late Edo and early Meiji periods, records around 40,000 visitors per year; the Kōchi Prefecture Memorial Museum for Sakamoto Ryōma (Kōchi Kenritsu Sakamoto Ryōma Kinenkan) has around 100,000 visitors a year—confirming once again the popularity of the hero "Ryōma". Then there is the Museum of the Bakumatsu and Meiji Periods (Bakumatsu to Meiji no Hakubutsukan) in Ibaraki Prefecture with around 10,000 visitors a year, and the Hara Kei Memorial Museum in Morioka (Hara Kei Kinkenkan), commemorating Hara Kei, the "first commoner" to become prime minister, with 8,000 to 10,000 visitors a year. As with the various peace museums, these institutions do not promote affirmative views of the war or serve the purposes of historical revisionism in any way. Their rationale is to attract tourists, not to serve as educational sites. While in many other countries there is lively debate over the merits of preserving a vital culture of memory vs. the commercialization of history (the "theme park" mentality), in Japan there is a tendency to avoid controversial episodes from the nation's history that might deter tourists and in effect exclude them from the "realms of memory" embodied in

---

roll-call was taken. The wood smells fresh and resinous, one can feel a refreshing wind playing over the spacious roll-call area, the barracks almost look inviting. The associations that came to mind were of a holiday camp rather than a tortured life." (Ruth Klüger, cited in Assmann 1999: 333)

these institutions. Historical museums have thus largely been deprived of their educational character or seek to divert visitors' attention to alternative topics of interest or historical eras other than the modern period.

As a result, many historical museums replicate the themes found in historical novels and television series, and the local tourism industry has done a remarkable job in keeping pace with the rapidly evolving historical trends that have swept the country. One of the major factors triggering these trends is the annual historical series produced by NHK discussed above, the *taiga dorama*, each of which portrays a famous historical character or grouping over 50 episodes. The town or district featured in the series invariably experiences a sharp rise in tourism during the year it is broadcast. In 2004, as record sales of Shinsengumi novels (not to mention relevant academic publications) were achieved; Kyōto, Hino and other cities associated with prominent members of the Shinsengumi mounted successful promotional campaigns that capitalized on the popularity of the series. In Kyōto, every souvenir shop displays the flag of the Shinsengumi outside, alerting visitors to the vast array of Shisengumi-related goods (*Shinsengumi guzzu*) within.

The NHK series has also promoted the growth of "Shinsengumi Festivals" in cities with links to this famous samurai association. When in 2002 the figure of feudal lord Maeda Toshiie took center stage in the NHK series, the city of Kanazawa—which Lord Maeda had governed—experienced a two-digit rise in income from tourism, according to the Kanazawa Chamber of Industry and Commerce (Kanazawa Shōkō Kaigisho 2002). This welcome publicity further strengthened the city's already robust tourism infrastructure which had included the partial rebuilding of the city's historic castle shortly before. Now, a brand new main tower forms the centerpiece of the old castle precincts which had served as the campus for Kanazawa University from 1949 to 1995.

All the factors explored in this chapter have contributed to the shaping of the contemporary historical consciousness of the Japanese. Reading historical novels; reading—and of course writing—autobiographies or recollections of the wartime period; visits to museums, whether during an obligatory school trip or as part of a private trip; and choosing television programs with historical content, are all facets of the Japanese inquiry into their national past. This inquiry is not always critical and does not always directly address the wartime past, as we have seen. Rather the "historical infrastructure" erected to support a particular understanding of the past provides the means to evade these issues. Perhaps surprisingly, however, it is equally clear that this trend towards the consumption of popular history has not contributed to an upsurge in historical revisionism, as the survey results discussed in chapter 3.2 demonstrate. It seems

Ill. 26: Shinsengumi Festival in Itabashi Ward, Tōkyō (April 2004) (Photo: Sven Saaler).

more likely that the popularity of certain episodes from Japanese history and the presentation of these as "bright chapters" of the national story in historical novels, television programs and museum displays has provided alternative historical narratives that in some way work to limit the influence of revisionist ideas, particularly affirmative views of the Asia-Pacific War. Thus, while interest in the "bright chapters" of the late Edo and the early Meij periods remains high, and these continue to provide material for commercial consumption, a "bright" view of the Asia-Pacific War, as constructed by historical revisionism, at present lies beyond the ken of the majority of the population. Not only is the affirmative view of the Asia-Pacific War failing to gain popular support but, as we saw in in chapter 3.2, since the 1980s the proportion of Japanese subscribing to an affirmative view of the war has been an astonishingly stable 15 to 17%. And among Japanese youth, this figure has recently fallen even lower.

While historical revisionism developed as a counter to the self-critical ("masochistic") view of wartime history, to the strong pacifist element in Japanese postwar identity, and to Marxist historiography, it stands in contradiction to popular perceptions of modern Japanese history which, while sometimes evasive about wartime issues, are rarely affirmative of the war itself. It is particularly the view of history associated with Shiba Ryōtarō, the "Shiba view of history" (*Shiba-shikan*), which must be credited with erecting a kind of populist bulwark against historical revisionism. Although, in the early days of their movement, historical revisionists like Fujioka Nobukatsu tried to capitalize on Shiba's popularity, the bestselling author's outspoken criticisms of the war were already well known among his readers and were an important factor in shaping popular awareness of historical issues. Shiba's critics have stressed that the Meiji period, which Shiba glorifies in his novels, already contained the seeds of ultranationalism and discrimination in Asia; they stress that the first Sino-Japanese War (1894/95) and the Russo-Japanese War (1904/05), the positive interpretation of which constitutes the center of the Shiba view of history, were important turning points in the making of an aggressive and expansionist Japan (Nakamura 1998; Kang 2003: 26; Tahara, Nishibe and Kang 2003: 90f). However, Shiba's simple dichotomy between a "bright Meiji" and a "dark Shōwa" period, and his interpretation of the Asia-Pacific War as an expansionist and aggressive war, have fed opposition to historical revisionism fully as much as liberal and Marxist historiography. Manga-writer Kobayashi Yoshinori, discussed at the beginning of this chapter, has attacked Shiba's view of history directly:

> There is of course glory (*eikō*) in wars that were won, but there is also glory in wars that were lost. (Kobayashi 1998: 311)

Through its double assault on postwar academic historiography, the self-critical view of history, and the pacifist thread in postwar Japanese identity on the one hand, and on the immensely popular "Shiba view of history" on the other, historical revisionism has greatly contributed to its own marginalization in society at large. Although the self-critical perspective and the Shiba view of history are in many ways incompatible (cf. Kang 2003: 26), both seem to offer more toward a consensus on Japan's modern history than the revisionist approach which, although responsible for the occasional sensational outburst, has so far failed to effect any fundamental changes in the historical consciousness of the Japanese.

Conclusions and Outlook

This overview of recent developments in Japanese discussion of their history, the politics of historical memory and the shaping of historical consciousness has shown that, far from remaining limited to academic history or history education, the "history textbook controversy" is a barometer of social and political debate in contemporary Japan. The controversy is closely linked to vital issues of the day such as the role of historical memory in the public sphere, reform of the education system, a new definition of Japan's role in the world, and the role of the military in Japanese society and politics. Underlying these specific issues are the broader questions of the relation of the citizen to the state and the importance of nationalism and patriotism in the quest for national integration. It is important to appreciate that the claims made by historical revisionism derive their significance from the politicized context in which they are made; rather than stemming from history as an academic discipline, they arise "directly from political antagonisms" (Abe 2004: 178).

By relying on historical revisionism and the "bright" narrative of national history it proposes—with the affirmative view of the war as its centrepiece—conservative politics aims at strengthening patriotism in society and fostering the allegiance of the citizen to the state. Some observers have placed this agenda within the context of a striving for an "Orwellian state" whose institutions reflect the slogan: "Who controls the past, controls the future; who controls the present controls the past." (cf. Nozaki and Inokuchi 2000) Against the "bright" historical narrative utilized by conservative politics, a strong liberal and leftist opposition in Japanese society at large is concerned to propagate critical views of history, denying the need to generate "pride" in the nation or "patriotism" in the first place. This deep rift in discussions on history and patriotism mirrors the polarized positions adopted on a raft of related political issues—revision (*kaisei*) of the Constitution vs. retention or protection (*goken*) of the existing text; revision of the Basic Law on Education vs. retention; loosening restrictions on the deployment of the SDF abroad vs. strict adherence to Article 9 of the Constitution, and so on. In all these issues, conservative politics faces strong resistance from societal opposition, and the discussions around them are closely linked, as we saw in chapter 1.5.2, to the controversies over the interpretation of Japanese wartime history as the central facet of the history textbook debate.

This societal (or extraparliamentary) opposition, which centers on academic historians and liberal media, lawyers and citizens organizations, frequently warns of a "drift to the right" (*ukeika*) (Takahashi 2003:

128f; 170f; Ōuchi 2003: 89–93; Tanaka 2002a: 211–214; Tawara 2001; Irie 2004: 201; Obinata 2004: 13; Umehara 2004: 72 and others) which will lead to a curtailment of citizens' rights or the increasing interference of the state in people's private lives. Recent legislation, such as the law designating a national flag and anthem and the enforcement of its use in school commencement and graduation ceremonies, provision for the expansion of state power in times of military crisis "in the vicinity of Japan" (*shūhen yūji*), the introduction of a computerized Basic Residential Register Network System (*Jūmin kihon daichō netto*, *jūki netto* for short) are placed in this context and opposed as inflating the role of the state vis-à-vis the individual. Issues such as the proposed revisions of the Constitution and the Basic Law of Education are next on the agenda. As I noted in the introduction, while this loose-knit opposition has not yet materialized as a substantial political opposition in the Diet, its influence in the wider society remains strong. Rather than looking at the distribution of seats in the Diet, the circulation figures of major newspapers in Japan offer a hint as to the strength of this unofficial opposition. While the newspaper with the largest daily circulation of slightly over 10 million copies, the *Yomiuri Shinbun*, is strongly conservative, the popular liberal *Asahi Shinbun* with around 8.3 million copies is only a little way behind. The second national daily with a liberal outlook, the *Mainichi Shinbun*, with a circulation of around four million, far outstrips the ultraconservative *Sankei Shinbun* with around two million copies.

The overlapping of conservative politics with historical revisionism on the one side and the extraparliamentary opposition with critical views of history on the other is a self-evident fact of political life in Japan. In a recently-published volume simply titled "Patriotism" (*aikokushin*) (Tahara, Nishibe and Kang 2003), this constellation is easily spotted in the basic ideological positions adopted by the contributors. While Kang Sang-jung, a Japanese of Korean descent (but born in Japan), strongly rejects the claim of the modern nation-state to the undivided loyalty of its citizens, Nishibe Susumu, a member of the revisionist Tsukuru-kai, argues that the commitment to the "common good", which he sees as largely synonymous with the state, is a duty for the citizen who also enjoys the state's protection. Kang, who also rejects the affirmative view of the war held by historical revisionists, stresses that for him, "nationalism is basically an illness. Love for one's home region (*aigōshin*) is unconnected with love of country (*aikokushin*)—rather the two are in conflict with each other." (Tahara, Nishibe and Kang 2003: 7, 184; cf. also Kang 2001: 56f) Nishibe on the other hand claims that his fellow Japanese must "preserve the essence of the country (*kokutai*)" and to that end "they must honor the special (*dokutoku*) values, traditions and the culture of their country."

(Tahara, Nishibe and Kang 2003: 5) The book's third author, Tahara Sōichirō, a popular moderator of television discussion programs on TV Asahi such as *Sunday Project* and *Asa made nama terebi* (Live until the morning), claims a neutral position and laments that in postwar Japan, patriotism and democratic thought seem to be irreconcilable: "Democrats are anti-establishment and anti-state, and patriots dislike democracy."[144] (Tahara, Nishibe and Kang 2003: 3) In the debates over Japan's wartime past, Tahara again aims at a middle position. In a book co-authored with Ishihara Shintarō, the rightist-populist governor of Tōkyō prefecture, he argues that Japan was guilty of being an aggressor towards Asia, but not to the United States (*Amerika ni taishite wa muzai, Ajia ni taishite wa yūzai*) (Ishihara and Tahara 2000: 62). However, in making this distinction, Tahara takes up one of the central revisionist arguments—the claim that the U.S. and Britain forced the war upon Japan and so were also responsible for its outbreak (*Bei-Ei dōzai shikan*).

While conservative politicians in Japan have advocated the affirmative views of the war formulated by historical revisionism throughout the postwar period, as we saw in chapter 1.5.1, since the 1990s, they have, for the first time, found some degree of popular support. Nonetheless, as I demonstrated in chapter 3, revisionist views have by no means gone uncontested. In society as a whole, such views are still in the minority, and Japanese academic historians, prompted by contemporary critiques of nationalism, also continue to challenge "the powerful repressive and appropriative functions of national History." (Duara 1995: 232f) Japanese postwar nationalism comes in many varieties (McVeigh 2004) and, as Oguma Eiji has pointed out, in the postwar period it again became a mass phenomenon during the high economic growth of the 1960s (Oguma 2002: chapter 13). However, the spread of this economic variant of nationalism clearly did not presuppose an affirmative, uncritical view of the war (as the figures collated in chapter 3.2 would indicate), and it is different in character from the statist nationalism now in the ascendant. The fact that the economic nationalism of the early postwar period was unconnected with historical revisionism probably reflects the failure of revisionist views to penetrate history education in schools and other popular representations of history which have contributed to the shaping of historical consciousness among the Japanese (see chapter 3.3). Not even the extensive media activities of the Tsukuru-kai since the 1990s and

---

[144] As Oguma Eiji has recently pointed out, in the early decades after the war the situation was very different: "patriotism" was openly advocated by the political left and was not considered incompatible with "democracy" (Oguma 2002: 103).

their influence in the sphere of public memory (explored in chapter 2) have thus far significantly affected the historical consciousness of the majority of Japanese, who remain quite self-critical on such questions as the Asia-Pacific War.

In response, the historical revisionism of the 21st century—as the name of its chief organization (the Society for the Creation of New History Textbooks) leaves in little doubt—has set its sights on history education in schools, and the textbook controversy has become the main battlefield for the wider debates over the role of the state in Japan. But in the textbook arena, too, historical revisionists face strong societal opposition, and it seems unlikely that the revised version of the Tsukuru-kai textbooks will be widely distributed when the next round of the approval and selection process, described in chapter 1.4, takes place in 2005. The coincidence with the 60th anniversary of the end of the war is likely to spark new levels of debate. There is no doubting that the claims of the Tsukuru-kai and the strength of its political connections carry sufficient potential for continuing conflict within Japan as well as for bilateral friction for years to come.

Popular resistance to an historical revisionism allied to or instrumentalized by politics seems to be rooted in the rejection of the claims of the state to impose an historical narrative of its own choosing upon its citizens. Such a rejection seems to be a universal tendency. As Jürgen Habermas has stressed of the German case, in modern states "politicians [...] founder when confronted with issues that concern the identity and self-understanding of the populace as a whole" (Habermas 1986: 49; cf. also Nagahara 1998: 7 for a similar comment from a Japanese historian). Criticizing former German Chancellor Helmut Kohl for his 1986 visit with U.S. president Ronald Reagan to a cemetery at Bitburg, where, amongst others, members of the Nazi SS were buried, Habermas adds:

> Given his intellectual makeup, the present chancellor [Helmut Kohl] is hardly suited for tasks of this sort. [...] The task of promoting social integration and self-awareness is no longer, today, the responsibility of the political system. For good reasons we no longer have a Kaiser or a Hindenburg. The public sphere should therefore refuse to tolerate such claims to spiritual-moral leadership among top elected officials. (Habermas 1986: 49)

The statistics presented in chapter 3 suggest that this process is underway in Japan, too—the affirmative view of the war, despite its strong promotion by conservative media and politicians, is being rejected by the wider society. The reasons for this, of course, are manifold. They include the international repercussions of the textbook controversy which largely lie outside the scope of this study; established popular perceptions of history, such as the "Shiba view of history" (see chapter 3.3); but also the inconsistencies apparent within the revisionist narrative itself—inconsistencies that are the product of a century's misdirected effort expended in constructing narratives and assembling facts which are in reality unrelated to one another, of constructing identities and retailing contradictory versions of history all of which, again, have resulted in a "high degree of nervousness regarding definitions of 'the nation'" in East Asia (Vickers 2002b: 644).

The strong popular resistance to revisionist textbooks also reflects a rising awareness that a nation's history must be considered in a global context and that a rejection of the importance of this context leads inevitably to isolation (Fujiwara 2002). One the one hand, Japanese historical revisionism should be considered in the larger framework of the processes that have been called globalization and internationalization, one manifestation of a nationalism that is gaining strength at exactly the moment that these processes are accelerating, as Kang Sang-Jung and Yoshimi Shun'ya have stressed (Kang and Yoshimi 2001). On the other, the repercussions of the continuing textbook controversy on Japanese foreign relations, and also on ordinary Japanese abroad, look set to continue as events during soccer matches at the "Asian Cup 2004 China" in Chungking—the capital of the Guomindang government after 1937 and target of major Japanese bombing campaigns over several years during the war—have demonstrated (Sugita 2004: Internet). While in Korea feelings have subsided a little recently [145] as the textbook controversy has temporarily gone off the boil, in the view of one astute observer, a "positive view of Japanese history and the policies [the Tsukuru-kai] urges on the Japanese government would, if ever adopted, set back immeasurably the process of rapprochement [...]. The regional consequences would be unpredictable but inevitably disturbing." (McCormack 2000: 69f)

The Japanese textbook controversy reveals the difficulties of restructuring a nationalism burdened by legacies of the past, above all in its role as an ideological vehicle for the militarism and national mobilization that issued in World War II. As a result, voices are regularly heard in Japan warning of a reversion to prewar patterns in recent nationalist rhetoric,

---

[145] A search of the subject database of the *Chosun Ilbo* (http://srch.chosun.com), one of Korea's major daily newspapers, turned up 210 articles on both "Japan" and "history" in 2001, 93 items in 2002, and 114 in 2003. Also, in terms of content, Korean newspapers have begun to show more understanding towards Japan in their coverage of Japanese affairs, while still criticizing Japanese politics. Intensive coverage is also given to pro-Korean voices in Japan.

particularly where loosening restrictions on the use of the military are concerned, as we saw in chapter 1.5.2. In the wake of similar discussions about the meaning of nationalism in the postwar period in Germany, some observers have come to the conclusion that the intensity and continuity of the debate signal that "nationalism no longer quite believes in itself." (Adorno 1986: 123) In Japan, however, researchers like Oguma Eiji have pointed out that nationalism has been generally accepted in postwar society. Oguma argues that "a complete negation of nationalism in a broad sense" in postwar Japan was hardly possible, not only for the government but also for the liberal-leftist camp heading the opposition (Oguma 2002: 826). Thus, according to Oguma, in postwar Japan democracy and nationalism were not always at loggerheads but rather coexisted over a long period. The recent textbook debate, however, suggests that strong resistance to *statist* nationalism will surface in a society which shows itself to be opposed to the monopolization of nationalism by the state, and the promulgation by the state of versions of the national narrative with a neonationalist or revisionist slant. This opposition is hardly likely to become weaker, but will remain a major force in the debates over Japanese history and civics textbooks in the years to come.

References

Newspapers

Asahi Shinbun
Chosun Ilbo
The Japan Times
The Korea Herald
Mainichi Shinbun
Sankei Shinbun

Monographs and Articles

Abe, Kin'ya (2004): *Nihonjin no Rekishi Ishiki* [The historical consciousness of the Japanese]. Tōkyō: Iwanami Shoten (= Iwanami Shinsho 874).

Adorno, Theodor W. (1986): What Does Coming to Terms with the Past Mean? In: Hartman, Geoffrey (ed.): *Bitburg in Moral and Political Perspective*. Bloomington: Indiana University Press, pp. 114–129.

Akazawa, Shirō (2002): Sensō giseisha no tsuitō to Yasukuni jinja [Mourning for war victims and the Yasukuni Shrine]. In: *Rekishi Hyōron* 628, pp. 2–14, 40.

Anderson, Benedict (1991): *Imagined Communities. Reflections on the Origin and Spread of Nationalism*. London, New York: Verso (Revised Edition).

Anderson, Benedict (1999): The Goodness of Nations. In: van der Veer, Peter and Hartmut Lehmann (eds.): *Nation and Religion. Perspectives on Europe and Asia*. Princeton: Princeton University Press, pp. 196–203.

Antoni, Klaus (1998): *Shintō und die Konzeption des Japanischen Nationalwesens (kokutai). Der religiöse Traditionalismus in Neuzeit und Moderne Japans*. Leiden, Boston, Köln: Brill (Handbuch der Orientalistik 8).

Arai, Shin'ichi (1994): 'Senbotsusha tsuitō heiwa kinen-kan' o tō [Questioning the 'Institution for Mourning the War Dead and Praying for Peace']. In: Arai, Shin'ichi (ed.): *Sensō Hakubutsukan*, pp. 2–27. Tōkyō: Iwanami Shoten (Iwanami Bukkuletto 328).

Arai, Shin'ichi (2001): 'Ushinawareta 10nen' to Rekishi Ninshiki Mondai [The 'lost decade' and the problem of historical consciousness]. In: Funabashi, Yōichi (ed.): *Ima, Rekishi Mondai ni dō Torikumu ka* [How Shall we Deal with the problem of history?]. Tōkyō: Iwanami Shoten, pp. 25–54.

Arendt, Hannah (1986): *Elemente und Ursprünge Totaler Herrschaft*. München and Zürich: Piper.

Asahi.com (1 May 2001): Yūkō no ba, towareta rekishi ninshiki [A place for exchange, historical consciousness challenged]. Internet: http://mytown.asahi.com/ishikawa (last accessed on 22 August 2001).

Asahi.com (2 May 2001): 'Himeyuri' kokuin ni munen [Grief over the inscription 'Himeyuri']. Internet: http://mytown.asahi.com/ishikawa (last accessed on 22 August 2001).

Asahi.com (4 May 2001): Sanpi 2-shi ni kiku [Questioning both sides about support and opposition]. Internet: http://mytown.asahi.com/ishikawa (last accessed on 22 August 2001).

AsiaSource (2003): *Japanese History Textbook Raises Concerns*. Internet: http://www.asiasource.org/news/at_mp_02.cfm?newsid=48253 (last accessed on 22 April 2004).

Assmann, Aleida (1999): *Erinnerungsräume. Formen und Wandlungen des Kulturellen Gedächtnisses*. München: C.H. Beck.

Assmann, Aleida (2001): Wie wahr sind Erinnerungen? In: Welzer, Harald (ed.): *Das Soziale Gedächtnis. Geschichte, Erinnerung, Tradierung*. Hamburg. Hamburger Edition, pp. 103–122.

Assmann, Aleida and Ute Frevert (1999): *Geschichtsvergessenheit, Geschichtsversessenheit. Vom Umgang mit deutschen Vergangenheiten nach 1945*. Stuttgart: Deutsche Verlags-Anstalt.

Assmann, Jan (1997): *Das Kulturelle Gedächtnis. Schrift, Erinnerung und Politische Identität in Frühen Hochkulturen*. München: Beck.

Barnard, Christopher (2001): Isolating Knowledge of the Unpleasant: the Rape of Nanking in Japanese high-school textbooks. In: *British Journal of Sociology of Education* 22:4, pp. 519–530.

BBK (Bōeichō Bōei Kenkyūjo) Rikugun-Rikugun-shō-Dai-nikki-rui-Mitsudai nikki, 28 December 1937 (*Saikin ni okeru kannai ippan chihō jōsei no ken*) (unpublished document).

BBK (Bōeichō Bōei Kenkyūjo) Rikugun-Rikugun-sh-Dai-nikki-rui-Rikushi kimitsu dai-nikki, 19 November 1938 (*Keizai-sen kyōchō shūkan jisshi yōkō no ken*) (unpublished document).

BBK (Bōeichō Bōei Kenkyūjo) Rikugun-Rikugun-shō-Dai-nikki-rui-Rikuman kimitsu dai-nikki, December 1938 (*Manshū-koku no taigai hōsaku ni kan-suru ken*) (unpublished document).

Bebel, August (1889): Rede im Deutschen Reichstag, 30.10.1889. In: *Stenographische Berichte über die Verhandlungen des Deutschen Reichstages*, 7. Legislaturperiode, 5. Session, Bd. 1. Berlin: Reichsdruckerei, pp. 44f.

Beier de Haan, Rosmarie (2000): Sensō o kataritsutaeru [Passing down stories of the war]. In: *Ritsumeikan Heiwa Kenkyū* 1, pp. 51–60.

Bhattacharya, Neeladri (2003): The Problem. In: *India-Seminar* 522 (Rewriting History. A Symposium on Ways of Representing Our Shared

Past). Internet: http://www.india-seminar.com/2003/522/522% 20the %20problem.htm (last accessed on 22 April 2004).

Billig, Michael (1995): *Banal Nationalism*. London. Sage.

Bodnar, John (2000): Pierre Nora, national memory, and democracy: A review. In: *Journal of American History* 87:3, pp. 951–963.

Borries, Bodo von (2001a): Geschichtsbewußtsein als System von Gleichgewichten und Transformationen. In: Rüsen, Jörn (ed.): *Geschichtsbewußtsein. Psychologische Grundlagen, Entwicklungskonzepte, Empirische Befunde*. Köln, Weimar and Wien: Böhlau, pp. 239–280.

Borries, Bodo von (2001b): Verknüpfung der Zeitebenen im Geschichtsbewußtsein? Zu Vergangenheitsdeutungen, Gegenwartswahrnehmungen und Zukunftserwartungen ost- und westdeutscher Jugendlicher 1992. In: Rüsen, Jörn (ed.): *Geschichtsbewußtsein. Psychologische Grundlagen, Entwicklungskonzepte, Empirische Befunde*. Köln, Weimar and Wien: Böhlau, pp. 281–315.

Borries, Bodo von et al. (2001): Jugendliches Geschichtsbewußtsein im Zeitgeschichtlichen Prozess – Konstanz und Wandel. In: Rüsen, Jörn (ed.): *Geschichtsbewußtsein. Psychologische Grundlagen, Entwicklungskonzepte, Empirische Befunde*. Köln, Weimar and Wien: Böhlau, pp. 317–404.

Buchholz, Petra (2003): *Schreiben und Erinnern. Über Selbstzeugnisse Japanischer Kriegsteilnehmer*. München: Iudicium (Iaponia Insula 10).

Buruma, Ian (1995): *The Wages of Guilt. Memories of War in Germany and Japan*. New York: Meridian.

Carpenter, Ted Galen (2004): China's Defense Budget Smoke and Mirrors. In: *The Washington Times* 15 March 2004, Internet: http://www.washtimes.com/upi-breaking/20040315-120805-4272r.htm (last accessed on 15 April 2004).

Cave, Peter (2002): Teaching the history of empire in Japan and England. In: *International Journal of Educational Research* 37, pp. 623–641.

Chidorigafuchi Senbotsusha Boen (2003): *Chidorigafuchi Senbotsusha Boen* [The Chidorigafuchi Cemetery for the War Dead]. Internet: http://homepage2.nifty.com/boen/ (last access on 27 July 2004).

Chung, Jae-Jung (1998): *Kankoku to Nihon: Rekishi Kyōiku no Shisō* [South Korea and Japan: The Ideology of History Education]. Tōkyō: Suzusawa Shoten.

Chung, Jae-Jung (2002): *Hirogaru Taiwa, Fukamaru Giron: Rekishi Ninshiki to Rekishi Kyōkasho Mondai no Saikin no Dōkō* [Broadening dialogue, deepening discussion: Recent developments in the study of historical consciousness and the history textbook debate]. Internet: http://www.jca.apc.org/asia-net/library/paper030701.shtml (last accessed on 15 May 2004).

Chung, Jae-Jung (2003a): Die Schatten der Vergangenheit im südkoreanisch-japanischen Verhältnis. In: Ducke, Isa and Sven Saaler (eds.): *Japan und Korea auf dem Weg in eine Gemeinsame Zukunft – Aufgaben und Perspektiven*. Munich: Iudicium (Monographien aus dem Deutschen Institut für Japanstudien 36), pp. 89–105.

Chung, Jae-Jung (2003b): South Korea-Japan History Reconciliation: A Progress Report. In: Horvat, Andrew and Gebhard Hielscher (eds.): *Sharing the Burden of the Past: Legacies of War in Europe, America, and Asia*. Tōkyō: The Asia Foundation, Friedrich-Ebert-Stiftung, 2003, pp. 107–114.

Chung, Jae-Jung (2004): *Kankoku to Nihon – Rekishi Kyōiku no Shisō* [Korea and Japan – the ideology of history education]. Unpublished Translation of Korean Publication.

Conrad, Sebastian (1999): *Auf der Suche Nach der Verlorenen Nation. Geschichtsschreibung in Westdeutschland und Japan, 1945–1960*. Göttingen: Vandenhoeck & Ruprecht (Kritische Studien zur Geschichtswissenschaft, 134).

Cornelißen, Christoph (2001): Das Studium der Geschichtswissenschaften. In: Corelißen, Christoph (ed.): *Geschichtswissenschaften*. Frankfurt am Main: Fischer Taschenbuch Verlag, pp. 9–25.

Cornelißen, Christoph, Lutz Klinkhammer and Wolfgang Schwentker (eds.) (2003): *Erinnerungskulturen. Deutschland, Italien und Japan seit 1945*. Frankfurt am Main: Fischer.

Crane, S. A. (ed.). (2000): *Museums and Memory*. Stanford, CA: Stanford University Press.

CSHC (Centre for the Study of Historical Consciousness) (2002): *Definition of Historical Consciousness*. Internet: http://www.cshc.ubc.ca/about.php (last accessed on 5 April 2004).

Dentsū Sōken and Yoka Kaihatsu Sentā (1995): *37ka-koku "Sekai Kachikan Chōsa" Repōto* [Report on the "Survey on social values in the world" covering 37 countries]. Tōkyō: Dentsū Sōken and Yoka Kaihatsu Sentā.

Dilworth, David and J. Thomas Rimer (eds.) (1977): *The Historical Fiction of Mori Ōgai*. Honolulu: University of Hawai'i Press.

Doak, Kevin M. (2003): Liberal nationalism in imperial Japan. In: Stegewerns, Dick (ed.): *Nationalism and Internationalism in Imperial Japan: Autonomy, Asian Brotherhood, or World Citizenship?* London, New York: RoutledgeCurzon, pp. 17–41.

Duara, Prasenjit (1995): *Rescuing History from the Nation: Questioning Narratives of Modern China*. Chicago: University of Chicago Press.

Duara, Prasenjit (2003): *Sovereignty and Authenticity. Manchukuo and the East Asian Modern*. Lanham et al.: Rowman & Littlefield.

Ducke, Isa (2003): Kann das Internet Berge versetzen? Transnationale Bürgerbewegungen und neue Medien. In: Ducke, Isa and Sven Saaler (eds.) (2003): *Japan und Korea auf dem Weg in eine Gemeinsame Zukunft – Aufgaben und Perspektiven.* Munich: Iudicium (Monographien aus dem Deutschen Institut für Japanstudien 36), pp. 195–214.

Ducke, Isa and Sven Saaler (eds.) (2003): *Japan und Korea auf dem Weg in eine Gemeinsame Zukunft – Aufgaben und Perspektiven.* Munich: Iudicium (Monographien aus dem Deutschen Institut für Japanstudien 36).

Etō, Jun and Kobori Keiichirō (eds.) (1986): *Yasukuni ronshū* [Articles on Yasukuni]. Tōkyō: Nihon Kyōbunsha.

Eguchi, Keiichi (1995): *Nihon no Shinryaku to Nihonjin no Sensōkan* [Japan's aggression and Japanese views of the war]. Tōkyō: Iwanami Shoten (Iwanami bukkuretto).

Evans, Richard J. (1989): *Im Schatten Hitlers?* Frankfurt am Main: Suhrkamp.

Fogel, Joshua (2000): Introduction: The Nanjing Massacre in History. In: Fogel, Joshua (ed.): *The Nanjing Massacre in History and Historiography.* Berkeley, Los Angeles and London: University of California Press, pp. 1–9.

Foljanty-Jost, Gesine (1979): *Schulbuchgestaltung als Systemstabilisierung in Japan.* Bochum: Studienverlag Brockmeyer.

Fuhrt, Volker (2002): *Erzwungene Reue. Vergangenheitsbewältigung und Kriegsschulddiskussion in Japan 1952–1998.* Hamburg: Verlag Dr. Kovac (Studien zur Zeitgeschichte, 24).

Fujitani, Takashi et al. (2001): Introduction. In: Fujitani, Takashi et al. (eds.): *Perilous Memories: the Asia-Pacific War(s).* Durham: Duke University Press, pp. 1–29.

Fujiwara, Kiichi (2001): *Sensō o Kioku Suru. Hiroshima, Horokōsuto to Genzai* [Remembering War: Hiroshima, the Holocaust and the present]. Tōkyō: Kōdansha.

Fujiwara, Kiichi (2002): Memory as Deterrence: The Moralization of International Politics. In: *Japan Review of International Affairs* 16:1, pp. 46–62.

Fulbrook, Mary (2004): Approaches to German contemporary history since 1945: Politics and paradigms. In: *Zeithistorische Forschungen/ Studies in Contemporary History,* Internet edition, vol. 1/1. Internet: http:// www.zeithistorische-forschungen.de/16126041-Fulbrook-1-2004 (last accessed on 1 March 2004).

Furaggushippu (1998): *Ryōma ga Yuku. CD-ROM-ban* [Ryōma on the Move. CD-ROM-version]. Tōkyō: Furaggushippu.

Furaggushippu (1999): *Yo ni Sumu Hibi. CD-ROM-ban* [The Days Passing by on Earth. CD-ROM-version]. Tōkyō: Furaggushippu.

Furaggushippu (2000): *Moe-yo ken! CD-ROM-ban* [Burn, Sword! CD-ROM-version]. Tōkyō: Furaggushippu.
Gellner, Ernest (1983): *Nations and Nationalism*. Oxford: Basil Blackwell.
Gerow, Aaron (2000): Consuming Asia, consuming Japan: the new neonationalistic revisionism in Japan. In: Hein, Laura and Mark Selden (eds.): *Censoring History: Citizenship and Memory in Japan, Germany, and the United States*. Armonk and London: M. E. Sharpe, pp. 74–95.
Giddens, Anthony (1987): *The Nation-State and Violence*. Berkeley: University of California Press (A Contemporary Critique of Historical Materialism, vol. 2).
Gold, Hal (1996): *Unit 731 Testimony. Japan's Wartime Human Experimentation Program*. Singapore: Yenbooks.
Gotōda, Masaharu (2003): Rekishi o wasurezu, rekishi o koete [Overcoming history while not forgetting it]. In: *Sekai* 718, pp. 179–181.
Ha, Jon-mon (2002): Kyōkasho mondai, Murayama danwa, Kan-Nichi kankei [The Textbook problem, the Murayama statement, and South Korean-Japanese relations]. In: *Sensō Sekinin Kenkyū* 36, pp. 76–85.
Habermas, Jürgen (1986): Defusing the Past. A Politico-Cultural Tract. In: Hartman, Geoffrey (ed.): *Bitburg in Moral and Political Perspective*. Bloomington: Indiana University Press, pp. 43–51.
Harada, Keiichi (2001): *Kokumingun no Shinwa* [The myth of the national army]. Tōkyō: Yoshikawa Kōbunkan (Nyū historī kindai Nihon 4).
Hardacre, Helen (1989): *Shintō and the State, 1868–1988*. Princeton: Princeton University Press.
Harootunian, Harry (1999): Memory, Mourning, and National Morality: Yasukuni Shrine and the Reunion of State and Religion in Postwar Japan. In: van der Veer, Peter and Hartmut Lehmann (eds.): *Nation and Religion. Perspectives on Europe and Asia*. Princeton: Princeton University Press, pp. 144–160.
Hata, Nagami (2002a): Koizumi shushō Yasukuni sanpai no seiji katei [The Political Process surrounding Prime Minister Koizumi's Visit to Yasukuni]. In: *Sensō Sekinin Kenkyū* 36, pp. 10–18.
Hata, Nagami (2002b): Kokka to irei. Nihon Izokukai to Yasukuni jinja o meguru sengo no shomondai [State and Mourning: The political implications of the Japan Bereaved Families' Organization and the Yasukuni Shrine in the postwar era]. In: *Rekishi Hyōron* 628, pp. 15–27.
Hatano, Sumio (1996): *Taiheiyō Sensō to Ajia Gaikō* [Japan's Asia Policy During the Pacific War: The Political conflict over "Asian Liberation"]. Tōkyō: Tōkyō Daigaku Shuppankai.
Heginbotham, Eric and Richard J. Samuels (2003): Japan. In: Ellings, Richard J. and Aaron L. Friedberg (eds.): *Strategic Asia 2002-03*. Seattle: The National Bureau of Asian Research, pp. 95–130.

Hein, Laura (2003): Citizens, Foreigners, and the State in the United States and Japan since 9/11. In: Hein, Laura and Daizaburo Yui (eds.): *Crossed Memories: Perspectives on 9/11 and American Power.* Tōkyō: Center for Pacific and American Studies, The University of Tokyo.

Hein, Laura and Mark Selden (eds.) (2000a): *Censoring History. Citizenship and Memory in Japan, Germany, and the United States.* Armonk and London: M. E. Sharpe.

Hein, Laura and Mark Selden (2000b): The Lessons of War, Global Power, and Social Change. In: Hein, Laura and Mark Selden (eds.): *Censoring History. Citizenship and Memory in Japan, Germany, and the United States.* Armonk and London: M. E. Sharpe, pp. 1–50.

Heiwa Kinen Jigyō Tokubetsu Kikin (2000): *Heiwa Kinen Jigyō Tokubetsu Kikin Shūshū Shiryō Shashin-shū* [A photographic Collection of material in the Exhibition Centre and Reference Library for Peace and Consolation]. Tōkyō: Heiwa Kinen Jigyō Tokubetsu Kikin.

Heiwa Kinen Jigyō Tokubetsu Kikin (2002): *Heiwa Kinen Tenji Shriyōkan* [The Exhibition Centre and Reference Library for Peace and Consolation]. Tōkyō: Heiwa Kinen Jigyō Tokubetsu Kikin.

Hobsbawm, Eric (1997): *On History.* New York: The New Press.

Hook, Glenn D. and Gavan McCormack (2001): *Japan's Contested Constitution. Documents and Analysis.* London und New York: Routledge.

Höpken, Wolfang (2003): Why Textbook Research? In: Horvat, Andrew and Gehard Hielscher (eds:) (2003): *Sharing the Burden of the Past: Legacies of War in Europe, America, and Asia.* Tōkyō: The Asia Foundation, Friedrich-Ebert-Stiftung, 2003, pp. 2–9.

Horvat, Andrew and Gehard Hielscher (eds:) (2003): *Sharing the Burden of the Past: Legacies of War in Europe, America, and Asia.* Tōkyō: The Asia Foundation, Friedrich-Ebert-Stiftung, 2003.

Hosoya, Chihiro and Magoroku Ide (1995): Sensō o kioku suru to iu koto, rekishi o kioku suru to iu koto [What it means to memorialize war and what it means to memorialize history]. In: *Sekai* 607, pp. 22–37.

Hudson, Mark J. (1999): *Ruins of Identity. Ethnogenesis in the Japanese Islands.* Honolulu: University of Hawai'i Press.

Iggers, Georg G. (1997): *Historiography in the Twentieth Century. From Scientific Objectivity to the Postmodern Challenge.* Hanover and London: Wsleyan University Press.

IISS (International Institute for Strategic Studies) (2004): *The Military Balance 2003–2004.* Oxford: Oxford University Press.

Ikezoe, Noriaki (2004): Bōsō suru 'Hinomaru' kyōiku ['Hinomaru' education runs out of control]. In: *Sekai* 726, pp. 62–69.

Inoue, Nobutaka (1999): *Jinja to Kamigami* [Shrines and Gods]. Tōkyō: Jitsugyō-no-Nihon-sha.

Irie, Yōko (2001): *Nihon ga 'Kami no Kuni' Datta Jidai* [The era when Japan was the 'Land of the Gods']. Tōkyō: Iwanami Shoten (Iwanami Shinsho 764).

Irie, Yōko (2004): *Kyōkasho ga Abunai. 'Kokoro no Nōto' to Kōmin, Rekishi* [Dangerous Textbooks: The 'notebook of the mind' and textbooks on civic studies and history]. Tōkyō: Iwanami Shoten (Iwanami Shinsho 886).

Ishida, Yūji (2002): *Kako no Kokufuku. Hitorā-go no Doitsu* [Overcoming the past. Germany after Hitler]. Tōkyō: Hakusuisha.

Ishihara, Shintarō and Tahara Sōichiō (2000): *Katsu Nihon* [The Japan that wins]. Tōkyō: Bungei Shunjū.

Itō, Nobutada (2002): 'Heiwa kinen' shisetsu to sensō tenji [Institutions for 'Praying for Peace' and War museums]. In: *Rekishi Hyōron* 621, pp. 25–35.

Jansen, Marius B. (1994): *Sakamoto Ryōma and the Meiji Restoration*. Stanford: Stanford University Press (originally published by Princeton University Press, 1961).

Jansen, Marius B. (2000): *The Making of Modern Japan*. Cambridge, Mass.: Belknap Press of Harvard University Press.

Jeismann, Karl-Ernst (1988): Geschichtsbewußtsein als zentrale Kategorie der Geschichtsdidaktik. In: Schneider, Gerhard (ed.): *Geschichtsbewußtsein und Historisch-Politisches Lernen. Jahrbuch für Geschichtsdidaktik* 1, pp. 1–24.

Jinja Honchō Kyōgaku Kenkyūjo (2000): 'Senbotsusha no irei ni kan suru ishiki chōsa' hōkoku [Report on the 'Survey of public awareness about Mourning the War Dead']. In: *Jinja Honchō Kyōgaku Kenkyūjo Kiyō* 5, pp. 173–203.

Jitsugen suru kai (2005nen taiga dorama ni Ryōma ga yuku o jitsugen suru kai) (2004): *NHK Taiga Dorama ni Ryōma ga Yuku o 2005nen Jitsugen ni Mukete*. Internet: www.ryoman.com (last accessed on 1 August 2004).

Jiyūshugi shikan kenkyūkai (2000): *Jiyūshugi Shikan Kenkyūkai Annai* [Understanding the Association for the Advancement of a Liberal View of History]. Internet: http://www.jiyuu-shikan.org/oversea/index.html (last accessed 10 December 2003).

Kajiyama, Masashi (2001): Kokutei kyōkasho mondai to "Taiyō" [The problem of state-issued textbooks and the magazine "Taiyō"]. In: Suzuki, Sadami (ed.): *Zasshi "Taiyō" to Kokumin Bunka no Keisei* [The magazine "Taiyō" and the shaping of popular culture]. Kyōto: Shibungaku Shuppan, 2001, pp. 409–434.

Kanazawa Shōkō Kaigisho (2002): *Keikyōkan ni Ondosa* [Different assessments of the economic situation]. Internet: http://www.kanazawa-cci.

or.jp/news/2002/02_11_07a/02_11_07a.html (last accessed on 4 November 2003).

Kang, Sang-jung (2001a): *Tsukuru-kai Kyōkasho no Haikei* [The background to the Tsukuru-kai textbook]. Presentation at the Symposium "9 June" organised by "Kodomo to kyōkasho zenkoku Net 21" (9 June 2001, Tōkyō).

Kang, Sang-jung (2001b): *Nashonarizumu* [Nationalism]. Tōkyō: Iwanami Shoten (Shikō no furontia).

Kang, Sang-jung (2003): *Han-nashonarizumu* [Anti-nationalism]. Tōkyō: Kyōiku Shiryō Shuppankai.

Kang, Sang-jung and Yoshimi Shun'ya (2001): *Gurōbaruka no Enkinhō. Atarashii Kōkyōkūkan o Motomete* [The Law of Perspective and Globalization: Working for a new Civil Order]. Tōkyō: Iwanami Shoten.

Katzenstein, Peter (1996): *Cultural Norms and National Security. Police and Military in Postwar Japan*. Ithaca: Cornell University Press.

Kawamoto, Shunzō (2002): Keizai, Rekishi Ninshiki de Nitchū ni ōki-na rakusa [Significant Differences between Japan and China in Economics and Historical Consciousness]. In: *Asahi Sōken Ripōto* 159, pp. 125–128.

Kimijima, Kazuhiko (2001): Atarashii rekishi shūseishugi hihan [A Critique of the new historical revisionism]. In: Uesugi, Satoshi et al.: *Iranai! 'Kami no Kuni' Rekishi – Kōmin Kyōkasho* [We don't need 'Land of the Gods' Textbooks for History and Civic Studies]. Tōkyō: Akashi Shoten, pp. 41–78.

Kinmonth, Earl H. (1999): The Mouse that Roared: Saitō Takao, Conservative Critic of Japan's 'Holy War' in China. In: *Journal of Japanese Studies*, 25:2, pp. 331–360.

Kitaoka, Shin'ichi (2000): *'Futsū no Kuni' e* [Towards becoming a normal country]. Tōkyō: Chūō Kōronsha.

Kleßmann, Christoph (2002): Zeitgeschichte als wissenschaftliche Aufklärung. In: *Aus Politik und Zeitgeschichte* B51–52, pp. 3–12.

Kleßmann, Christoph (2003): Zeitgeschichte als wissenschaftliche Aufklärung. In: Sabrow, Martin et al. (eds.): *Zeitgeschichte als Streitgeschichte. Grosse Kontroversen seit 1945*. München: Beck, pp. 240–262.

Kobayashi, Yoshinori (1998): *Sensō-ron* [War]. Tōkyō: Gentōsha.

Kobayashi, Yoshinori (ed.) (2002a): *Washizumu* [Washism]. Tōkyō: Gentōsha.

Kobayashi, Yoshinori (2002b): *Shin Gōmanizumu Sengen 11: Terorian Naito* [New Manifesto of Arrogantism 11: Terrorian Nights]. Tōkyō: Shōgakukan.

Kobayashi, Yoshinori and Nishibe Susumu (2002): *Hanbei to iu Sahō* [An attitude called anti-Americanism]. Tōkyō: Shōgakukan.

Kobori, Keiichirō (1998): *Yasukuni Jinja to Nihonjin* [The Yasukuni Shrine and the Japanese]. Tōkyō: PHP Kenkyūjo (PHP Shinsho, 52).

Kondō, Takahiro (2001): 20nen no kensō to chinmoku [20 years of uproar and silence]. In: Funabashi, Yōichi (ed.): *Ima, Rekishi Mondai ni dō Torikumu ka* [How will we cope with the problem of history now?]. Tōkyō: Iwanami Shoten, pp 81–102.

Koselleck, Reinhart (2002): *The Practice of Conceptual History. Timing History, Spacing Concepts.* Stanford: Stanford University Press.

Kyōkasho Repōto 2002 (2002) [Textbook Report 2002]: Tōkyō: Shuppan Rōren Kyōkasho Taisaku Iinkai.

Kyōkasho Repōto 2003 (2003) [Textbook Report 2003]: Tōkyō: Shuppan Rōren Kyōkasho Taisaku Iinkai.

Kyōkasho Repōto 2004 (2004) [Textbook Report 2004]: Tōkyō: Shuppan Rōren Kyōkasho Taisaku Iinkai.

Lakshmi, Rama (2002): Hindu rewriting of history texts splits India. In: *International Herald Tribune*, 15 October 2002, Internet: http://www.iht.com/cgi-bin/generic.cgi?template=articleprint.tmplh&ArticleId=73673 (last accessed on 22 April 2004).

Lokowandt, Ernst (1981): *Zum Verhältnis von Staat und Shinto im Heutigen Japan: eine Materialsammlung.* Wiesbaden: Harrassowitz.

Maeda, Tetsuo (ed.) (2002): *Iwanami Shōjiten Gendai no Sensō* [The Iwanami Dictionary Wars Today]. Tōkyō: Iwanami Shoten.

Maeno, Tōru (2003): *Shin Rekishi no Shinjitsu* [The Truth of Japanese History. New]. Tōkyo: Keizaikai, 2003.

Mainichi Interactive (2001): *KSD Jiken* [The KSD Incident]. Internet: http://www.mainichi.co.jp/eye/feature/article/ksd/200107/0702-6.html (last access on 15 June 2002).

Makita, Tetsuo (2000): Nihonjin no sensō to heiwa-kan. Sono jizoku to fūka [Continuity and change in views on war and peace amongst the Japanese]. In: *NHK Hōsō Kenkyū to Chōsa* 2000:9, pp. 2–19.

Marshall, Byron K. (1994): *Learning to be Modern: Japanese Political Discourse on Education.* Boulder: Westview Press.

Matsui, Kōji (2003): Sofuto pawā e no tenkan o [Turning towards 'soft' power]. In: *Asahi Shinbun* 12 August 2003, p. 6.

Matsuyama, Yōichi et al. (1981): Jidō, seito no rekishi ninshiki no kiso chōsa [A preliminary Investigation into the historical Understanding shown by children and school pupils]. In: *Tsukuba Daigaku Gakkō Kyōikubu Kiyō* 3, p. 25–43.

McCormack, Gavan (2000): The Japanese Movement to 'Correct' History. In: Hein, Laura and Mark Selden (eds.): *Censoring History. Citizenship and Memory in Japan, Germany and the United States.* Armonk and London: M. E. Sharpe. pp. 53–73.

McCormack, Gavan (2001a): *The Emptiness of Japanese Affluence.* Revised Edition. Armonk and London: M. E. Sharpe.
McCormack, Gavan (2001b): *Japan's Afghan Expedition.* Internet: http://www.iwanami.co.jp/jpworld/text/Afghanexpedition01.html (last accessed on 15 May 2004).
McVeigh, Brian J. (2004): *Nationalisms of Japan. Managing and Mystifying Identity.* Lanham et al.: Rowman and Littlefield.
Mill, John Stuart (1958): *Considerations on Representative Government.* Edited by Currin V. Shields. New York: The Liberal Arts Press.
Mishima, Ken'ichi (1999): Die Schmerzen der Modernisierung als Auslöser kultureller Selbstbehauptung – Zur geistigen Auseinandersetzung Japans mit dem "Westen". In: Hijiya-Kirschnereit, Irmela (ed.): *Überwindung der Moderne? Japan am Ende des Zwanzigsten Jahrhunderts.* Frankfurt am Main: Suhrkamp, pp. 86–122.
Mishima, Ken'ichi (2000): Fandamentarizumu hihan no kufū. Nishio Kanji no baai [A Device for Critiquing Fundamentalism: The Case of Nishio Kanji]. In: *Rekishgaku Kenkyū* 744, pp. 17–29.
Miyachi, Masato (2004): *Rekishi no Naka no Shinsengumi* [The Shinsengumi in history]. Tōkyō: Iwanami Shoten.
MOFA (Ministry of Foreign Affairs) (1995): *Statement by Prime Minister Tomiichi Murayama "On the occasion of the 50th anniversary of the war's end".* Internet: http://www.mofa.go.jp/announce/press/pm/murayama/9508.html (last accessed on 22 April 2004).
Monbu Kagakushō (1989): *Chūgakkō Gakushū Shidō Yōryō* [Guidelines for Study in Junior High Schools]. Internet: http://www.mext.go.jp/b_menu/shuppan/sonota/890303.htm (last accessed on 8 April 2004).
Monbu Kagakushō (1999): *Gimu Kyōiku Shogakkō no Kyōikuyō Tosho no Mushō ni kan-suru Hōritsu* [The Law on the Free Provision of Textbooks for Schools in the Level of Compulsory Education]. Internet: http://www.mext.go.jp/b_menu/houdou/11/09/990908a/990908l.htm (last access on 27 July 2004).
Morris, Ivan (ed.) (1963): *Japan 1931–1945. Militarism, Fascism, Japanism?* Boston: D.C. Heath and Company.
Morris-Suzuki, Tessa (2003): Globale Erinnerungen, nationale Darstellungen: Nationalismus und die Revision der Geschichte. In: Richter, Steffi and Wolfgang Höpken (eds.): *Vergangenheit im Gesellschaftskonflikt. Ein Historikerstreit in Japan.* Köln, Weimar, Wien: Böhlau, 2003, pp. 27–53.
Mosse, George L. (1990): *Fallen Soldiers. Reshaping the Memory of the World Wars.* New York and Oxford: Oxford University Press.
Mukae, Ryuji (1996): Japan's Diet Resolution on World War Two. Keeping History at Bay. In: *Asian Survey* XXXVI, pp. 1011–1030.

Murai, Atsushi (2001): Kentei koso ga nejire no kongen [The Approval System is the Root of Distortion]. In: *Sekai* 689, pp. 118–112.

Muramatsu, Michio (1987): In Search of National Identity: The Politics and Policies of the Nakasone Administration. In: *Journal of Japanese Studies* 13:2, pp. 307–342.

Nakamura, Masanori (1998): The History Textbook Controversy and Nationalism. In: *Bulletin of Concerned Asian Scholars* 30:2, pp. 24–29.

Narita, Ryūichi (2003): *Shiba Ryōtarō no Bakumatsu – Meiji: 'Ryōma ga Yuku' to 'Saka no ue no Kumo' o Yomu* [The Bakumatsu-Meiji period of Shiba Ryōtarō: Reading 'Ryōma ga yuku' and 'Saka no ue no kumo']. Tōkyō: Asahi Shinbunsha (Asahi Sensho 728).

National Committee (National Committee for the 50th Aniversary of the End of World War II) (1995): *A Celebration of Asian Nations' Symbiosis*. Tōkyō: Shūsen Gōjūshūnen Kokumin Iinkai.

Nelson, John (2002): Tempest in a Textbook. A Report on the New Middle-School History Textbook in Japan. In: *Critical Asian Studies* 34:1, pp. 129–148.

Nelson, John (2003): Social Memory as Ritual Practice: Commemorating Spirits of the Military Dead at Yasukuni Shinto Shrine. In: *Journal of Asian Studies* 62:2, pp. 443–467.

Net (= Kodomo to Kyōkahso Zenkoku Netto 21) (ed.) (2000): *Kyōkasho Kōgeki no Uso o Kiru* [We put an end to the lies of the textbook offensive], Tōkyō: Aoki Shoten.

NHK (1996) (NHK Hōsō Kenkyūbu): Sekai no terebi wa sengo 50shūnen o dō tsutaeru ka [How international television broadcast the 50th anniversary of the war]. In: *Hōsō Kenkyū to Chōsa* 1996:10, pp. 2–23.

NHK (2000) (NHK Hōsō Bunka Kenkyūjo) [NHK Broadcasting Culture Research Institute]) (ed.): *Gendai Nihon no Ishiki Kōzō* [The structure of awareness among contemporary Japanese]. Tōkyō: 2000 (NHK Books, 880).

NHK (2004): *Taiga Dorama Ichiran* [Overview of the Annual Historical Series]. Internet: http://www.nhk.or.jp/pr/marukaji/m-taiga.htm (last accessed on 27 June 2004).

Nichibenren (Nihon bengoshi rengōkai) (2002): *Kyōiku Kihon-hō no Arikata ni kan-suru Chūkyōshin e no Shimon Oyobi Chūkyōshin de no Giron ni tai-suru Ikensho* [Statement on the advice of the Chūkyōshin and the discussion in the Chūkyōshin over the present state of the Basic Law on education]. Internet: http://www.nichibenren.or.jp/jp/katsudo/sytyou/iken/data/2002_24.pdf (last accessed on 10 May 2004).

Nishibe, Susumu (2000): *Kokumin no Dōtoku* [The Morals of the Nation]. Tōkyō: Sankei Shinbun Nyūsu Sābisu/Fusōsha.

Nishibe, Susumu et al. (2001): *Atarashii Kōmin Kyōkasho* [The New Civics Textbook]. Tōkyō: Fusōsha.
Nishihara, Hiroshi (2004): Kyōshi ni okeru 'shokumu no kōkyōsei' to wa nani ka [What does 'public office' mean in the case of a teacher?]. In: *Sekai* 725, pp. 74–82.
Nishikawa, Nagao (1995): *Kokumin Kokka-ron no Shatei. Aruiwa: 'Kokumin' to iu Kaibutsu ni Tsuite* [Theories of the Nation-State, Or: A Monster called 'Nation']. Tōkyō: Kashiwa Shobō.
Nishio, Kanji (1994): *Kotonaru Higeki – Nihon to Doitsu* [Different tragedies – Japan and Germany]. Tōkyō: Bungei Shunjū.
Nishio, Kanji (1999): *Kokumin no Rekishi* [History of the Nation]. Tōkyō: Sankei Shinbun Nyūsu Sābisu/Fusōsha.
Nishio, Kanji (2001): *Kankoku no Hitobito e no Tegami* [Letter to the Korean People]. Internet: http://www.tsukurukai.com/02_about_us/01_opi_03.html (last accessed on 20 April 2004).
Nishio, Kanji et al. (eds.) (2001): *Atarashii Rekishi Kyōkasho* [The New History Textbook]. Tōkyō: Fusōsha.
Nora, Pierre (1989): Between Memory and History. Les Lieux de Mémoire. In: *Representations* 36, pp. 7–25.
Nora, Pierre (2002): The Reasons for the Current Upsurge in Memory. In: *Transit. Europäische Revue*, vol. 22. Internet: http://www.iwm.at/t-22txt3.htm (last accessed on 7 July 2004).
Nozaki, Yoshiko (2002): Japanese politics and the history textbook controversy, 1982–2001. In: *International Journal of Educational Research* 37, pp. 603–622.
Nozaki, Yoshiko and Inokuchi Hiromitsu (2000): Japanese Education, Nationalism, and Ienaga Saburō's Textbook Lawsuits. In: Hein, Laura and Mark Selden (eds.): *Censoring History. Citizenship and Memory in Japan, Germany, and the United States*. Armonk and London: M. E. Sharpe, pp. 97–126.
NSKK (Nihon Shakai-ka Kyōiku Kenkyūkai) (1971): *Rekishi Ishiki no Kenkyū* [Research on Historical Consciousness]. Tōkyō: Daiichi Gakushū-sha.
Obinata, Toshio (2004): Kindai Nihon no Sensō to Kokumin Tōgō [War and National Integration in Modern Japan]. In: Obinata, Toshio and Yamada Akira (eds.): *Kindai Nihon no Sensō dō Miru ka* [How do we see the wars of modern Japan?]. Tōkyō: Ōtsuki Shoten (Kōza Sensō to Kindai 3), pp. 13–92.
Obinata, Toshio et al. (1999): *Kimitachi wa Sensō de Shineru ka: Kobayashi Yoshinori 'Ssensō-ron' Hihan* [Can you Really Die in War? A Critique of Kobayashi Yoshinori's 'On War']. Tōkyō: Ōtsuki Shoten.
Oguma, Eiji (1996): Shinwa o kowasu chi [The Knowledge that destroys myths]. In: Kobayashi, Yasuo and Funabiki Tateo (eds.): *Chi no Moraru*

[The Ethics of Knowledge]. Tōkyō: Tōkyō Daigaku Shuppankai, pp. 71–86.
Oguma, Eiji (1998): *'Nihonjin' no Kyōkai* [The Boundaries of the Japanese]. Tōkyō: Shin'yōsha.
Oguma, Eiji (2002): *'Minshu' to 'Aikoku'* ['Democracy' and 'Patriotism']. Tōkyō: Shin'yōsha.
Oguma, Eiji and Ueno Yōko (2003): *'Iyashi' no Nashonarizumu. Kusa no ne Hoshu Undō no Jisshō Kenkyū* [Nationalism as 'Pain Reliever': An Empirical Study of the Conservative Grassroots Movement]. Tōkyō: Keiō Gijuku Daigaku Shuppankai.
Ōnuki, Atsuko (2003a): Instrumentalisierung der Geschichte und Nationaldiskurse. Das Beispiel der Schulbuchdiskussion in Japan. In: Richter, Steffi and Wolfgang Höpken (eds.): *Vergangenheit im Gesellschaftskonflikt. Ein Historikerstreit in Japan.* Köln, Weimar, Wien: Böhlau, pp. 133–149.
Ōnuki, Atsuko (2003b): Die erzählte Nation: Geschichte als Mittel der Selbstbehauptung und der performative Effekt der Geschichtsschreibung. In: Amelung, Iwo et al. (eds.): *Selbstbehauptungsdiskurse in Asien. China – Japan – Korea.* München: Iudicium (Monographien aus dem Deutschen Institut für Japanstudien 34), pp. 109–123.
Orr, James (2001): *The Victim as Hero: Ideologies of Peace and National Identity in Postwar Japan.* Honolulu: University of Hawai'i Press.
Ortmanns-Suzuki, Annelie (1989): Japan und Südkorea: Die Schulbuchaffäre. In: *Japanstudien. Jahrbuch des Deutschen Instituts für Japanstudien* 1, pp. 135–182.
Ōuchi, Hirokazu (2003): *Kyōiku Kihon-hō Kaisei-ron Hihan* [A Critique of the Argument for a Revision of the Basic Laow of Education]. Tōkyō: Hakutakusha.
Petersen, Susanne (2001): Die Schulbuchprozesse. Geschichtspolitik in japanischen Schulbüchern. In: *Periplus. Jahrbuch für Außereuropäische Geschichte*, pp. 59–82.
PFFPC (The Public Foundation for Peace and Consolation) (2002): *Exhibition and Reference Library for Peace and Consolation.* Tōkyō: The Public Foundation for Peace and Consolation.
Pye, Michael (2003): Religion and Conflict in Japan with Special Reference to Shinto and Yasukuni Shrine. In: *Diogenes* 50:3, pp. 45–59.
Reichel, Peter (1999): *Politik mit der Erinnerung. Gedächtnisorte im Streit um die Nationalsozialistische Vergangenheit.* Frankfurt am Main: Fischer Taschenbuch Verlag.
Rekishigaku Kenkyūkai (ed.) (2000): *Rekishi ni Okeru 'Shūseishugi'* ['Revisionism' in history]. Tōkyō: Aoki Shoten.

Rekishigaku Kenkyūkai (ed.) (2001): *Machigai-darake no 'Atarashii Rekishi Kyōkasho'* [The 'New History Textbook' that is full of mistakes]. Tōkyō: Rekishigaku Kenkyūkai.

Rekishi Kentō Iinkai [History Examination Committee] (ed.) (1995): *Daitōa Sensō no Sōkatsu* [Summary of the Greater East Asian War]. Tōkyō: Tentensha.

Rekishi Kyōikusha Kyōgikai (ed.) (2000): *Shinpan. Heiwa Hakubutsukan, Sensō Shiryōkan Gaidobukku* [Guidebook to Peace Museums and War Collections. New Edition]. Tōkyō: Aoki Shoten.

Rekishi Kyōikusha Kyōgikai (ed.) (2002): *Q&A Motto Shiritai Yasukuni Jinja* [Q&A – I want to know more about the Yasukuni Shrine]. Tōkyō: Ōtsuki Shoten.

Renan, Ernest (1967) [1882]: Qu'est-ce qu'une nation? In: Vogt, Hannah (ed.): *Nationalismus Gestern und Heute*. Opladen: C. W. Leske.

Richter, Steffi (2001): Nicht nur ein Sturm im Wasserglas: Japans jüngster Schulbuchstreit. In: *Internationale Schulbuchforschung* 23, pp. 277–300.

Richter, Steffi (2003): Zurichtung von Vergangenheit als Schmerzlinderung in der Gegenwart. In: Richter, Steffi and Wolfgang Höpken (eds.) (2003): *Vergangenheit im Gesellschaftskonflikt. Ein Historikerstreit in Japan.* Köln, Weimar, Wien: Böhlau, pp. 1–26.

Richter, Steffi and Wolfgang Höpken (eds.) (2003): *Vergangenheit im Gesellschaftskonflikt. Ein Historikerstreit in Japan.* Köln, Weimar, Wien: Böhlau.

Roy, Kumkum (2003): What happened to Confucianism? In: *India-Seminar* 522 (Rewriting History. A Symposium on Ways of Representing Our Shared Past). Internet: http://www.india-seminar.com/2003/522/522%20kumkum%20roy.htm (last accessed on 22 April 2004).

Ruesen, J. (2001): *What is Historical Consciousness? – A Theoretical Approach to Empirical Evidence*. Paper presented at the conference "Canadian Historical Consciousness in an International Context: Theoretical Frameworks", University of British Columbia, Vancouver, BC.

Rüsen, Jörn (2001): Einleitung. Geschichtsbewußtsein thematisieren – Problemlaten und Analysestrategien. In: Rüsen, Jörn (ed.): *Geschichtsbewußtsein. Psychologische Grundlagen, Entwicklungskonzepte, Empirische Befunde*. Köln, Weimar and Wien: Böhlau, pp. 1–13.

Saaler, Sven (2002a): *Pan-Asianism in Modern Japanese History: A Preliminary Framework*. Tōkyō: German Institute for Japanese Studies (DIJ Working Papers 02/4).

Saaler, Sven (2002b): Zur Popularisierung und Visualisierung von Geschichte in Japan. Ein Beitrag zur aktuellen Diskussion um Erinnerungskultur. In: *Beiträge zur Japanforschung. Festgabe für Peter Pantzer zu seinem sechzigsten Geburtstag*. Bonn: Bier'sche Verlagsanstalt, pp. 257–279.

Saaler, Sven (2003a): Implikationen der Debatte um japanische Geschichtslehrbücher für die japanisch-koreanischen Beziehungen. In: Ducke, Isa and Sven Saaler (eds.) (2003): *Japan und Korea auf dem Weg in eine Gemeinsame Zukunft – Aufgaben und Perspektiven*. Munich: Iudicium (Monographien aus dem Deutschen Institut für Japanstudien 36), pp. 123–149.

Saaler, Sven (2003b): Neuere Entwicklungen in der japanischen Schulbuchdebatte. In: Pohl, Manfred and Iris Wieczorek (eds.): *Japan 2003. Politik und Wirtschaft*. Hamburg: Institut für Asienkunde, pp. 259–287.

Sakai, Tetsuya (1991): Tōa Shin-chitsujo no seijigaku. Takahashi Kamekichi no shoron o chūshin ni [The political science of the New Order in East Asia: A preliminary approach to Takahashi Kamekichi]. In: *Kokusai Seiji* 97, pp. 51–66.

Sakai, Toshiki (2003): Die gemeinsamen Forschungen zur Verbesserung der Geschichtslehrbücher in Japan und Südkorea. In: Ducke, Isa and Sven Saaler (eds.) (2003): *Japan und Korea auf dem Weg in eine Gemeinsame Zukunft – Aufgaben und Perspektiven*. Munich: Iudicium (Monographien aus dem Deutschen Institut für Japanstudien 36), pp. 123–149.

Sarkar, Sumit (2003): The Limits of Nationalism. In: *India-Seminar* 522 (Rewriting History. A Symposium on Ways of Representing Our Shared Past). Internet: http://www.india-seminar.com/2003/522/522%20sumit%20sarkar.htm (last accessed on 22 April 2004).

Selden, Mark (2003): Confronting World War II: The Atomic Bombing and the Internment of Japanese-Americans in U.S. History Textbooks. In: Horvat, Andrew and Gehard Hielscher (eds:) (2003): *Sharing the Burden of the Past: Legacies of War in Europe, America, and Asia*. Tōkyō: The Asia Foundation, Friedrich-Ebert-Stiftung, 2003, pp. 60–68.

Senghaas, Dieter (1994): *Wohin Driftet die Welt?* Frankfurt am Main: Suhrkamp.

Sen'yūren (Zenkoku Sen'yūkai Rengōkai) (2002): *Yasukuni Jinja to Chidorigafuchi Senbotsusha Boen* [The Yasukuni Shrine and the Chidorigafuchi Cemetery for the War Dead]. Internet: http://www.senyu-ren.jp/omou/19.htm (last accessed on 30 July 2003).

Seraphim, Franziska (1996): Der Zweite Weltkrieg im öffentlichen Gedächtnis Japans: Die Debatte zum fünfzigsten Jahrestag der Kapitulation. In: Hijiya-Kirschnereit, Irmela (ed.): *Überwindung der Moderne? Japan am Ende des Zwanzigsten Jahrhunderts*. Frankfurt am Main: Suhrkamp, pp. 25–56.

Shiba, Ryōtarō (1997): *Kono Kuni no Katachi 4* (The shape of this country, vol. 4). Tōkyō: Bungei Shunjū (Bungei Bunko Shi–1–64).

Shimazu, Naoko (2001): The Myth of the 'Patriotic Soldier': Japanese Attitudes Towards Death in the Russo-Japanese War. In: *War & Society* 19:2, pp. 69–89.

Shintō Seiji Renmei [Shintō Association of Spiritual Leadership] (2003): *Kudan no Sakura wa Naite-iru!* [The Cherry Blossoms in Kudan Weep!]. Tōkyō: Shintō Seiji Renmei.

Shōwakan (2002): *Senchū Sengo no Kurashi. Shōwakan* [Life in the war and postwar periods: The Shōwa Hall]. Tōkyō: Shōwakan.

Shūsen Gojūshūnen Kokumin Iinkai [People's Committee for the Commemoration of the 50th Anniversary of the End of the War] (ed.) (1995): *Daitōa Sensō no Shinjitsu o Tsutaete* [Conveying the real truth about the Greater East Asian War]. Tōkyō: Shūsen Gojūshūnen Kokumin Iinkai.

Shushō Kantei (2002): *Chidorigafuchi Senbotsusha Boen ni tsuite* [On the Chidorigafuchi Cemetery for the War Dead]. Internet: http://www.kantei.go.jp/jp/singi/tuitou/dai2/siryo2_1.html (last accessed 1 August 2004).

Shushō Kantei (2003a): *Tsuitō, Heiwa Kinen no tame no Kinenhi-nado Shisetsu no Arikata o Kangaeru Kondankai* [Discussion Group to Consider Memorials and Other Sites for the Commemoration of the War Dead and Praying for Peace]. Internet: http://www.kantei.go.jp/jp/singi/tuitou/kaisai-dex.html (last accessed 1 August 2004).

Shushō Kantei (2003b): *Hōkokusho* [Report]. Internet: http://www.kantei.go.jp/jp/singi/tuitou/kettei/021224houkoku.html (last accessed 1 August 2004).

Soysal, Yasemin Nuhoglu (2000): Identity and Trasnationalization in German School Textbooks. In: Hein, Laura and Mark Selden (eds.): *Censoring History. Citizenship and Memory in Japan, Germany, and the United States*. Armonk and London: M. E. Sharpe, pp. 127–149.

Steinbach, Peter (1999): Zeitgeschichte und Massenmedien aus der Sicht der Geschichtswissenschaft. In: Wilke, Jürgen (ed.): *Massenmedien und Zeitgeschichte*. Kontanz: UVK-Medien (Schriftenreihe der Deutschen Gesellschaft für Publizistik- und Kommunikationswissenschaft, vol. 26), pp. 32–52.

Stille, Alexander (2002): Textbook Publishers Learn to Avoid Messing With Texas. In: *The New York Times* 29 June 2002. http://www.nytimes.com/2002/06/29/arts/29TEXT.html (last accessed on 22 April 2004).

Straub, Jürgen (2001): Über das Bilden von Vergangenheit. Erzähltheoretische Überlegungen und eine exemplarische Analyse eines Gruppengesprächs über die 'NS-Zeit'. In: Rüsen, Jörn (ed.): *Geschichtsbewußtsein. Psychologische Grundlagen, Entwicklungskonzepte, Empirische Befunde*. Köln, Weimar and Wien: Böhlau, pp. 45–113.

Sugita, Yone[yuki] (2004): *Historical Lessons from Asian Cup*. Internet: http://www.japantoday.com/e/?content=comment&id=620 (last accessed on 12 August 2004).

Suny, Ronald G. (2001): History. In: Motyl, Alexander J. (ed.): *Encyclopedia of Nationalism*. San Diego: Academic Press, pp. 335–358.

Tahara, Sōichirō and Kobayashi Yoshinori (2002): 'Nihon no sensō' wa shinryaku sensō ka, kaihō sensō ka [Were 'Japan's wars' wars of aggression or wars of liberation?]. In: *Sapio*, 23 October 2002, pp. 96–100.

Tahara, Sōichirō, Nishibe Susumu and Kang Sang-Jung (2003): *Aikokushin* [Patriotism]. Tōkyō: Kōdansha.

Takahashi, Tetsuya (2001): *Rekishi/Shūseishugi* [History/Revisionism]. Tōkyō: Iwanami Shoten (Shikō no Furontia).

Takahashi, Tetsuya (ed.) (2002): *'Rekishi Ninshiki' Ronsō* [The Debate about 'Historical Consciousness']. Tōkyō: Sakuhinsha.

Takahashi, Tetsuya (2003): *'Kokoro' to Sensō* [The 'heart' and war]. Tōkyō: Shōbunsha.

Takahashi, Tetsuya and Miyake Akiko (2003): Kore wa 'kokumin seishin kaizō undō' da [This is the 'movement for renewing the morale of the people']. In: *Sekai* 712, pp. 33–47.

Takayama, Hiroyuki and Fujita Tsunehisa (1995): Rekishi ninshiki ni okeru 'sekai ishiki' no taiyō to gakushū-jō no kadai [The present state of 'world consciousness' regarding Historical Understanding and Learning to solve Problems]. In: *Kyōto Kyōiku Daigaku Kyōiku Jisshi Kenkyū Nenpō* 11, pp. 51–66.

Tanaka, Hidemichi (2004): *Kokumin no Minasama e* [To all members of the nation]. Internet: http://www.tsukurukai.com/02_about_us/01_opi_01.html (last accessed on 14 April 2004).

Tanaka, Masaaki (2001): *Pāru Hanji no Nihon Muzai-ron* [Justice Pal's plea that Japan be found not guilty]. Tōkyō: Shōgakukan (Shōgakukan Bunko 533).

Tanaka, Nobumasa (2002a): *Yasukuni no Sengo-shi* [The Postwar History of Yasukuni]. Tōkyō: Iwanami Shoten (Iwanami Shinsho 788).

Tanaka, Nobumasa (2002b): Arata-na senshi ni soroeru kokuritsu tsuitō shisetsu [An institution preparing for the mourning of new war dead]. In: *Shūkan Kin'yōbi* 425 (30 August 2002), pp. 22–25.

Tanaka, Nobumasa (2003): Kokka wa naze senshisha o tsuitō suru no ka [Why does the state mourn for the war dead?]. In: *Rekishi Chiri Kyōiku* 650, pp. 58–63.

Tanaka, Yuki (1996): *Hidden Horrors. Japanese War Crimes in World War II*. Boulder: Westview Press.

Tanaka, Yuki (2002): *Japan's Comfort Women. Sexual Slavery and Prostitution During World War II and the US Occupation*. London: Routledge (Asia's Transformations 11).

Tawara, Yoshifumi (2000): *Junior High School History Textbooks: Whither "Comfort Women" and the "Nanking Massacre"?* http://www.iwanami.co.jp/jpworld/text/textbook01.html (last accessed on 15.11.2001).

Tawara, Yoshifumi (2001): *Abunai Kyōkasho. 'Sensō Dekiru Kuni' o Mezasu 'Tsukuru-kai' no Jittai* [The dangerous textbook: The truth about the 'Tsukuru-kai' and the 'war-capable nation' it aims to create]. Tōkyō: Gakushū no tomo-sha.

Tawara, Yoshifumi (2002): Kinrin shokoku jōkō no sakujo yōkyū ya 'naisei kanshō'-ron no futōsei [The demand to delete the 'paragraph on neighbouring countries' and the argument alleging 'interference in internal affairs' are unreasonable]. In: *Kyōkasho Repōto* 46, pp. 23–29.

Tawara, Yoshifumi (2004): Kyōiku kihon-hō 'kaisei' o mokuromu hitobito [Those aiming at 'reform' of the Basic Law of Education]. In: *Sekai* 725, pp. 115–122.

Toby, Ronald (2001): Three Realms/Myriad Countries: An "Ethnography" of Other and the Re-bounding of Japan, 1550–1750. In: Chow, Kai-wing, Kevin M. Doak und Poshek Fu (eds.): *Constructing Nationhood in Modern East Asia*. Ann Arbor: The University of Michigan Press, pp. 15–45.

Torpey, John (2001): *The Pursuit of the Past: A Polemical Perspective*. Paper presented at the conference "Canadian Historical Consciousness in an International Context: Theoretical Frameworks", University of British Columbia, Vancouver, BC.

Tsukuru-kai (Atarashii rekishi kyōkasho o tsukuru-kai/Japanese Society for History Textbook Reform) (1996): *Declaration*. Internet: http://www.tsukurukai.com/02_about_us/01_opi_02.html (last accessed on 10 December 2003).

Tsukuru-kai (Atarashii rekishi kyōkasho o tsukuru-kai) (ed.) (1997a): *Atarashii Nihon no Rekishi ga Hajimaru* [A new Japanese history begins]. Tōkyō: Gentōsha.

Tsukuru-kai (Atarashii rekishi kyōkasho o tsukuru-kai) (1997b): *Atarashii Rekishi Kyōkasho o Tsukuru-kai Shuisho* [The reasons for founding the Society for the Creation of New History Textbooks]. Internet: http://www.tsukurukai.com/02_about_us/01_opinion.html (last accessed on 10 December 2003).

Tsukuru-kai (Atarashii rekishi kyōkasho o tsukuru-kai) (2004a): *Jigyaku* [Masochism]. Internet: http://www.tsukurukai.com/02_about_us/01_opinion.html (last accessed on 10 April 2004).

Tsukuru-kai (Atarashii rekishi kyōkasho o tsukuru-kai) (2004b): *Kawamura Bunkashō ni 'Kinrin Shokoku Jōkō' Sakujo o Mōshiire* [Demanding the deletion of the 'paragraph on neighbouring countries' from Minister of Education Kawamura]. Internet: http://www.tsukurukai.com/01_top_news/file_news/news_040413_1.html (last accessed on 10 May 2004).

TV Tokyo (2004): *Ryōma ga Yuku* [Ryōma on the Move]. Internet: http://www.tv-tokyo.co.jp/ryoma/ (last accessed on 15 July 2004).

Uesugi, Satoshi (2002): *Monbu Kagakushō ni Totte 'Tsukuru-kai' Kyōkasho Mondai to wa Nan-datta-no-ka* [What did the 'Tsukuru-kai' textbook question mean for the Ministry for Education and Science?]. Internet: http://www.h2.dion.ne.jp/~kyokasho/nandatta.html (last accessed on 6 April 2004).

Uesugi, Satoshi (2003a): *'Tsukuru-kai' no Ima* [The Tsukuru-kai now]. Internet: http://www.h2.dion.ne.jp/~kyokasho/0_conb07.htm (last accessed on 25 April 2004).

Uesugi, Satoshi (2003b): *Nihon ni Okeru 'Shūkyō Uyoku' no Taitō to 'Tsukuru-kai' 'Nippon Kaigi'* [The emergence of the 'religious right' in Japan and the 'Tsukuru-kai' and 'Nippon kaigi']. Internet: http://www.h2.dion.ne.jp/~kyokasho/nandatta.html (last accessed on 6 April 2004).

Uesugi, Satoshi et al. (eds.) (2001): *Iranai! 'Kami no Kuni' Rekishi – Kōmin Kyōkasho* [We don't need 'Land of the Gods'-style textbooks for history and civic studies]. Tōkyō: Akashi Shoten.

Umehara, Takeshi (2004): Yasukuni jinja wa Nihon no dentō kara itsudatsu shite-iru [The Yasukuni Shrine is a deviation from Japanese tradition]. In: *Sekai* 730, pp. 72–78.

Vickers, Edward (2002a): Introduction: history, politics and identity in East Asia. In: *International Journal of Educational Research* 37, pp. 537–544.

Vickers, Edward (2002b): Conclusion: Deformed relationships – identity politics and history education in East Asia. In: *International Journal of Educational Research* 37, pp. 643–651.

Wababayashi, Bob Tadao (2000): The Nanking 100-Man Killing Contest Debate: War Guilt Amid Fabricated Illusions, 1971–75. In: *Journal of Japanese Studies* 26:2, pp. 307–340.

Wakabayashi, Bob Tadao (2001): The Nanking Massacre. Now You See It,… In: *Monumenta Nipponica* 56:4, pp. 521–544.

Wakamiya, Yoshibumi (1995): *Sengo Hoshu no Ajia-kan* [Views of Asia held by Postwar Conservatives]. Tōkyō: Asahi Shinbunsha (Asahi Sensho 541).

Watanabe, Osamu (2002): Dai-san-ji kyōkasho kōgeki katsuyō no haikei – Gurōbaru gunji taikoku-ka no shin-dankai [The background to the third attack on our textbooks – the latest stage towards becoming a global military power]. In: *Kyōkasho Repōto* 46, pp. 4–9.

Wehler, Hans-Ulrich (1988): *Entsorgung der Deutschen Vergangenheit? Ein Polemischer Essay zum 'Historikerstreit'*. München: Beck.

Weiner, Michael (1994): *Race and Migration in Imperial Japan*. London, New York: Routledge (The Sheffield Centre for Japanese Studies Routledge Series 10).

White, Hayden (1973): *Metahistory. The Historical Imagination in Nineteenth-Century Europe*. Baltimore and London: The Johns Hopkins University Press.

Yagyū, Kunichika (2003): Der Yasukuni-Schrein im Japan der Nachkriegszeit. Zu den Nachwirkungen des Staatsshintō. In: Cornelißen, Christoph, Lutz Klinkhammer und Wolfgang Schwentker (eds.): *Erinnerungskulturen. Deutschland, Italien und Japan seit 1945*. Frankfurt am Main: Fischer, pp. 243–253.

Yakabi, Osamu (2002): 'Okinawa' o meguru ronsō, rongi [Discusssions and debates about 'Okinawa']. In: Takahashi, Tetsuya (ed.) (2002): *'Rekishi Ninshiki' Ronsō* [The Debate about 'Historical Consciousness']. Tōkyō: Sakuhinsha, pp. 87–89.

Yamabe, Masahiko (2002): Jūgonen Sensō-ka no Hakubutsukan no Sensō Tenji [War exhibitions in museums during the 15-year war]. In: Suzuki, Ryō and Takagi Hiroshi (eds.): *Bunkazai to Kindai Nihon*. Tōkyō: Yamakawa Shuppansha, pp. 143–167

Yamada, Akira (2002): Kyōkasho mondai kara rekishi ninshiki, rekishi kyōiku o kangaeru [Thinking about Historical Consciousness and History Education from the Perspective of the Textbook Problem]. In: *Jinmin no Rekishigaku* 151, pp. 1–10.

Yamaguchi, Takashi (2001): *Kanazawa ni Shutsugen Shita 'Daitō-A Seisen-hi'* [The 'Great Monument to the Holy War in Greater East Asia' erected in Kanazawa]. Internet: http://www.asahi-net.or.jp/~ew5m-asi/awiis/8/8.htm (last accessed on 22 July 2004).

Yang, Daqing (1999): Convergence or Divergence? Recent Historical Writings on the Rape of Nanjing. In: *American Historical Review* 1999:6, pp. 842–865.

Yang, Daqing (2000): The Challenges of the Nanjing Massacre: Reflections on Historical Inquiry. In: Fogel, Joshua (ed.): *The Nanjing Massacre in History and Historiography*. Berkeley, Los Angeles and London: University of California Press, pp. 133–179.

Yang, Daqing (2001): The Malleable and the Contested: The Nanjing Massacre in Postwar China and Japan. In: Fujitani, Takashi et al. (eds.): *Perilous Memories: the Asia-Pacific War(s)*. Durham: Duke University Press, pp. 50–86.

Yaskukuni Jinja Shamusho (1992): *Yasukuni jinja o Yori Yoku Shiru Tame ni* [Towards a better understanding of the Yasukuni Shrine]. Tōkyō: Yasukuni Jinja Shamusho.

Yaskukuni Jinja Shamusho (2002): *Yasukuni Dai-hyakka* [The Great Yasukuni Encyclopedia]. Tōkyō: Yasukuni Jinja Shamusho.

Yokota, Kōichi (2004): Kōteki sanpai 'seikyō bunri gensoku' ihan de aru [The official visit is a violation of the 'principle of separation of politics and religion']. In: *Sekai* 730, pp. 79–85.

Yoshida, Takashi (2000): A Battle over History: The Nanjing Massacre in Japan. In: Fogel, Joshua (ed.): *The Nanjing Massacre in History and Historiography*. Berkeley, Los Angeles and London: University of California Press, pp. 70–132.

Yoshida, Yutaka (1994): Nihonjin no Sensōkan [Japanese Views of the War]. In: *Sekai* 599, pp. 22–33.

Yoshida, Yutaka (1995): *Nihonjin no Sensōkan* [Japanese Views of the War]. Tōkyō: Iwanami Shoten.

Yoshida, Yutaka (1997): Heikan suru nashonarizumu [Exclusive Nationalism]. In: *Sekai* 633, pp. 74–82.

Yoshida, Yutaka (2002): Sengo 'Nihonjin' no Rekishi Ninshiki/Sensōkan no hen'yō [Changes in Historical Consciousness and Japanese attitudes to War in the Postwar Era]. In: Takahashi, Tetsuya (ed.) (2002): '*Rekishi Ninshiki' Ronsō* [The Debate about 'Historical Consciousness']. Tōkyō: Sakuhinsha, pp. 32–39.

Yoshimi, Yoshiaki (1987): *Kusa no ne no Fashizumu* [Grass-Roots Fascism]. Tōkyō: The University of Tokyo Press.

Yoshimi, Yoshiaki and Kawada Bunko (eds.): '*Jūgun Ianfu' o meguru 30 no uso to shinjitsu* [30 Lies and Truths Concerning the Comfort Women Issue]. Tōkyō: Ōtsuki Shoten.

Yoshizawa, Tatsuhiko (2001): Kyōkasho saitaku no genba de susumu 'kyōshi-hazushi' [Teachers are being Shut out of the Textbook Adoption Process]. In: *Sekai* 690, pp. 122–128.

Zaidan Hōjin Chidorigafuchi Senbotsusha Boen Hōshakai (ed.) (1989): *Chidorigafuchi Senbotsusha Boen sōken sanjūnen-shi* [The history of the Chidorigafuchi Cemetery for the War Dead since its foundation 30 years ago]. Tōkyō: Zaidan Hōjin Chidorigafuchi Senbotsusha Boen Hōshakai.

Zeitgeschichte-online (2004): *Die Fernsehserie "Holocaust" – Rückblicke auf eine "betroffene Nation"*. Internet: http://www.zeitgeschichte-online.de/md=FSHolocaust-Inhalt (last accessed on 6 June 2004).

Appendix

1. "Resolution to Renew the Determination for Peace on the Basis of Lessons Learned from History"
(adopted by the House or Representatives on 9 June 1995)

The House of Representatives resolves as follows:

On the occasion of the 50th anniversary of the end of World War II, this House offers its sincere condolences to those who fell in action and victims of wars and similar actions all over the world.

Solemnly reflecting upon many instances of colonial rule and acts of aggression in the modern history of the world, and recognizing that Japan carried out those acts in the past, inflicting pain and suffering upon the peoples of other countries, especially in Asia, the Members of this House express a sense of deep remorse.

We must transcend the differences over historical views of the past war and learn humbly the lessons of history so as to build a peaceful international society.

This House expresses its resolve, under the banner of eternal peace enshrined in the Constitution of Japan, to join hands with other nations of the world and to pave the way to a future that allows all human beings to live together.

(cited in Mukae 1996: 1012)

2. "On the occasion of the 50th anniversary of the war's end"
(statement by Prime Minister Murayama Tomiichi [*Murayama danwa*] on 15 August 1995)

The world has seen fifty years elapse since the war came to an end. Now, when I remember the many people both at home and abroad who fell victim to war, my heart is overwhelmed by a flood of emotions.

The peace and prosperity of today were built as Japan overcame great difficulty to arise from a devastated land after defeat in the war. That achievement is something of which we are proud, and let me herein express my heartfelt admiration for the wisdom and untiring effort of each and every one of our citizens. Let me also express once again my profound gratitude for the indispensable support and assistance extended to Japan by the countries of the world, beginning with the United States of America. I am also delighted that we have been able to build the friendly relations which we enjoy today with the neighboring countries of the Asia-Pacific region, the United States and the countries of Europe.

Now that Japan has come to enjoy peace and abundance, we tend to overlook the pricelessness and blessings of peace. Our task is to convey to younger generations the horrors of war, so that we never repeat the errors in our history. I believe that, as we join hands, especially with the peoples of neighboring countries, to ensure true peace in the Asia-Pacific region—indeed, in the entire world—it is necessary, more than anything else, that we foster relations with all countries based on deep understanding and trust. Guided by this conviction, the Government has launched the Peace, Friendship and Exchange Initiative, which consists of two parts promoting: support for historical research into relations in the modern era between Japan and the neighboring countries of Asia and elsewhere; and rapid expansion of exchanges with those countries. Furthermore, I will continue in all sincerity to do my utmost in efforts being made on the issues arising from the war, in order to further strengthen the relations of trust between Japan and those countries.

Now, upon this historic occasion of the 50th anniversary of the war's end, we should bear in mind that we must look into the past to learn from the lessons of history, and ensure that we do not stray from the path to the peace and prosperity of human society in the future.

During a certain period in the not too distant past, Japan, following a mistaken national policy, advanced along the road to war, only to ensnare the Japanese people in a fateful crisis, and, through its colonial rule and aggression, caused tremendous damage and suffering to the people of many countries, particularly to those of Asian nations. In the hope that no such mistake be made in the future, I regard, in a spirit of humility, these irrefutable facts of history, and express here once again my feelings of deep remorse and state my heartfelt apology. Allow me also to express my feelings of profound mourning for all victims, both at home and abroad, of that history.

Building from our deep remorse on this occasion of the 50th anniversary of the end of the war, Japan must eliminate self-righteous nationalism, promote international coordination as a responsible member of the international community and, thereby, advance the principles of peace and democracy. At the same time, as the only country to have experienced the devastation of atomic bombing, Japan, with a view to the ultimate elimination of nuclear weapons, must actively strive to further global disarmament in areas such as the strengthening of the nuclear non-proliferation regime. It is my conviction that in this way alone can Japan atone for its past and lay to rest the spirits of those who perished.

It is said that one can rely on good faith. And so, at this time of remembrance, I declare to the people of Japan and abroad my intention to make good faith the foundation of our Government policy, and this is my vow.

(MOFA 1995)

3. Numbers of war dead worshipped at the Yasukuni Shrine

Restoration wars 1853–1868	7.751
Southwest war (Satsuma Rebellion) 1877/78	6.971
Taiwan expedition 1877	1.130
Sino-Japanese war 1894/95	13.619
Boxer rebellion 1900	1.256
Russo-Japanese war 1904/05	88.429
World War I and Siberian Intervention 1918–1925	4.850
Sainan Incident	185
Manchurian Incident 1931	17.175
China Incident (Second Sino-Japanese War) 1937–1945	191.218
Greater East Asia War 1941–1945	2.133.760
Total	2.466.344

4. Visits of Japanese Prime Ministers to the Yasukuni Shrine
(total number of visits in brackets)

Shidehara Kijūrō (2)	23.10.1945, 20.11.1945
Yoshida Shigeru (5)	18.10.1951, 17.10.1952, 23.04.1953, 24.10.1953, 24.04.1954
Katayama Tetsu (0)	
Ashida Hitoshi (0)	
Hatoyama Ichirō (0)	
Ishibashi Tanzan (0)	
Kishi Nobusuke (2)	24.04.1957, 21.10.1958
Ikeda Hayato (5)	10.10.1960, 18.06.1961, 15.11.1961, 04.11.1962, 22.09.1963
Satō Eisaku (11)	24.04.1965, 21.04.1966, 22.04.1967, 23.04.1968, 22.04.1969, 18.10.1969, 22.04.1970, 17.10.1970, 22.04.1971, 19.10.1971, 22.04.1972

Tanaka Kakuei (5)	08.07.1972, 23.04.1973, 18.10.1973, 23.04.1974, 19.10.1974
Miki Takeo (3)	22.04.1975, **15.08.1975**, 18.10.1976
Fukuda Takeo (4)	21.04.1977, 21.04.1978, **15.08.1978**, 18.10.1978,
Ōhira Masayoshi (3)	21.04.1979, 18.10.1979, 21.04.1980
Suzuki Zenkō (9)	**15.08.1980**, 18.10.1980, 21.11.1980, 21.04.1981, **15.08.1981**, 17.10.1981, 21.04.1982, **15.08.1982**, 18.10.1982
Nakasone Yasuhiro (10)	21.04.1983, **15.08.1983**, 18.10.1983, 05.01.1984, 21.04.1984, **15.08.1984**, 18.10.1984, 21.01.1985, 22.04.1985, 1**5.08.1985**
Takeshita Noboru (0)	
Uno Sōsuke (0)	
Kaifu Toshiki (0)	
Miyazawa Kiichi (0)	
Hosokawa Morihiro (0)	
Hata Tsutomu (0)	
Murayama Tomiichi (0)	
Hashimoto Ryūtarō (1)	29.07.1996
Obuchi Keizō (0)	
Mori Yoshirō (0)	
Koizumi Jun'ichirō (3)	13.08.2001, 21.04.2002, 14.01.2003, 01.01.2004

5. Responses to Opinion Survey by Author on Japanese History (chapter 3.2)

	Total	total (%)	female	female (%)	male	male (%)	n/a
Q: Do you think the war of 1931–1945 was a war of aggression or not?							
Yes, a war of aggression	385	47,2	176	38,9	159	60	50
No, not a war of aggression	39	4,8	21	4,6	16	6	2
No interest	7	0,9	4	0,9	1	0,4	2
I don't know (insufficient knowledge)	315	38,6	221	48,8	65	24,6	29
I don't know (I can't judge)	58	7,1	31	6,8	23	8,7	4
No answer	12	1,5	0	0	1	0,4	11
Other	0	0	0	0	0	0	0
Total	816	100,1	453	100	265	100,1	98

Do you think the war of 1931–1945 was an unavoidable war or not?							
Yes, war was unavoidable	99	12,1	41	9,1	41	15,5	17
No, war was not unavoidable	361	44,2	169	37,3	150	56,6	42
No interest	7	0,9	4	0,9	1	0,4	2
I don't know (insufficient knowledge)	279	34,2	202	44,6	54	20,4	23
I don't know (I can't judge)	58	7,1	37	8,2	19	7,2	2
No answer	12	1,5	0	0	0	0	12
Other	0	0	0		0		0
Total	816	100	453	100,1	265	100,1	98
Do you think Japan still has continuing responsibility for the war?							
Yes, Japan still bears responsibility	540	66,2	296	65,3	180	67,9	64
No, Japan no longer has responsibility	62	7,6	28	6,2	29	10,9	5
Japan was not responsible for the war	27	3,3	12	2,6	13	4,9	2
I don't know (insufficient knowledge)	78	9,6	55	12,1	13	4,9	9
I don't know (I can't judge)	92	11,3	60	13,2	28	10,6	5
No answer	17	2,1	2	0,4	2	0,8	13
Other	0	0	0		0		0
Total	816	100,1	453	99,8	265	100	98

Monographien aus dem Deutschen Institut für Japanstudien

Bd. 1: Harumi Befu, Josef Kreiner (Eds.): *Otherness of Japan. Historical and Cultural Influences on Japanese Studies in Ten Countries.*
1992, ²1995 ISBN 3-89129-481-6 342 S., kt.

Bd. 2: Erich Pauer (Hg.): *Technologietransfer Deutschland – Japan von 1850 bis zur Gegenwart.*
1992 ISBN 3-89129-482-4 330 S., geb.

Bd. 3: Shigeyoshi Tokunaga, Norbert Altmann, Helmut Demes (Eds.): *New Impacts on Industrial Relations – Internationalization and Changing Production Strategies.*
1992 ISBN 3-89129-483-2 492 S., geb.

Bd. 4: Roy Andrew Miller: *Die japanische Sprache. Geschichte und Struktur.* Aus dem überarbeiteten englischen Original übersetzt von Jürgen Stalph *et al.*
1993 ISBN 3-89129-484-0 XXVI, 497 S., 24 Tafeln, geb.

Bd. 5: Heinrich Menkhaus (Hg.): *Das Japanische im japanischen Recht.*
1994 ISBN 3-89129-485-9 XVI, 575 S., geb.

Bd. 6: Josef Kreiner (Ed.): *European Studies on Ainu Language and Culture.*
1993 ISBN 3-89129-486-7 324 S., geb.

Bd. 7: Hans Dieter Ölschleger, Helmut Demes, Heinrich Menkhaus, Ulrich Möhwald, Annelie Ortmanns, Bettina Post-Kobayashi: *Individualität und Egalität im gegenwärtigen Japan. Untersuchungen zu Wertemustern in bezug auf Familie und Arbeitswelt.*
1994 ISBN 3-89129-487-5 472 S., geb.

Bd. 8: Gerhard Krebs, Bernd Martin (Hg.): *Formierung und Fall der Achse Berlin-Tōkyō.*
1994 ISBN 3-89129-488-3 256 S., geb.

Bd. 9: Helmut Demes, Walter Georg (Hg.): *Gelernte Karriere. Bildung und Berufsverlauf in Japan.*
1994 ISBN 3-89129-489-1 521 S., geb.

Bd. 10: Josef Kreiner (Ed.): *Japan in Global Context. Papers presented on the Occasion of the Fifth Anniversary of the German Institute for Japanese Studies, Tōkyō.*
1994 ISBN 3-89129-490-5 123 S., geb.

Bd. 11: Josef Kreiner (Ed.): *The Impact of Traditional Thought on Present-Day Japan.*
1996 ISBN 3-89129-491-3 236 S., geb.

Bd. 12: Josef Kreiner, Hans Dieter Ölschleger (Eds.): *Japanese Culture and Society. Models of Interpretation.*
1996 ISBN 3-89129-492-1 361 S., geb.

Bd. 13: Josef Kreiner (Ed.): *Sources of Ryūkyūan History and Culture in European Collections.*
1996 ISBN 3-89129-493-X 396 S., geb.

Bd. 14: Aoki Tamotsu: *Der Japandiskurs im historischen Wandel. Zur Kultur und Identität einer Nation.* Aus dem japanischen Original übersetzt von Stephan Biedermann, Robert Horres, Marc Löhr, Annette Schad-Seifert.
1996 ISBN 3-89129-494-8 140 S., geb.

Bd. 15: Edzard Janssen, Ulrich Möhwald, Hans Dieter Ölschleger (Hg.): *Gesellschaften im Umbruch? Aspekte des Wertewandels in Deutschland, Japan und Osteuropa.*
1996 ISBN 3-89129-495-6 272 S., geb.

Bd. 16: Robert Horres: *Raumfahrtmanagement in Japan. Spitzentechnologie zwischen Markt und Politik.*
1996 ISBN 3-89129-496-2 267 S., geb.

Bd. 17/1: Shūzō Kure: *Philipp Franz von Siebold. Leben und Werk.* Deutsche, wesentlich vermehrte und ergänzte Ausgabe, bearbeitet von Friedrich M. Trautz. Herausgegeben von Hartmut Walravens.
1996 ISBN 3-89129-497-2 LXVI, 800 S., geb.

Bd. 17/2: Shūzō Kure: *Philipp Franz von Siebold. Leben und Werk.* Deutsche, wesentlich vermehrte und ergänzte Ausgabe, bearbeitet von Friedrich M. Trautz. Herausgegeben von Hartmut Walravens.
1996 ISBN 3-89129-497-2 XXX, 899 S., geb.

Bd. 18: Günther Distelrath: *Die japanische Produktionsweise. Zur wissenschaftlichen Genese einer stereotypen Sicht der japanischen Wirtschaft.*
1996 ISBN 3-89129-498-0 253 S., geb.

Bd. 19: Gerhard Krebs, Christian Oberländer (Eds.): *1945 in Europe and Asia – Reconsidering the End of World War II and the Change of the World Order.*
1997 ISBN 3-89129-499-9 410 S., geb.

Bd. 20: Hilaria Gössmann (Hg.): *Das Bild der Familie in den japanischen Medien.*
1998 ISBN 3-89129-500-6 338 S., geb.

Bd. 21: Franz Waldenberger: *Organisation und Evolution arbeitsteiliger Systeme – Erkenntnisse aus der japanischen Wirtschaftsentwicklung.*
1999 ISBN 3-89129-501-4 226 S., geb.

Bd. 22: Harald Fuess (Ed.): *The Japanese Empire in East Asia and Its Postwar Legacy.*
1998 ISBN 3-89129-502-2 253 S., geb.

Bd. 23: Matthias Koch: *Rüstungskonversion in Japan nach dem Zweiten Weltkrieg. Von der Kriegswirtschaft zu einer Weltwirtschaftsmacht.*
1998 ISBN 3-89129-503-0 449 S., geb.

Bd. 24: Verena Blechinger, Jochen Legewie (Eds.): *Facing Asia – Japan's Role in the Political and Economical Dynamism of Regional Cooperation.*
2000 ISBN 3-89129-506-5 328 S., geb.

Bd. 25: Irmela Hijiya-Kirschnereit (Hg.): *Forschen und Fördern im Zeichen des Ginkgo. Zehn Jahre Deutsches Institut für Japanstudien.*
1999 ISBN 3-89129-505-7 270 S., geb.

Bd. 26: Harald Conrad, Ralph Lützeler (Eds.): *Aging and Social Policy. A German-Japanese Comparison*
2002 ISBN 3-89129-840-4 353 S., geb.

Bd. 27: Junko Ando: *Die Entstehung der Meiji-Verfassung. Zur Rolle des deutschen Konstitutionalismus im modernen japanischen Staatswesen.*
2000 ISBN 3-89129-508-1 273 S., geb.

Bd. 28: Irmela Hijiya-Kirschnereit (Hg.): *Eine gewisse Farbe der Fremdheit. Aspekte des Übersetzens Japanisch-Deutsch-Japanisch.*
2001 ISBN 3-89129-509-X 316 S., geb.

Bd. 29: Peter J. Hartmann: *Konsumgenossenschaften in Japan: Alternative oder Spiegelbild der Gesellschaft?*
2003 ISBN 3-89129-507-3 628 S., geb.

Bd. 30: Silke Vogt: *Neue Wege der Stadtplanung in Japan. Partizipationsansätze auf der Mikroebene, dargestellt anhand ausgewählter* machizukuri-*Projekte in Tōkyō.*
2001 ISBN 3-89129-841-2 312 S., geb.

Bd. 31: Birgit Poniatowski: *Infrastrukturpolitik in Japan. Politische Entscheidungsfindung zwischen regionalen, sektoralen und gesamtstaatlichen Interessen.*
2001 ISBN 3-89129-842-0 417 S., geb.

Bd. 32: Gerhard Krebs (Hg.): *Japan und Preußen.*
2002 ISBN 3-89129-843-9 356 S., geb.

Bd. 33: René Haak, Hanns Günther Hilpert (Eds.): *Focus China – The New Challenge for Japanese Management.*
2003 ISBN 3-89129-844-7 223 S., geb.

Bd. 34: Iwo Amelung, Matthias Koch, Joachim Kurtz, Eun-Jung Lee, Sven Saaler (Hg.): *Selbstbehauptungsdiskurse in Asien: China – Japan – Korea.*
2003 ISBN 3-89129-845-5 438 S., geb.

Bd. 35: Andrea Germer: *Historische Frauenforschung in Japan. Die Rekonstruktion der Vergangenheit in Takamure Itsues „Geschichte der Frau"* (Josei no rekishi).
2003 ISBN 3-89129-504-9 425 S., geb.

Bd. 36: Isa Ducke, Sven Saaler (Hg.): *Japan und Korea auf dem Weg in eine gemeinsame Zukunft: Aufgaben und Perspektiven.*
2003 ISBN 3-89129-846-3 232 S., geb.

Bd. 38: René Haak, Dennis S. Tachiki (Eds.): *Regional Strategies in a Global Economy. Multinational Corporations in East Asia.*
2004   ISBN 3-89129-848-X   294 S., geb.

Bd. 39: Sven Saaler (ed.): *Politics, Memory and Public Opinion. The History Textbook Controversy and Japanese Society.*
2004   ISBN 3-89129-849-8   202 S., geb.